**Dr Vibha Chauhan** taught English lit[...] College and is at present Principal [...] University. She has co-written, with Sa[...] a biography; and written *Ganga Jamuna Beech*, a novel in Hindi. She translated *Paar Pare* (*Beyond Black Waters*) by Joginder Paul and co-translated, with Khalid Alvi, *Angarey: Nine Stories and a Play*.

**Dr Khalid Alvi**, poet, critic and Urdu scholar, taught Urdu literature at Zakir Husain Delhi College. He is the author of twelve books. Many of his works have been translated into German, Persian and Uzbek. He also edited *Furtherance*, an English journal, and *Shahkaar*, an Urdu monthly.

# MANTO
## *Saheb*

Friends and Enemies
on the Great Maverick

Translated by
**VIBHA CHAUHAN**
and **KHALID ALVI**

SPEAKING
**TIGER**

SPEAKING TIGER PUBLISHING PVT. LTD
4381/4 Ansari Road, Daryaganj,
New Delhi–110002, India

ISBN: 978-93-88070-25-6
eISBN: 978-93-88070-27-0

10 9 8 7 6 5 4 3 2 1

Typeset in Garamond Premier Pro by SÜRYA, New Delhi
Printed at Sanat Printers, Kundli

# Contents

# My Twin

## Saadat Hasan Manto

MUCH HAS ALREADY BEEN WRITTEN AND SAID ABOUT
Manto. Some in his favour but most roundly condemn him.
If one were to pay attention to the opinions expressed about
Manto as a whole, they would make it extremely difficult for
any person with even an iota of wisdom to hold a favourable
opinion about him. I decided to write this article but I still do
feel that it is tough to express any opinion about Manto. Not
for me, though. I can make this claim only because I have had
the good fortune of knowing him quite intimately. The truth
of the matter is that I am exactly like Manto. Actually, I am like
Manto's twin.

I have no serious objection to the things that have been
written about Manto but I feel that much of what has been
expressed is far from truth. Some portray him as a devil and
others call him a bald angel, a ganja farishta. Just a moment...
Let me make sure that the good-for-nothing fellow is not
listening to us on the sly... No, no, it's fine. I just remembered
that this is when he sits and drinks. He is in the habit of
drinking bitter spirits after six in the evening.

We were born at the same time and I think we will also die
at the same time; but it could also happen that Sadaat Hasan
dies but Manto lives on. This suspicion has always caused a
great deal of pain to me because I have done all I could to
sustain my friendship with him. If he lives on but I kick the
bucket, it will be as though the shell of the egg is safe and
sound but the egg white and the yoke have faded out.

Now, I have no desire to stretch this preface further. I must
plainly let you know that I have never met anyone more crafty

and devious than Manto. One, two, Mantoo!* In short, Manto can stand in for three. In other words, he alone is as good as three people. Actually, Manto is an expert at triangles but what is also true is that this triangle is still incomplete... Of course, these hints about Manto can be understood only by those who have some modicum of wisdom.

As things go, I have known Manto from the moment he was born. We were born at the same time on 11 May 1912. But he tried to live life like a tortoise. What I mean is that it becomes impossible to discover the tortoise if it decides to tuck its head into its shell... But, then, I am his twin after all and have also managed to scrutinize all his actions very closely.

Fine then, I will now tell you how this big-headed, arrogant man was fashioned into a writer. Critics write elaborate articles as evidence of being well-informed and all-knowing. They quote from Schopenhauer, Freud, Hegel, Nietzsche, Marx; but the fact is that they are completely distanced from the real world.

Manto's writing is a consequence of the mutual contradiction between two aspects of his life. His father, may God grant him mercy, was a very stern and severe man, and his mother was extremely tender-hearted. You can well imagine the condition of that pellet of wheat which would have emerged after being pulverized between two such grindstones.

Now let me talk about his schooldays. He was a very intelligent and mischievous boy. He would have been at the most three-and-a-half feet tall in those days. He was his father's last born. He did receive affection from his parents but he never got the opportunity to meet his three step-brothers, who were much older than him and were studying abroad. He

*Manto often said that the correct pronunciation of his name rhymed with two. Also, in colloquial language, a person indulging in 'one two' is understood as being a cunning and crafty person.

deeply desired that his brothers meet him and treat him like their younger brother. However, he got this love and regard from them only after he had been accepted as an eminent short-story writer in the world of literature.

So now, let me talk to you about him as a short-story writer. To put it briefly, he is a fraud of the first order. His first story titled 'Tamasha' was about the Jallianwala Bagh massacre. He did not get this story published under his name and therefore escaped arrest.

After this his erratic mind became obsessed with the idea of studying further. It is interesting to note here that he passed his 'entrance', the high-school exam, only after two failed attempts. That was not all! He finally managed to scrape through with a third division—and you would be truly bowled over by the fact that he failed his Urdu exam.

People now accept him as a great Urdu writer and I can't help laughing when I hear this because the truth is that he does not know Urdu even today. He chases words like a hunter, running with his net to trap butterflies, does. They, however, keep escaping and he fails. It is because of this that one sees a dearth of beautiful words in his writings. He is uncivilized and seems to be wielding a baton instead of a pen. Nonetheless, he too has been knocked around innumerable times by the baton and what one cannot take away from him is the fact that he has borne all these beatings with a smile.

There is, however, a difference between the thrashings that Manto received and those he bestowed. The latter are not merely the flaunting of brawn or brute force, devoid of culture and finesse. In fact, these are well-mastered, elegant tricks of the trade—like banot and faket, those graceful yet invincible styles of accomplished wrestlers. Manto is that distinctive individual who refuses to walk the straight path, choosing, instead, to balance himself on the tightrope. People keep expecting him to slip any moment but this ruffian Manto has not lost his footing even once. Well, he may sometime or the other fall flat on his face, never again to get up, but I do know that he will in, these last moments, announce quite loudly and clearly to everyone: 'I fell only to destroy the belief that one need not despair if one falls.'

I have already mentioned that Manto is a fraud of the top order. The most unshakable evidence of this is that he often asserts that it is not he who thinks about the story, it is the story that seeks him out. This kind of posturing is certainly a fraud. I know for a fact that when he has to write a story, his condition is exactly like that of a hen about to lay an egg. He, however, lays this egg not in hiding but in front of everybody—with his friends sitting around him and his three daughters creating a racket.

Manto sits on his favourite chair, pulls his feet up, folds his knees and begins to lay the eggs that later crack open, bringing out stories that run around squawking like chickens.

His wife is really distressed and often tells him, 'Forget all this story-writing. Just open up a shop...'

But the shop in Manto's mind is packed with stuff that is very different from what one finds in any other. He often thinks that if he were to open one, he himself would turn into a cold storage with all his emotions and writings kept there, frozen.

Manto might get very offended when he reads what I have written. And I must confess that I cannot get rid of this apprehension even as I carry on writing. It is possible to put up with many other facets of Manto's personality but it is impossible to face his anger. He truly becomes a fiend when he is incensed but, thankfully, that lasts for only a few moments. But those few moments! Only God can be our saviour then!

He does act hoity-toity when it comes to writing stories but since I am his twin, I know better than anybody else that all of it is also sheer fraud. He himself once wrote that his pockets are packed with innumerable stories. The truth, in fact, is quite the contrary. When he does decide to write a story, he thinks about it through the night but does not hit upon anything; he then gets up early, at five, and tries to squeeze out a story from newspaper reports but still does not succeed. He then goes for a bath and tries to cool down his frenzied head so that it becomes capable of some thought and contemplation. He fails once again and, out of sheer irritation, starts quarrelling with his wife; when this does not work either, he walks out of the house to eat paan. The paan lies on his table but the theme of the story still evades him. Finally, he picks up the pen or pencil in sheer vengeance, writes 786 on the sheet of paper, puts down the first thought that comes to his mind, and that becomes the opening of his story. Stories like 'Babu Gopinath', 'Hatak', 'Mummy' and 'Mozel' are outcomes of such fraud.

It is quite strange that people carry the impression that he is both obscene and an atheist. I too have often felt that he probably belongs to those categories since he frequently chooses to write about very base and degenerate matters. Moreover, the language in which he expresses these ideas may be considered objectionable. But I also know that before starting a story, Manto writes 786—Bismillah—on top of the sheet of paper. This gentleman who often repudiates the existence of God becomes a chaste Muslim on paper. This Manto is a kagazi Manto, a paper Manto, whom you can easily split open like kagazi badam, those almonds with thin shells. Except this: he is a man who cannot be crushed, even with iron hammers.

Now let me say something about Manto's personality. I will use very few words to describe him. He is a crook... A liar... A garrulous teller of tales.

He often takes advantage of his wife's naïveté and has fobbed off hundreds of rupees off her! For instance, when he gives her some money, let's say eight hundred rupees, he keeps a sly watch to find out where she keeps it and, the very next day, he plucks out a hundred-rupee note. When the poor thing discovers her loss, she reprimands the servants.

It is generally believed that Manto is an honest man but I am not willing to accept this proposition. He is a liar, that too of the worst kind. Earlier, his family used to entirely believe him because his lies had the special 'Manto touch' but it later dawned on his wife that Manto lied to her on many occasions. Actually, Manto lies rarely but now the trouble is that his family is convinced that he only lies all the time, like the black mark a woman makes on her cheek with kajal, hoping to pass it off as a genuine beauty spot.

He is poorly educated, in the sense that he has never studied Marx; neither has he ever set eyes on any of Freud's works; and he knows Hegel only by name. But the most interesting thing is that people, especially critics, have declared that he has been influenced by all these thinkers. As far as I know, it is impossible for Manto to be influenced by any other scholar. He feels that all those who preach in any form are truly idiots; one should not even try to preach. People should attain knowledge through their own experience. He has deliberated so much with himself that he has transformed into the kind of thought and philosophy that can be grasped only by the wise. The absurd comments he makes off and on make me laugh.

I can tell you with complete conviction that Manto, who has been charged with obscenity in many lawsuits, is obsessive about cleanliness, but I also cannot stop myself from saying that he is a self-centred man who never stops thumping, scouring, scrubbing and cleaning himself as well.

# The Diviner of the Human Heart

## Krishan Chander

TALL, A LITTLE BENT. FAIR. PROMINENT VEINS ON THE back of the hand. A significant Adam's apple. Gangling legs with outsized but far from gawky feet. Exasperation clearly writ on a face which reflects a singular kind of sophistication and refinement. An edginess in the voice. A restlessness to write. A kind of bitterness in behaviour. And hasty steps. These are some conspicuous traits that catch our eye when we meet Sadaat Hasan Manto for the first time. However, soon, a very different kind of impression begins to override this first one. The shape of Manto's forehead, like his intellect, is very impressive and unique. We often find a similarity between the shape of the foreheads of sharp and intelligent people and those of the devils one sees in paintings by some Western artists. It is interesting to see how they share similar physical attributes: an expansive forehead with the hairline at the temples gradually receding as it moves behind the ear. But Manto's forehead is not at all like that of the devil. It is rectangular. Like a cinema screen, it is narrow at the base and widens out at the top. His hair is long, straight and thick. His eyes have a peculiar, intense gleam that exists alongside a kind of bluntness which peeps through them. His wisdom has that special quality that is born only after a close brush with mortality. I have never asked Manto about this aspect of his life. I have, however, heard from some others that he has been a victim of tuberculosis or some other equally dangerous ailment... Anyhow, the searing pain in his large, passionate and bewildered eyes is evidence that Manto has travelled far beyond the ultimate experience of life, into the realm of death, before turning back and returning to this world again. It is possible that his suffering may have been the consequence of a love affair and not a medical condition— though love too is often considered a malady. Whatever be the case, the experience was certainly not a losing proposition for Manto. He may have been burnt by fire but the ultimate outcome was that it transformed Manto into sterling gold.

Manto is a Kashmiri Pandit like Jawaharlal Nehru and Iqbal. His family settled in Amritsar many years ago. Both his older brothers left India and migrated abroad. One of them is a barrister in Kenya as well as a member of Kenya's Legislative Council. I have met Manto's brother and found him to be a religious, moral man, a virtuous practising Muslim. Manto is everything that his brothers are not. As far as his forbears are concerned, Manto does have regard but not love for them. There was such an insurmountable disagreement regarding manners, conduct and perspective between Manto and his brothers that he left home at a very young age to seek a new life for himself. Places like Aligarh, Lahore, Amritsar, Bombay, and Delhi have seen Manto in his many different incarnations: Manto the aficionado of Russian literature; Manto the connoisseur of Chinese literature; Manto the victim of hostility and pain; the unappreciated Manto; the maligned Manto; the Manto who haunted infamous establishments, drinking houses, brothels; as well as the domesticated Manto; the Manto who was ever ready to help his friends; the most famous writer of Urdu, Manto. These places have seen different shades of Manto's life and Manto too was intimately acquainted with different manifestations of all these places. Manto has burnt himself like the candle in order to closely observe life.

Manto is like the Shiva of Urdu literature who himself prepared and drank the cup of life's poison. Thereafter, he tore apart the overlapping layers of different facets of this poison and depicted them in his writings. People recoil from it and are afraid to accept what Manto writes, but cannot deny the truth and discernment in his observations. Shiva's throat had turned blue from the poison and Manto too has lost his health because of it. His life is now completely dependent on medicines and injections. But what is also true is that nobody but Manto could have drank the poison and digested and absorbed it as well. Any other man would have gone mad but such is the mettle of Manto's mind that it managed to soak in all, like those ascetics who start with cannabis and gradually move on to lethal venoms, getting their tongues bitten by snakes.

Manto's sharp, razor-edged writing and his surgical tongue are evidence that Manto's asceticism has reached its pinnacle. I had read Manto's stories before I met him. The language and expression, the lexis of these stories are so peculiar and incisive that one is completely won over by them. I probably read stories like 'Shoo-shoo', 'Khusihya' and 'Diwali ke Diye' in *Musavvir* and also conveyed my appreciation of these stories in my letters to Manto. That was when Manto lived in Bombay. He was the editor of the weekly *Musavvir*, and was also writing the story, scenes and dialogues for the film *Keechad*. After Premchand, it is Manto who had moved on from literature to films. But then it is probably not correct to say this because he actually achieved literary fame only after finishing his first innings in films. Manto is thus probably the only writer who moved from films to literature, laid the foundation of his fame, and then turned and entered the film world once again. Everything about him is amazing.

I read Manto's story 'Laalten' after having read the stories I mentioned above. The story is about Batote, a place in Kashmir, where Manto had gone to recover from some chronic illness. I feel that a large part of this story is autobiographical. The agony suffused in the minor details and climax of the story seems to represent the authentic experience of the romantic Manto. After this story, it seems like somebody had snatched away gentleness and tenderness from Manto's stories, or perhaps he himself drove these traits out. I feel Manto repeatedly strives to do this because of some pain and emotional turmoil that he is constantly confronting and grappling with. 'Go away, leave!' he seems to declare. 'Life is too brutal to let such emotions survive. It is better for you to just go away.' His stories often create the impression that these emotions have been driven out of them with clear and deliberate vehemence. He sometimes teases them like a child, and at other times mocks them in such an obnoxious way that most people fail to get a glimpse of the tenderness and an eternal yearning that lies buried under the bitterness, poison and sarcasm of Manto's writing. A yearning, a hunger, that can never be satisfied. Manto has been starving since the beginning of time. Each one of his stories is a plea as well as a declaration of his love for humanity. You must not be misled by his mannerisms. He continues to insist, 'I have no love for human beings. I can feel affection for a diseased dog but never for any human being.'

He will claim over and over again: 'I have no faith in friendship, benevolence, or affection. The only thing I believe in is alcohol. All this business of the Progressive movement is complete rubbish. I am certainly not a Progressive writer. I am just Manto or perhaps not even that.'

He says all this sometimes to mock, and at other times to shock and aggravate others. He says these things perhaps to deceive himself too but his eyes convey a completely different message. His pen, too, tells a very different story and it is our good fortune that he holds as little sway over his pen as he does over his tongue. He tries hard to camouflage his empathy for the agony of human beings, his love for them, and his progressive outlook. He uses the brush to colour his stories with mockery and derision but his pen refuses to be reined in by him and we find that, in all his stories, love for humanity boils over from the background.

I had begun editing *Naye Zawye*, a collection of short stories. I asked Manto to contribute and he soon sent his story. I feel that this story continues to be one of the best stories in Urdu to date. As far as the wider realm of literature is concerned, it can be placed on the same standard as Rajinder Singh Bedi's 'Krishna' and Hyatullah Ansari's 'Aakhri Koshish'. It is possible that such good stories will never again be written in Urdu. I have read the masterpiece 'Yama' and many other French stories on the same subject. I have conducted a detailed study of the characters of *Umrao Jaan*. But across all these novels and stories, I have not come across any character that can stand on the same footing as the heroine of 'Hatak'. Manto quite gradually, one by one, peels the layers off the life of a prostitute embedded in contemporary social structures. He dismantles them in such a masterly manner that not just the body but even the soul of the prostitute in the story is stripped of all its wrappings and stands naked and exposed in front of us. Manto has unclothed her with such brutality and ruthlessness that we look through her as though she were a piece of transparent glass. Manto paints this hideous sketch with revolting colours and yet he manages to create a kind of beauty that is unique. Not that it makes prostitution look irresistible. Neither does it arouse pity for Sugandhi and the life she lives. It makes us accept as true Sugandhi's innocence, her artlessness, she as a woman, her life, her longings, her pain. And it is this singular quality that turns a piece of writing into literature.

After 'Hatak' many of Manto's stories were published in different magazines and his brilliance as a short-story writer spread like lightning and touched the hearts of readers. It was around this time that I was called to join All India Radio and

I left Lahore and came to Delhi. I had been there for less than
a month when I received a letter from Manto saying that he
too was coming to Delhi and would stay with me. I had found
a small house near Tees Hazari as well as a servant to take care
of domestic chores and so I was quite comfortable. I had come
back home from office at about six in evening and was strolling
outside my house when I saw a gentleman—tall, a little bent,
fair—coming towards me with a leather bag under his arm.
He looked at me and started smiling. All at once, both of us
recognized each other.

'You are Krishan Chander,' said the newcomer.

'Manto,' I responded, and we embraced each other.

Manto was wearing a long coat. He entered the room,
took off his overcoat and chucked the leather bag on to the
sofa. He then bent his legs and sat on a chair in the position
in which Kanhaiyalal sits in films while playing the role of a
pick-pocket. I could not control my laughter when I saw him
sitting in that posture.

I told him, 'Here, have a cigarette.' It was a cheap variety.

'La haula wa la quwwata!' Manto exclaimed, 'Is this what
you smoke? I am surprised! How can you write such good
stories after smoking these! Smoking such cigarettes, you can
only be a clerk in an office! Krishan Chander M.A., can you
understand what I am saying? Here, smoke this 555 and forget
that those cigarettes even exist.'

The servant brought some fresh, warm phulki on a plate. I
said that they had been cooked in the pure ghee that I had got
from Punjab.

'Phulki, and cooked in ghee!' Manto shrieked, 'La haula
wa la quwwata! Look here man, you are worthless! Look
bhai, which idiot cooks phulki in pure ghee? The best way to
fry them is in dalda, not ghee. Just wait for my wife to arrive
and then I will offer you real phulki. Crisp and spicy, which

taste like the Ghaatan from Bombay. Have you ever been to Bombay?'*

'It is the first time ever that I have come even to Delhi. I have not the foggiest idea of the world beyond.'

'Come to Bombay. Just cut out this radio business. Here, drink.'

Manto then took out a bottle of whisky, Solan No. 1, from the pocket of coat he was wearing. He plucked out the cork from the bottle and said, 'Hurry up. Ask for the glasses. It's getting late.'

I had never had even a drop of whisky till then but Manto's expression was so unyielding and his gestures so aggressive that I felt there was a real danger I would be murdered if I refused. I remained completely unruffled and asked for two glasses. Manto started pouring out the whisky and then asked me, 'Which whisky do you drink?'

I said, 'Brandy or any other good English whisky.'

'Which English whisky? Whisky is not English, its Scotch, Scottish! The bloody English have no idea how to distill alcohol. How do they even dream of ruling over India?'

The advertisement for an imported whisky brand flashed in my memory and I hastily said, 'Don't be vague, ask for Haig.'

'Nonsense,' Manto said, 'Solan No. 1 is the best. The first benefit is that it is less expensive, and besides that, it is much more enjoyable than Haig and gives a better kick. You must never drink Haig from now. Drink only Solan No. 1. Understand?'

'I will never drink Haig now.'

'Should I pour some more?' Manto asked, looking at my glass that was almost a quarter full.

---

*Ghaatan is a name given to members of an Adivasi community which, at the time Manto was writing, formed a large part of the migratory labour population. An unnamed Ghaatan girl is the chief character in Manto's story 'Boo'.

I said, 'No more... As you wish... Pour some more.'

'So, do you want a Patiala peg?' Manto looked at me with surprise.

I quickly said, 'Yes.'

The truth is that I had no idea what a Patiala peg was. I only wanted to be let off the hook.

'You're quite an impressive drinker,' said Manto and looked at me with suspicious eyes.

The first drink was enough to knock me out. I did not drink after that. And because he could see my condition after the first drink, Manto didn't insist either. I made a clean breast of the fact that I was drinking for the first time. After Manto learned this, he began to enumerate the advantages of drinking.

'The pleasures of sin exist in alcohol. The delights that women can bring exist in alcohol. The honey of literature exists in alcohol. The freedom from mundane chores exists in alcohol. How long will you not allow yourself to be sullied? You have to create literature, not teach school children. If you don't experience life, commit no offences, do not come in close proximity with death, don't taste the spice of agony, don't drink Solan No. 1—tell me, how the hell do you think you can write?'

Manto too was knocked out of his senses after he finished the bottle. After that, his major problem was why I was Krishan Chander, M.A. and why not just plain and simple Krishan Chander. He then began to tease me by repeatedly addressing me as, 'Krishan Chander M.A.... Krishan Chander M.A....'

I too started teasing him to settle scores and said, 'You must first tell me, what you are. Minto or Manto? What, for God's sake is Manto? Mintoo? Minto? Manto...?'

And he continued to repeat, 'Krishan Chander M.A.... Krishan Chander M.A....'

We kept repeating this for a while and then fell asleep. I

slept on the sofa and Manto fell asleep sitting on the chair. I found him sleeping in the same position when I got up in the morning. The bottles were lying in disarray on the table, the glasses were empty and the rotis had gone stale.

I woke Manto. 'Get up.'

As soon as he did he said, 'If I could get a little whisky now, I could wash out the taste from my mouth. Did you know that the only way to kill off the taste of whisky from one's mouth is to have a couple of drinks? Do you understand? Get some whisky for me. After that I have to go to All India Radio.'

'Why?' I asked.

'I have been called to write plays.'

'But you were talking about me going to Bombay to work for films.'

'Forget it. Films be damned. Stop this nonsense. Ask for the whisky.'

He then opened his leather bag and took out the script of a story. He gave it to me and said, 'Read this. I don't show my stories to anyone. Absolutely nobody, not even if he was my own father. I am showing it only to you though you too are not that good a writer. But there is a special quality, something unique, in your stories. I accept that. Do you understand, Krishan Chander, M.A.?'

We worked together for two years at the radio station. Upendranath Ashk too joined us later. I was one of the play producers and Manto and Ashk used to write plays. I had to constantly try and maintain a kind of equilibrium between the two. Both were good writers and egotists of the same degree. The outcome was that many good plays were written for the radio during that time. Moreover, these were original plays and not translations from other languages. They were creations of bright and unrestrained intellects. These plays may be seen as those which popularized modern plays in Urdu literature. In fact, after this, Upendranath Ashk decided to devote all his energies and talents to the world of theatre.

Those were happy days. The three of us used to have frequent literary discussions and arguments. Stories got written; plays were penned down; essays were read out to each other. After some time, Bedi too joined us. Then came Ahmed Nadeem Qasimi, and after that Noon Meem Rashid. This congregation launched a new chapter in the world of Urdu literature. Nadeem wrote his long opera. Bedi was attracted to theatre for the first time. Rashid's *Mavara** was also published during this time. Devendra Satyarthi too meandered in and presented himself. He and Manto got along like a house on fire for the first couple of days but Manto's cutting and sardonic personality was at complete odds with Satyarthi's sugary demeanour. They could not get along for too long. Manto later attacked Satyarthi in one of his stories.** Satyarthi countered this with his story 'Naye Devta'. Manto was deeply affected by the story and its impact on him was evident for about two or three days, after which he dismissed the whole affair by saying, 'It's fine, all this business about "Naye Devta". Let's think no more of it.'

I too did not raise the issue. Manto used to often say to me, 'This is what I don't like about you. I want to quarrel with you, but you always manage to walk over. I really dislike this impertinence.'

I would reply, 'Why? Is it not enough that you have Ashk to quarrel with?'

The conflict between Ashk and Manto were a regular feature. They used to spar about almost every topic under the sun. They would often discover and debate such fine literary points that it left no scope for anybody to ever get bored.

---

*A collection of poems. Krishan Chander wrote the preface to the book.

**The story was called 'Tarraki Pasand'.

Manto had an Urdu typewriter and he typed out all his plays on it. He would insert the paper, sit down and start typing right away. Manto believed that no other machine is as sensitive as the typewriter and often said, 'Well-rounded letters, gleaming like pearls, materialize out of this uncontaminated, dust-free machine. It is very different from writing with a pen; a nib that is sometimes worn out, sometimes the ink is not enough, or sometimes the paper is too thin. A typewriter is as important for a writer as a wife for a husband, but here are Upendranath Ashk and Krishan Chander. Still scratching their pens on paper. Look here gentlemen! Do you think it is ever possible to create great literature with a pen costing eight annas? You are real asses! Idiots!'

I did not respond but two or three days later we spotted Ashk-saheb walk in with an Urdu typewriter tucked under his arm. The gentleman kept the typewriter on Manto's table and starting running his fingers over the keys.

'Listen,' Manto said, 'it's pointless to have only an Urdu typewriter. One must have an English typewriter too. Krishan, have you seen an English typewriter? I have one the likes of which you will not be able to find in the whole of Delhi. I will bring it one day and show it to you.'

Ashk bought not just the English typewriter but a Hindi one as well. When he came to office, the office attendant would follow him carrying his three typewriters. Ashk used to cross Manto's table on the way to his room to clearly underscore the point that he had three typewriters while Manto had only two. Manto got so annoyed that he sold off his English typewriter. Actually, he wanted to get rid of his Urdu typewriter too but that would have affected his work and so he decided to keep it. But for how long could he have been harassed by the three typewriters, and so he eventually sold off his Urdu machine as well. His rationale for doing so was: 'Say what you may, the machine can never replace the pen. The relation that exists between the paper, pen and the mind can never be achieved with the typewriter. And then the wretched thing makes such a racket with its continuous khat-khat... There is such a marvellous flow in the pen. It seems like the ink is being released straight from the mind and spreading across the surface of the paper. Oh! This Sheaffer pen is so beautiful! Have you ever seen such sleek and lustrous beauty? Just like a young Christian lass from Bandra!'

Ashk was badly stung and said, 'Do you have any principles at all? You were an enthusiast and an admirer of the typewriter until yesterday. You showered such praise on it. Today when I possess three typewriters, you have started praising the pen! Is this fair? I have spent one thousand rupees.'

Manto broke out into loud laughter.

One day, Manto walked up to me looking very pleased with himself. Handing a letter to me he said, 'Look here bhai, here's a letter from Ahmed Nadeem Qasimi. He has conveyed his regards to you too.'

I read the letter, which was delightful, but I also realized that Manto had asked me to read it because it expressed great admiration for Manto as a short-story writer. The last sentence of the letter was: 'You are the monarch of story writing.'

After reading the letter, I opened my drawer and took out another letter. This was also by Ahmed Nadeem Qasimi and I had received it that very day. I handed it to Manto and said, 'Bhai, the same gentleman has written a letter to me too. You must read this as well.'

The letter carried high praise for me as a short-story writer and the last sentence of the letter was, 'You are the sovereign monarch of story writing.'

I said, 'Manto, you are merely the monarch, I am the sovereign monarch of short-story writing. Superior to you! What do you have to say for that?'

Both of us started laughing. Nadeem had played a good trick on both of us. Manto then said, 'Let's both of us write to him and call him here.'

Those were the days when educated girls from respectable families were reluctant to participate in radio plays. When I came to Delhi, I found only three or four girls who were willing to work for us. However, that was also the time when a new kind of play, with its focus on the middle and high classes in contemporary society, was beginning to take shape. This brought in its wake the realization that our group was too narrow and needed to be expanded. I worked hard and managed to put together a group of ten or twelve girls who used to regularly participate in our productions.

One day Manto asked me, 'Listen bhai, how many girls can you get for your play?'

'What do you mean by how many? As many as you want.'

'Now, don't start bragging. I want to know from you.'

'Why do you need to ask? Write a play with as many women characters as you deem fit. I will manage to get them.'

'It's settled then. I will write a play with only women characters. There will be twenty-six or twenty-seven of them.'

'And you must call it *Ek Mard*.'

The drama was written and broadcast. We also managed to find a girl for every character.

There was thus an ongoing contest in everything that was done. If I wrote a good story, so did Manto and Ashk. And Rashid would pen down a poem. If Manto wrote a play, it became essential for Ashk to write one too, and then I too followed suit and tried to write one. All my plays, including *Sarai ke Bahar*\*, were conceived and written during this phase. Those days of companionship between Manto and me were

---

\*A very well-known drama by Krishan Chander. He later picturized it with his brother Mahendra Nath in the lead.

happy days. We were always cheerful despite the financial troubles that weighed on us. We wrote a lot, wrote with originality and enthusiasm, not with hearts that are wilted and insensitive.

It was during this time that Manto wrote his best dramas and stories. There was a mind-boggling flow to his pen. He used to write a new play or story every second or third day. Regardless of all the squabbling and the wrangling that went on among us, we worked amazingly well as a team. We stayed together day and night, thinking of ways and means to enhance the quality of our programmes. The radio artists were especially fond of Manto. He rarely came for our rehearsals but when he did, he spread such fun and hilarity with his sparkling jokes and witticisms that its impact stayed on for long after he left. These artists worked extremely hard and with unimaginable dedication to telecast Manto's plays that became immensely popular with the public. The extent of their commitment is evident from the fact that Manto dedicated one of his collections of radio plays to these radio artists.

It was around this time that Manto and I got together to write a story for *Banjara*. This was my first attempt at doing anything connected with films. We sold this story to some distributor in Delhi because we wanted the money to get new suits stitched for ourselves and had no hopes of receiving any money from a publisher in the near future. However, the most interesting aspect of this event turned out to be not our suits but a completely new experience that I had.

The seth to whom we sold our story heard it and said, 'The story is very good. We will buy it but Manto-saheb, you have turned the mill manager into a really evil man. You should present him as a good person otherwise it will have a bad impact on the workers.'

'Fine,' Manto said, 'we will turn him into a good man.'

I was flabbergasted and looked at Manto in utter complete shock. Actually, I was just about to respond to the seth by saying, 'That's not possible,' when Manto stopped me with a gesture.

The seth had not finished. He had other ideas as well and said, 'And then there is this manager's wife. She could have an unmarried sister who falls in love with the hero. She could be the vamp. How would that be, Manto-saheb?'

'That's good! That's good!' Manto said.

I was taken aback once more. Was this the same Manto who refused to change a line or even a single word at somebody's suggestion? His stories had to be published exactly as he turned them in, or else he took them back. Was this the same Manto?

I started looking at him with complete astonishment.

When we came out after our meeting with the seth, Manto said, 'Look here bhai, this is not literature. This is film. The educated, civilized and people with literary sensibilities have no control over it. The people who will assess our stories are the ones like Maulana Salauddin, Kaleemullah and Hamid Ali Khan, not people like Saaru-bhai, Tokarji Patel, or Mangu-Bhangu-Jangu and Brothers. It is child's play for us to turn mother into sister, sister into lover, and lover into vamp for films. Do you understand? Serve literature and make money from films. Now tell me, do you want the suit or not?'*

'I do.'

'Then the story for the film will definitely be changed.'

'Of course bhai, certainly,' I said.

Manto remains a Kashmiri Pandit even today as far as his temperament, physique and devotion is concerned. He is quite similar to Ashk in many ways. I realize that he will be deeply offended by this but this is not far from the truth. Ashk is

---

*Maulana Salauddin, Kaleemullah and Hamid Ali Khan were editors of various magazines.

also a Brahmin, a pandit. Both of them are tall and slim. Both
are hypochondriacs and are obsessed with the idea of taking
injections. Both have the stubbornness of Brahmins, their
intellect, as well as their impatience and exasperation. Both
of them are very talkative. Of course, Manto's conversation
has a strong dose of his distinctive humour. One may discuss
anything under the sun with him and discover his ability to
present a completely new perspective regarding it. To avoid
that which is commonly accepted has become a special feature
of his personality and he cannot abandon it now under any
circumstances. If you praise Dostoevsky, he will eulogize
Somerset Maugham. If you commend something about
Bombay, he will go into raptures about Amritsar. If you appear
to be an admirer of the merits of Jinha or Gandhi, he will
establish and affirm the outstanding personality of the cobbler
on his street. If you desire to have a dish of meat and paalak,
he will advise you to eat daal. If you express a wish to get
married, he will insist that you remain a bachelor. If you are an
exponent of bachelorhood, he will argue in favour of marriage
and persuade you to get married. If you express your obligation
for any favour he may have done you, be sure that you will be
abused. If you abuse him, you will discover that he has been
going around looking for a job for you. Manto's friendship,
enmity and vengeance are as peculiar as his personality. And
what is very clearly visible in both is the presence of many
different shades of genuine humanism.

His inflexibility, bluntness and acrimony are a kind
of protective armour with which he shields his internal
tenderness. His attempt to demonstrate how he is completely
different from everybody else is actually evidence of the fact
that he is just like all of us. In truth, he is much more deeply
wounded, more vulnerable, and more compassionate than any
of us. People have seen Manto laughing, drinking, mocking

his friends, denying the facts and realities of life in his usual sarcastic manner but I have seen Manto weep too. He does not cry either for the sorrows of the world or for his own miseries. He has neither suffered the agony of love, nor the anguish of any dangerous illness. He wept when he lost his one-and-a-half-year-old son.

I had rushed to his house as soon as I received the news. Manto stared at me with bloodshot eyes as if to say, 'You have come now, when he is dead and gone and we are taking him to be buried? Where were you before this? Maybe my child could have been saved if you had come earlier...'

His throat was choked and his eyelids swollen. He said, 'Krishan, I am not scared of death. I have not been affected by anybody's death but this child... I am not saying this because he is my son. I am saying this because... Just look at him... He looks so innocent, fresh, so sweet even now. I feel that it is a big tragedy when a new and unsullied idea meets a premature death. Each infant is like an idea. Why did it shatter? I have just seen the spark of life leave his body. I may die, you may die, old, young and middle-aged people may die... People keep dying, but this child... Nature should not have killed a new idea so rashly, with such haste.'

And then he broke down and started weeping bitterly. The armour of cynicism that he had built up all around himself was smashed to smithereens.

After that day, I never saw him weeping but those tears had transported me deep into that bottomless ocean within Manto where literature gets created. This ocean is dark green and golden. Its water is salty and many dangerous animals like sharks and octopuses lie waiting in its depths. But along with them, one also sees here multi-coloured, delightful rocky cliffs covered with green, velvety moss and the pure, shiny pearls spread out on them. It is only once that I have had a glimpse of this extraordinary panorama. You have seen the pearls that Manto brings out after diving deep into the depths of his heart. These are frozen drops of Manto-blood which he polishes with his sarcasm and cynicism before presenting them to you. You must not be taken in by Manto's style, for what he presents to you are pure and unadulterated pearls. It is our country's misfortune that it has not recognized their worth. Hindustan is considered to be a storehouse of literature, culture and the fine arts but, across centuries, we have been extremely callous towards our great artists without ever becoming conscious of our grave transgression. I have the example of Sehgal in my mind. When Sehgal passed away, we did not hear even a word of regret from the so-called eminent persons. These same people are the ones who whine about the condition of art and culture in our country. Just try and find out if they know the names and circumstances of major artists, writers, painters, singers and you will find that they will lose their voices and will try to justify their ignorance by blaming their busy schedules.

Clothes are not a major obsession for Manto. What he is fond of is a good home, good food and good alcohol. You will always find his home clean, orderly and well-decorated. He has the habit of working in clean and dust-free surroundings. Cleanliness, precision and refinement are special traits of Manto's temperament. The kind of disorder and grubbiness one usually finds in the homes of writers is completely non-existent in Manto's home. You will not find anything out of place or crooked. The only crooked thing there is the mind of the man of the house. But even here, one soon discovers patterns that are revealed only at the end of his stories. Manto's stories are a reflection of his temperament and his surroundings. Manto stitches the costume of his stories with extreme care. One does not find even a small crease. There isn't a single careless stitch. The hemming is perfect and after all this is done, it is ironed in the most perfect way. Manto's stories are tidy and uncluttered, and their language polished yet simple. Nonetheless, his stories have peculiar shades and a distinctive craftsmanship. Manto's metaphors are unique and devoid of succulence, cadence and uncertainty. He is not a devotee of beauty in literature but of geometry. For him, everything must be in correct proportion. He is conscious of the meanings as well as the limits of his metaphors. He aspires to impact the reader not through some unconscious idea of the beautiful but through a well-organized and well-balanced geometrical diagram.

Manto is very firmly rooted to the ground. In fact, he is so deeply embedded that even the tiny bugs which creep under the grass reveal all their special qualities to him. Those who are limited by their superficial vision will fail to either understand or commend Manto's sharp eye and its minute observations. There is no doubt, however, that on some occasions his exceptionally strong ego does prove treacherous to him. What also happens at times is that he is not able to successfully strike an equilibrium between life and literature as it exists in the region that is spread out between the bugs in the grass and the clouds floating in the skies. At these times Manto slides back into his own peculiar, personal temperament and becomes obdurate. This, however, happens rarely. Most of his literary works achieve the high goal of humanism; and within their garb of simplicity, truth and cynicism one discovers the vigour and the potential of generating the kind of beauty and tenderness that the human heart yearns to experience even until this day.

Manto was deeply influenced by Russian literature in his initial years. The fact is not in the least surprising since we find that not just Progressive writers but even writers who have been conservative in their approach have reaped the benefits

of the legacy of Russian literature. Nonetheless, in a short
time, Manto discovered a style of writing which was entirely
and distinctively his own. You will find many people who
imitate the writing style of Abbas, Ashk, Ismat and Krishan
Chander but nobody has been successful in imitating Manto's,
and to some extent, Bedi's style of writing. There is only one
Manto and only one Bedi in Urdu literature. Besides these
two exceptions, you are likely to find overlaps and similarities
between the works of most other writers. This is especially
true when it comes to the frankness with which Manto has
used his pen to articulate the issue of sexuality. As far as I
know, it is difficult to come across any other instance of this
kind of writing in all our literature, including that of Hindi,
as well as the translations that I have read from Marathi,
Gujarati and Bengali. To begin with, Manto first stripped off
the concept as well as the mantle of shame. He then combed
off the layers of filth, and then continued to scrub, wash and
polish the real subject to such an extent that today all of us
recognize the power of sex, its complexity, and its sway. We
are obliged to Manto for imparting this kind of sex education
to all of us. He granted us this sex education at the cost of his
youth and health. Manto has looked at the criminal world of
Bombay, including its chawls, its alcohol dens and its brothels,
very keenly. He himself sank knee-deep into it in his quest for
truth through this grime and muck. His clothes did get soiled
but his conscience remained free of all contamination and the
strongest evidence of this is the agony that lies hidden in his
stories. It is difficult to find as strong a supporter of the dignity
of women, their modesty and domesticity, as Manto is. He
becomes very restless when he sees a woman lose her honour,
her place in the family and her reputation; and then he, with
great impatience, begins to investigate the reasons behind such
occurrences. And when after close observation he repeatedly

discovers that the same patterns, the same social structures and systems are the cause, he loses his temper and wants to strike and attack them. Manto does not believe in pleading and appealing. He believes in striking and slapping. All his stories end with a slap; a slap so hard on the faces of his readers that it badly unsettles them and they begin to berate Manto roundly. Manto, however, does not stop. He never will. What critics call Manto's sadism is actually a much altered version of his wounded humanity and it is this that you will find in his mannerisms, conversation, writings and routine life.

There are many events in Manto's life that cannot be stated or written during his lifetime but there is one incident that I cannot help mentioning. It occurred when I was an employee at Shalimar Pictures, Poona, and had gone to Bombay to participate in a Progressive Writers' Association conference. Quite unexpectedly, I met Manto on the train. We were together for about ten minutes. After talking about this and that, Manto asked me, 'Listen bhai, I had sent a girl to "Sh" in Poona. She wanted to become an actress. Do you know what happened to her?'

I told him, 'That girl is with "P" these days,' and then added, 'you too perhaps have your own experience about her.'

Manto became very serious and said, 'La haul wa la quwwata! My experience is limited only to prostitutes. I don't ever go close to these respectable girls.'

This was Manto's distinctive style. He kept quiet for a while and then said, 'She looked really modest and decent to me. But then the need for a full stomach can crush anybody.'

After that, he was quiet for a long time and I began to get a feel of the qualms, shame and the inner purity that existed within him. He wanted to see the woman as entirely spotless, pure and revered. He wanted to clean off the filth from what he considered the source of life, creation and beauty. Can anybody call this approach anything but wholesome, decent and virtuous? We are left with little choice but to put our faith in Manto's literary honesty and become a supporter of his sincerity. At least, I have full faith in it. It is, of course, an entirely different matter that Manto may write a couple of stories just to contradict me. He has the ability to do so but this response is not evidence of his versatility or literary capability. A considerable part of his talent reflects his desire to enhance the beauty of human existence and sensitivity for the pain of humanity. This is the distinctive hallmark of his writing and can never be ever be erased or forgotten.

# Manto, My Enemy

## Upendranath Ashk

PEOPLE ASSUMED MANTO WAS MY ENEMY. THERE WAS always some dispute, fight or argument going on between us and there is no doubt that we hurt each other severely in the time we spent together. Krishan Chander wrote a sketch of Manto for the series *Naye Adab ke Memar* (The Architects of Contemporary Writing) published by Kutab Publishers. In that essay, he happened to mention the ongoing row between Manto and me and brought our antagonism into the public sphere. This became common knowledge, and a friend of mine mentioned it to me and said he would never forgive me if I did not write about Manto. But today, when Manto is longer in this world, I wonder if we really were foes. And when I look back to reflect over the last fifteen or twenty years, I can't help but think that we would have been good friends had our first interaction not started with hostility.

Our temperaments contrasted as starkly as do heaven and earth. Since childhood, Manto was an active participant of the gambling groups that would meet above the houses of Deenu and Fazlu, the potters. Manto saw card games like Flash even in his dreams and I had never as much as even touched a pack of cards. He was a heavy drinker and as for me, forget drinking, the first time I ever smoked a cigarette was in 1942 when I was thirty-two. He was a regular visitor to the flesh bazaars of Katra Ghoomiya, Hira Mandi or Foras Road and I had not so much as even sneaked a look at them. The fact is that my mother had filled my heart with hatred for these three things since childhood. The accomplishments of my respected father in all these three areas were so outstanding that I really do feel that the next two generations of my family can hold their heads high; they neededn't add anything more to these spheres of activity. It was because of my father's exploits that the condition of our household became deplorable and we spent our childhood in utter poverty. It made me so cold and rigid that even though I don't now consider smoking and drinking as undesirable as I did earlier, I cannot let myself go and freely indulge in them. Whenever my father had a drink or two, he would declare, 'Save nothing. Not even pennies. Not even for the shroud.' He lived in the present and never worried about or planned for the future. As a reaction, I had planned out my entire life in childhood. And Manto nursed a deep aversion to my abstinence, my calculation, planning, careful spending and stability. And he often expressed his dislike in harsh and blunt words. Manto had called me to work in Filmistan in Bombay. About two or three days after my arrival, Manto and I were seated in a Victoria, on our way to Grant Road. Manto had had a drink. Suddenly he told me in English, 'I like you though I hate you.'

A year and a half later we were sitting in the canteen at Filmistan. It was lunchtime and as usual, a few friends like Raja Mehdi Ali Khan and Vacha were sitting at the table with Manto. I, along with friends from my unit, was sitting at the table next to his. I am not sure how it happened but the discussion turned to kapaal kriya, the ritual of cracking the skull of the corpse on the pyre. Manto gnashed his teeth and said, 'I will perform Ashk's kapaal kriya when he dies.'

I was admitted to KEM Hospital. The doctors had declared my illness tuberculosis. Raja Mehdi Ali Khan came to meet me and said, 'Manto has been calling you names, saying that the fellow would not have fallen ill had he not been miserly.'

While travelling towards Grant Road, Manto had said, 'I like you though I hate you.' I had responded by saying that I too felt the same. The truth, however, is that I had said that merely for the sake of making a sharp, timely response and I have actually never nursed any hatred for Manto. As far as Manto was concerned, despite the dislike that he off and on expressed against me, and despite the contrariness of our dispositions, I know well that the two of us would have been good friends had I not flippantly passed a critical comment without having seen, known or read his writing seriously.

It was around 1938 or 1939 that Manto's story 'Khushiya' was published in a magazine. Rajinder Singh Bedi and I used to sit and discuss and write together in those days. He would read his stories to me and I would do the same. We would also often talk about and discuss stories by other contemporary writers and, as often happens with the young, our opinions were rather harsh and categorical. Bedi asked me my opinion about 'Khushiya'.

I had still not either read or met Manto. *Sarguzasht-e-Aseer*, Manto's translation of Victor Hugo's novel, *The Last Days of the Condemned* had already been published. I am not sure how true it is but I had heard that Manto had travelled to Lahore looking for a publisher for his translation of Russian stories. Anyway, these were the only two things I knew about Manto before the publication of 'Khushiya'. I had begun to write before Krishan, Manto and Bedi did and was older than them too. By that time some of my well-known stories like 'Daachi', 'Konpal' and 'Qafas' had already been published. I also considered translators inferior to writers and so Manto had little significance in my scheme of things. Obviously, I was already biased against the writer before I read 'Khushiya'. Moreover, I did not much like it. It enjoys prominence amongst Manto's stories and it is also true that he develops the central idea very well. However, my objection to the story was that the character of Khushiya is neither real nor credible and springs entirely out of the writer's imagination. One of my friends was a regular visitor of those lanes and by-lanes and I had learnt a great deal about the life and culture of those areas. I knew for a fact that pimps are the first to establish physical relations with prostitutes like Khushiya's Kanta, and so I was certain that the character of Khushiya was unreal and unconvincing. I had unconsciously nursed these ideas in my mind at the time when Bedi asked for my opinion. Those were carefree days and I still had not developed the habit of seriously weighing my words. I would impulsively say whatever came to my mind. I was on this track when I pronounced my judgment on the story to Bedi: 'It's worthless.'

I made the comment and forgot about it but Bedi committed it to memory. After some time Bedi joined All India Radio in Delhi. Manto was already working there. As was his habit, Manto would tease Bedi. I am not quite certain how and in what context it happened but Bedi mentioned my opinion about 'Khushiya' to Manto.

After he came back from Delhi, Bedi told me about how he had met Manto and added, 'I have communicated your opinion to Manto.'

I had not the slightest idea at that time that Manto's and my paths would ever cross and so I paid no heed to the information that Bedi had given me. However, it was in 1940 when I went to All India Radio on Krishan Chander's invitation that I realized for the first time the magnitude of the impact that my remark had had. Friends had expressed joy at my appointment and hoped that Manto would now be tackled in a befitting manner. Though we had still not come face to face, people had already begun to see Manto and me as opponents.

I discovered this on my second day of work. It was after a great ordeal and tribulation that I had come to Delhi and my very soul shuddered at the thought of confronting somebody head on. I had decided that at first opportunity, I would try to convince Manto that people just wanted to have fun at somebody else's expense and there was no reason why we should provide them the occasion. I, however, failed miserably. Firstly, because Manto was highly respected and held sway over the office. His word was treated as command. Secondly, Manto had already made up his mind to humiliate me. In those days the office of All India Radio was located in a huge bungalow on Alipur Road. The bigger rooms were for the Station Director, Programme Director and the Music Department. From among the smaller rooms (which must have been the bungalow's bathrooms) one was given to Rashid, the second to Krishan and the third to Manto. These rooms were next to each other. I can clearly recall that I was once sitting in Krishan's room—he had gone to the studio that was in a bungalow across the road. I was writing a feature when Manto strolled in. After talking casually about this and that he began to talk about 'Khushiya' and said, 'I know you didn't like that story.'

I tried to sidestep the issue but Manto was not one to give up easily.

'What is it that you did not like about it?'

I tried to drive home the point that I had joined the office as the Hindi Advisor and we had no reason to compete against each other. He must continue to work without getting disturbed and allow me to do the same. There is no point in arguing with each other and becoming a spectacle for others, though this is what they would love most, I said to him.

But Manto did not allow the issue to end there. He gestured with his hand to interrupt me and repeated his question. He also probably said something harsh too. Having no option, I said, 'The story is good but not real.'

'Why is it not real?'

I articulated my objection: 'An idea came to your mind and

you positioned yourself in the place of the pimp and wrote what your own response would have been in the situation. Actually, if Khushiya had been the pimp and Kanta had stood there naked in front of him, he would have immediately pounced upon her. What you have written is the way an educated writer may think and behave, not an illiterate pimp.'

I said something like this loudly, with a great deal of emphasis. Manto was quiet for a moment and then said with bitter exasperation, 'Yes. Yes, I am that pimp. Manto is that pimp. Do you have any idea about writing stories? What is it that you write yourself?'

But at that moment either Krishan came back or Advani, the Station Director, called me. I am not sure what happened but the topic was closed.

The issue, however, was never settled. Manto could never put behind him my reservation about his story that had led to the argument in Delhi. Many years later, the journal *Naqoosh* published the proceedings of a symposium on Urdu writers in a special edition. I have been writing Urdu stories for the last eight years. Unfortunately, most of them have been translations of the Hindi original. My friends and some other people connected with Urdu writing had forgotten me but Manto had not put me out of his mind. He did not forget to allude to my objection as well as his own response regarding 'Khushiya' at the symposium.

After that I tried my best to avoid any confrontation with Manto. I even carried my table to the second storey. All efforts were in vain. Whenever I was on the ground floor, or went there to see friends, Manto would look at me with deep contempt and express his extreme dislike of me in one way or the other. The image of that time is clearly imprinted on the canvas of my mind. Krishan Chander was in charge of drama. I was the Hindi Advisor. Hindi was not considered a significant language at that time and so there was not much work to be done. Consequently, I used to often have free time during which I managed to pen down a few plays.

Manto's usual style of working was to sit down in front of his Urdu typewriter and ask Krishan, 'So bhai, which theme should the play be written on?'

Manto would start typing as soon as he got the topic and by evening, he would hand over the script to Krishan. Manto was extremely proud of his ability and often declared that he could write plays on any topic under the sun. He was always surrounded by theatre artists like Ghulam Mohammad, Randhir (who is now an actor in films) and Taj Mohammad. Manto used to read out his plays to them even as he wrote. They would listen to him and exclaim, 'Manto-saheb, you are the king of plays!' And glug down tea at his expense.

He bonded with Javed and Hasrat because they all drank together. Advani was quite compliant when dealing with him because one of Manto's relatives was the Secretary of Information and Broadcasting. The words 'Manto-saheb' resounded in the corridors all the time and his suggestions were treated as commands. Manto was always surrounded by friends or flatterers. During lunchtime, people sometimes congregated either in Manto's or Krishan's room. I also sometimes went and stood there. Manto never allowed me to speak. He never failed to pass some or the other insulting remark about me. It is true that people never supported him against me but I would still get deeply distressed.

Finally, one day, I said to Krishan, 'Look here, you must talk to Manto. He quite pointlessly troubles me regularly even though I try my best to take no notice of it.'

'So, you also go ahead and trouble him,' Krishan said. 'I am sure he will not pay any attention to what I tell him.'

And that day I went to office determined to vex Manto in

some or the other way. His story 'Dhuaan' had been published a few days earlier and I had loved it. Manto had written with extreme finesse and delicacy about a very sensitive issue. But I was bent upon causing mischief. I had closely observed different aspects of Manto's egotism over a period of time and had therefore worked out a suitable strategy. I went to Manto's room soon after reaching. He too had just arrived. I went up to him and said, 'I read your story "Dhuaan".'

'What do you think of it?'

'It's good. Now you should write something about the libido.'

Manto stayed quiet for a few moments and, further widening his already large eyes, said, 'What do you mean?'

I did not respond to his question and merely repeated what I had said earlier, 'Now you should write something about the libido.'

Ismat had still not written 'Lihaaf' at the time. Manto actually would have loved to react by saying, 'And what kind of stories do you write?'

The only hitch was that he had declared a few days ago that he had not read any of my stories. So he said, 'I know what gibberish you produce. I have read your plays.'

'Forget about my plays because I am still learning to write them, but you are considered to be the king of plays. I know very well the bizarre things you do. You have stolen the plot from Maugham's story "Rain" for *Karwat*. Your play *Rooh ka Natak* is a complete translation of the original text and you have not so much as acknowledged it. (I had mentioned the name of the writer of the original text at that time.) I may not be writing good plays but at least they are original. Their good and bad points are mine, not stolen from someone else.'

Manto was incensed but I refused to wait there and went to Krishan's room. Manto was just about to begin writing his play. What I had said made it not only difficult for him to write, it also made it impossible for him to continue to sit in his room. He followed me into Krishan's chamber. He tried hard to talk to me about the art of writing stories. I evaded this and went to the studio instead. Manto followed me into the studio too but I managed to give him the slip once again.

That same evening, Vishwamitra Adil came to meet Manto with his friend and his brother-in-law, Mr Madan Mohan Bhalla. He told me that Manto had given him a collection of his stories and had abused me roundly saying, 'Who does this damn Ashk think he is! He does not even know the a-b-c-d of what a story is. His article on the art of writing stories in *Adab-e-Lateef* is pure nonsense...'

Manto continued to abuse me for three days. I could hear everything that was being said in my room upstairs. The spectators were gleeful and never missed an opportunity to tell me in detail everything that Manto said. But I continued to remain silent and smiled to myself thinking that the situation had turned out exactly as I had imagined. At the same time, I also regretted doing something merely to fulfill the expectations of friends without really desiring to do so.

I liked Manto's stories. I had read some very good ones after 'Khushiya'. I had really liked 'Naya Kanoon', 'Mantra', 'Shoo-shoo', 'Darpok', 'Mausam ki Shararat', 'Hatak', and 'Mrs D'Costa'. But for as long as I was in Delhi, not once did I praise Manto's stories in his presence. Manto had a sharp sense of discretion and even though flattery brought him a momentary pleasure, he lacked genuine respect for his flatterers. It was also quite strange that while Krishan was responsible for getting me to Delhi—where Manto already was—he always argued in Manto's favour in case of any altercation between him and me. Manto took advantage of Krishan's support, but the truth was that he had scant respect for him. In fact, he often showered abuse on him too. Manto was perpetually surrounded by flatterers in those days and my ego prevented me from creating the impression of being a part of that group. It was this that stopped me from praising Manto's stories even when I sincerely liked them. It was my conscious decision to disregard Manto's good stories and quite enthusiastically criticize the weaker, unconvincing ones. In short, there existed an ongoing battle between the two of us.

Obscenity was considered to be progressive in those days and Ahmed Ali, Ismat and Manto were the major torchbearers of this approach. While Krishan was not an open votary, he had worked out a formula for his stories which were peppered with obscenities even as they carried the usual ingredients of romance and progressive social satire. My understanding was that there were many other significant social problems that were no less critical than the marketing and violation of women's bodies. I failed to understand the rationale of the Progressive writers of the time choosing to write only about subjects that were obscene, and these bewildered educated young men making the rounds of the world of tawaifs. Whenever I told Krishan that this was not progressive writing, he would say, 'You are merely jealous since you cannot write in the way in which people like Manto and Ismat do.'

He of course included himself in that group.

I cannot fully recall if somebody suggested the theme or I thought of it myself, but it so happened that both Manto and I ended up writing stories on the thoughtlessness of employers who have sex in the presence of servants. Manto's story was titled 'Blouse' and my story was 'Ubaal'. Both stories were published in the same issue of the monthly, *Saqi*. Friends really enjoyed reading 'Ubaal'. Krishan too praised it. Later, an English translation of the story was also published and much liked by readers. 'Blouse' and 'Ubaal' represent both mine and Manto's writing at the time. The element of obscenity is more or less analogous in both stories—they bring to light the consequences of the sexual recklessness of employers which are visited upon servants. However, while the climax in 'Blouse' is unrealistic and fictionally convincing, that of 'Ubaal' subtly includes the issue of wider social tragedy within the explicit tragedy of the servant. The story may thus be seen as a sample of how social realism is represented in fiction.

It was because of my ongoing argument with Manto that I had written a story of this kind. Even though the story was much appreciated, I did not venture to write anything like that ever again. Not because I condemn such stories but because they do not agree with my taste and predilection.

Manto in his sketch of Bari-saheb* has shown him as a person who turned his back on hostile situations without confronting them. But as much as I have seen and understood Manto, I feel that some characteristics of Bari-saheb had rubbed off on him too. It is of course an entirely different matter that he himself may have been quite unaware of this aspect of his personality. The circumstances under which Manto had suddenly disappeared from Delhi were quite similar to the ones under which he ran away from Bombay to Pakistan. I was the reason for his fleeing Delhi and it was because of Nazeer Ajmeri that he left Bombay. The truth, however, is that Manto was himself responsible for his running away. He used to be perfectly content as long as he successfully routed somebody in a quarrel, but when the others aimed the same guns at him he could not take it and would flee the battlefield. Manto has criticized Nazeer Ajmeri while writing about his decision to leave Bombay saying, 'I have pondered a great deal but have

---

*Abdul Bari Aleeg, a teacher, journalist, writer and a member of the Progressive Writer's Movement. Manto acknowledged Bari-saheb as a mentor.

still not understood anything much. Finally, I said to myself, "My dear Manto, you will never find clear road for yourself... Just stop your car... Go, take that side alley." And I walked through the side alley and came to Pakistan...'

I was shocked when Manto suddenly disappeared from Delhi. While it is true that there was a rumour doing the rounds that he had found work in films, it was about two years later that Manto himself told me that he had no promise of a job when he left Delhi through that side alley after not finding a clear road. Just like he escaped Bombay a few years later.

Throughout his life, my father remained an adamant devotee of the idiom, 'Don't leave behind even loose change, not even for the shroud.'

His other favourite catchphrase was, 'If there is life, there will be struggle.'

And he proffered the advice generously to his sons too. As he had no doubt that at least one of his sons would achieve the distinction of being the fiercest, most violent fighter, he spent immense energy teaching everybody different ways of dealing with quarrels with opponents. The most important point he wanted to drive home was that only somebody who can tolerate being beaten will be able to beat others. It is much more difficult to put up with being beaten than to beat up others. So, do get beaten up but never allow the one who has beaten you to go scot free. I had delicate health since childhood and could hardly have got into physical fights like my father and brothers. However, the idea did strike root in my mind and whenever I have been beaten by someone in this battle of life I have made sure—after being initially overthrown—to eventually trounce and defeat him.

I had to deal with Manto on two occasions, the first time in Delhi and then in Bombay. I hurt him in Delhi but, in Bombay, we were eventually evenly poised.

Our relationship soured further after our confrontation regarding 'Dhuaan'. Manto was in top form and while Krishan was not harsh to me, he acted as Manto's armour and that diluted the power of my attack. But it was during this period that Manto's relationship with Rashid was destroyed because of his ego. Rashid was accepted as the architect of free verse and Manto intensely disliked it. Around this time, *Mavara*, a collection of poems by Rashid, with a foreword by Krishan Chander, was published. Manto ridiculed both of them. He wrote the drama *Neeli Ragen* in which he incorporated many words from Rashid's songs and tore them apart.

For some time Manto continued to jeer at free verse and make fun of Rashid's unusual similes. He then discovered some new interest and everything seemed to have blown over. Rashid, however, did not forget this.

Manto wrote a play and gave it to Rashid to read.

'How is it?' Manto asked him.

'It has been typed out really well.'

Rashid said this with his special sarcastic smile and Manto smouldered and burnt till he had, to put it in his own words, 'become a kebab'.

After this, Manto continued to curse Rashid and his poetry for many days. He also persuaded a friend of his to publish an article on Rashid's poetry.

My position as the Hindi Advisor provided me with the opportunity of spending a lot of time with Rashid. An unending discord had sprung up between Manto and Rashid, but Manto could not harm me much since Rashid was my neighbour too. Manto, however, left no stone unturned in embarrassing me. It was probably around 1942 that Rashid was promoted to Programme Director. After this, the first thing that Rashid did was to get Krishan transferred to Lucknow. He got the orders passed when Krishan was absent from office. The fact of the matter was that with the exception of Rashid, Krishan was the most competent person in office. All Programme Assistants used to seek Krishan's help in planning their schedule. Obviously, they also listened and abided by whatever he said. Even the Programme Director often sought Krishan's advice and help in many things and so none of them ever interfered with his work. There were many things that Krishan got cleared by the Director straightaway. Rashid was quite dictatorial and found it difficult to accept Krishan bypassing or ignoring him and so he got him transferred. I was, however, very disconcerted by the manner in which Krishan had been transferred to Lucknow. Rashid had made certain accusations against Krishan in his absence. Krishan was immediately transferred since Rashid personally knew Bokhari- saheb. I expressed my displeasure to Rashid but that only resulted in him becoming angry with me as well.

After Rashid became Programme Director, Manto managed to get over to his side the other Programme Director, Surendra Chopra. Manto presented a good suit to him on his birthday and won him over. Since Advani was happy with me, he asked me to take charge of Krishan's work till the new Programme Assistant joined. Manto's play was scheduled and I was to produce it. I clearly remember how Manto would regularly come to the studio for the rehearsals, even though he generally took very little interest in his plays.

It was around this time that a Programme Assistant for Hindi arrived from Lucknow to take over Krishan's position. He was a really ugly, tall and bulky young man with a flat nose. Advani called him and me to his room one morning and told him to learn the ropes from me. Krishan's room had only enough space for a table and two chairs. After the meeting, I took Krishan's chair and began the day's work. Soon, Manto caught hold of that Programme Assistant from Lucknow and explained to him that since he was the Programme Assistant, he should be sitting in Krishan's chair and not me. This man from Lucknow held quite a high opinion about himself and this made the situation no better. He had not liked being asked to learn about his job from me. He had consulted Rashid, too, who informed him that I was just an artist and that he was the one responsible for the entire Theatre Department. If something went wrong there, he would be held responsible for it. I had no idea what was transpiring. I was sitting in Krishan's chair, going through the day's work, concentrating on the script, when Manto came with the Programme Assistant from Lucknow. He pointed at my chair and said, 'That is your chair.'

He then pointed to the other chair and said, 'You come here.'

I lifted my eyes and saw the authority in the eyes of the Programme Assistant and a victorious gleam in Manto's. I grasped the situation in a split second.

'I am going to the room upstairs,' I said, 'you come up there in case you need anything.'

And I walked away, blinded by anger. When I discussed all this with Rashid I discovered that he had already met the new Programme Assistant. Rashid also believed that the new person must learn on the job himself through trial and error. He too had not approved of the fact that Advani had asked me to work in Krishan's place without consulting him. Actually, I myself was not at all eager to take up the post of Programme Assistant and had already refused it once earlier when Jugal-saheb had asked me to take it up. But it was an entirely different matter to be asked to leave once I had taken it up. I was deeply offended that this happened in front of Manto and that too basically due to his own maneuverings. I first felt that I should go to Advani since he was the one who had sent me there. Then I reconsidered the situation and concluded that Advani would not be able to do much. The glow of victory in Manto's eyes bored a deep wound in my heart. The idea of resigning from the job also crossed my mind in its agitated state, but then I felt like laughing at the absurdity of the thought. I was, however, still annoyed and when I went to my room upstairs, the gleam in Manto's eyes flashed through my mind once again. Only God knows that if Manto had not turned up with that Programme Assistant from Lucknow that day, and his eyes would not have had that gleam, I would not have done all that I did and Manto would not have had to leave Delhi.

That day I found it difficult to work even after going back to my room. The jagged memory of my humiliation continued to stab me. I was angry with Rashid and with that Programme Assistant from Lucknow but I was angriest with Manto. The gleam I had seen in his eyes was evidence enough of the fact that the one who had humiliated me was neither Rashid nor that Programme Assistant but Manto. I made up my mind to settle scores with him for the conspiracy he had hatched. An additional reason for my anger was that, as long as I had worked in Krishan's place and produced Manto's plays, I had made a conscious attempt not to alter even a single word written by him and produce the plays as best as possible.

I am not sure if my ancestors were trained in Chanakya's ashram, or our family was in some way related to him, or I had heard my father relate stories about this high priest throughout my childhood, I had begun to think like him. Anyhow, I find that my ability to think, plan and comprehend becomes much sharper when I am trapped in a difficult situation. And I have never forgiven people—be they equals or superiors—who have insulted me and have always avenged the insult. I have not only emerged from tough situations, I have always surged ahead.

I pondered the situation and came to the conclusion that the

Programme Assistant from Lucknow must be quite the idiot. While it was true that Manto was the one who had provoked him, surely there could be no doubt about the foolishness of a man who could be swayed and influenced by Manto! Even at that time I was quite well known in the world of Hindi literature. It is difficult to believe that he would not have known me by name. If he had even a modicum of intelligence, he would have talked to me in private and certainly never in a dictatorial tone. I finally concluded that I must use that idiot himself as my weapon. I went down after sometime and found the Programme Assistant sitting proudly, his flat nose screwed up, nostrils flared, narrating anecdotes about his exploits in Lucknow. Manto, quite contrary to his usual behaviour, was sitting quietly, his feet on the chair, his knees folded and encircled with his arms, listening to his boasting. I went to the room and kept standing. There was no chair for me to sit on. After some time, Mr Chopra's peon arrived to call Manto away. I then said to that man from Lucknow, 'I just found out that you are a Hindi person. This station was in dire need of a Hindi Programme Assistant.'

And I invited him for tea to my house in the evening.

In those days I used to live in the Tees Hazari area which has some hilly ranges and a pleasant forest nearby. It was a wet evening. I offered some tea to the idiot and then took him to the ridge. The clouds had gathered and it was drizzling lightly. He continued to praise himself endlessly about how he wrote plays and about how Chab-saheb, the Station Director in Lucknow, had told him that nobody could write scripts as well as he could, and how he pulled strings to get him the position of Programme Assistant. I too boosted his ego and gave an additional shot in the arm by praising his personality. I also drove home the point that people would remain in awe of him only if he was able to establish his authority right at the start, since the artists could quite easily pull wool over anybody's eyes. I also told him that it was the responsibility of the Progamme Assistant to carefully read and vet all plays which were to be broadcasted. He declared that he would not allow even a single word to be broadcasted without reading and vetting it.

'I will write my plays in Devanagari now since you know Hindi and are here,' I said to him. 'And I could read out to you the ones written in the Urdu script. You can hear them and then weigh their worth before broadcasting them because you will be held responsible and scolded in the meeting if any substandard play is cleared and broadcasted.'

This resulted in me being further enlightened about his qualities through another torrent of self-praise that issued forth. In short, he was quite happy when he went back.

The schedule used to be prepared three months in advance and Krishan had finalized it before leaving. I used to write plays once a month or, sometimes, once in two months. Manto's two or three plays were broadcasted every month. Manto's play was next in line. As far as I can remember, it was titled *Awara*. I have forgotten the plot but I do remember that like Manto's other plays, this too had been written in a day. It was the very next day that the Programme Assistant from Lucknow brought out the script and called me in. I took him to the studio and began to read it to him. He hardly had any knowledge about language or playwriting. While reading out the script, I often said, 'So then, saheb, how would it work if we substitute this word with that?'

And he responded, 'Yes, yes, that's better.'

I kept changing words and idioms with a red pencil. I also circled a few words and told him, 'Rashid-saheb is dead against using such words.'

I knew from my experience of more than a year that I did

not need to change anything in the script. All I needed to do was circle words in red and the Programme Assistant would surely change the words himself. Thus, the onus of making changes would fall on him. So, I edited the climax of Manto's play and proposed three climaxes instead.

What followed was exactly what I had hoped for. In order to make an impression on Rashid, that man from Lucknow told him that he had read Manto's play, mulled over it with great effort, and felt that it was half-baked. And that Rashid must have a look at the script and clear it for broadcasting. Rashid was nursing an old resentment against Manto and felt that he had found a suitable opportunity to avenge himself. So he altered the words which I had circled in red.

Manto was ready to commit murder after he discovered that his play had been vetted. He went to the Director's room and gave both Rashid and the Programme Assistant from Lucknow a piece of his mind, declaring that the play should be broadcasted without any alterations or not at all.

I used to sit upstairs in the English announcer Noby Clarke's room. The ventilator of Advani's room fell straight in my line of vision. Manto was screaming so loudly in Advani's room that I stood near the ventilator and bent down for a view of the room. Rashid was saying that he had read the play and if it was to be broadcasted at all it would be with the alterations in place, or it would not be broadcasted. He was not ready to be held liable for deviations from the schedule. If we can evaluate the writings of outsiders, he said, why should the same not be done for the writings of our own artists? Manto was agitated like a caged tiger, almost roaring and repeating that the play would be broadcast without alterations, or not at all.

I experienced a wicked pleasure when I saw him so deeply traumatized. Manto had abused me so often; he had put barriers on my path to progress; he had lied to me and cheated me of forty rupees when he sold his Urdu typewriter to me; and to top it all had announced how he had managed to fool me. I felt compensated for everything in the agitation I saw him going through.

'A strong blow from a smart man is better than a hundred punches by an idiot,' I said to myself and turned away from the ventilator.

I don't clearly remember what decision Advani finally took. He probably decided not to interfere with the Programme Assistant's jurisdiction and left it to him to settle the issue. Anyhow, I was suffused with a devilish contentment as I came back and sat on my chair. I stretched my legs out on the table and drew a deep breath of satisfaction.

But despite this exhilaration and satisfaction, a strange feeling of pain and gloom took hold of me. Manto's distress, the creases on his beautiful forehead, his bulging eyes, all of this flashed through my mind, along with the realization that I was the reason for it all. I, who was actually fond of Manto; I, who wanted to sit with him; I, who was a much bigger fan of his stories than his other so-called admirers; I, who had dedicated *Charwahe*, a collection of my stories, to him a few months earlier.

A copy of *Charwahe* is lying in front of me as I write this. The dedication says:: 'For Manto, whom I immensely like sometimes and dislike at others.'

How accurately it reflects my feeling for Manto at that time!

The issue of the play was presented in the meeting the next day. The Programme Assistant from Lucknow, on Rashid's advice, submitted a written critique of the drama. This was the first time that a play yet to be broadcast was being discussed and criticized in a meeting at All India Radio. But Rashid had raised this issue in the meeting since substituting the play under consideration with another in case of its rejection was a deviation from the routine schedule. The Programme Assistant from Lucknow had already prepared a critique that he read out straight away. Never before had Manto been criticized, and that too in a full and open meeting. Manto was not at all accustomed to hearing criticism in this manner. He said a few unkind things about the understanding and the judgment of the Programme Assistant from Lucknow. Manto did not think twice before saying harsh things. I lost my cool once again and voiced my agreement with the criticism stating that I too had had a look at the play. I highlighted its weaknesses quite effortlessly since I was the one who had edited it.

I have now forgotten what exactly Manto said but I remember that he made some derogatory remarks about my ability, which in short meant that I had no knowledge about technique. He also asked me, 'Can you write something better than this and produce it in front of me?'

I responded very sharply: 'I can spend at least the next decade teaching you how to write plays. Just come up to my room and I will show you how plays ought to be written. And I can also show you how this play can be improved.'

The matter would have become further aggravated but Advani-saheb came out of his room when he heard the commotion. Finally, it was decided that only the revised version of the play would be broadcast and since the matter concerned our own artist, there would be no 'deviation' from the schedule.

Manto did not stay in the office after the meeting. He picked up his typewriter and went away. He did not come to the office the next day too. The office received a phone call from Khursheed-saheb, Secretary of Information and Broadcasting, that if Manto's play was broadcast at all, it should be faithful to his original script or else it should be entirely scrapped.

I do not clearly remember the sequence of events.
Khursheed-saheb had probably asked for the play and sent the
message after seeing it. Since Rashid was determined not to
disturb the schedule and get only the revised play broadcasted,
Manto had got the whole thing done through Khursheed-
saheb.

Manto did not come to office even on the fourth day. He
had asked for the script of the play to be returned to him. It
was on the fourth, fifth, or perhaps the seventh day that we
heard he had gone away to Bombay to join a film company at
a salary of five hundred rupees a month.

Sitting in the Victoria on Grant Road, Manto had told me
that he had not found a job in Bombay and had had a very
tough time there. He had left his wife behind in Delhi. It was
after some time that he got a job for three hundred and fifty
rupees in Filmistan and it was perhaps his friend Nazeer who
travelled to Delhi and fetched his family to Bombay.

'That script which was made red all over by you is still with
me,' Manto suddenly said.

In short, just as I was angry neither with Rashid nor with
that Programme Assistant from Lucknow but with Manto,
Manto too was angry with me and not with either of the other
two. He had found out that I was the one who had edited his
play.

'What are your plans now?' I asked him.

Manto was quiet.

'Look here. What happened in Delhi must be left behind.
I will not accept the job in Filmistan if we continue with our
quarrels. I earn three hundred and fifty rupees there but I am
comfortable. If the same nuisance continues here too it is
pointless even if I get five hundred.'

'No! No! Nothing like that will happen here,' he said and

then went on to complete his statement by adding in English, 'I like you, though I hate you.'

I went to Manto's house that day and said to Safia-bhabhi, 'Please keep in mind it is Manto who called me here. I have come only after he sent me two telegrams. Manto has already let me know that he has preserved the copy of *Awara* and has still not forgotten the incident that occurred in Delhi. We constantly quarrelled in Delhi and provided great entertainment to our colleagues. Now he has called me to Bombay. You must persuade him not to trouble me here. If he does, I too will trouble him and this will end up with both of us getting troubled.'

Both Manto and Safia-bhabhi assured me that nothing like that would be repeated and I accepted the job though I had still not signed the contract. When I thought about the whole situation I decided that as far as possible I would not allow things to reach a point where I would have to quarrel with Manto. I met all my acquaintances in Bombay to find out as much as possible about Sashadhar Mukherjee, the overall in-charge of Filmistan. I also tried to get information about how the place functioned. I took special care to meet people who had earlier worked with Manto but had left the place. I discovered three or four important facts:

Mukherjee, the boss at Filmistan, was like the sadist police inspector of old days who would make people labour like slaves under the power of their whip.

Filmistan was solely under Manto's command.

A year earlier, when Shahid Latif had first proposed my name, Manto had opposed my coming to Filmistan, saying, 'Ashk is a very dangerous man.'

All the dialogue writers in Filmistan wrote out the same scene. Manto read everybody's dialogues, rejected them all, and then wrote them out himself. Of course, that was undoubtedly the best. It was Manto's style of functioning that had left no option for Shahid Latif and Santoshi but to leave Filmistan. Even though Shahid Latif was the one who had brought Manto to Filmistan.

The question was that if Manto considered me dangerous less than a year ago, then how could I have become harmless now? It was Manto himself who asked me to come to Bombay. I had refused when I got Manto's first letter but a month later he sent me a telegram asking me to come for the interview, adding that the second-class fare would be paid by the company. I agreed since Kaushalya too had to go to Bombay for her training. I thought that even if nothing comes out of the trip to Bombay, it will be a break and an outing. However, despite having taken the decision to go there, I kept wondering why Manto had called me to Bombay. I had arrived at an understanding at that time but that had to undergo some amendments after I met Manto and learned of the situation there. Nonetheless, my basic assumptions did not change. Since this narrative has a psychological aspect, and that happens to be very interesting as well, I feel that I must at least touch upon it.

I have already said earlier that I did not hate Manto. It is essential to spend time together before one can begin to hate or love another. I had never met Manto before I went to Delhi and when I did meet him for the first time, I liked him as far as his features and personality were concerned: fair complexion, a slender body, a broad forehead, sharp nose, and a sarcastic smile that seemed ready to offend. This image of Manto is the one that I still carry in my mind.

In the meantime, I had read 'Mantra', 'Naya Kanoon' and perhaps 'Mrs D'Costa' too and really liked them. Manto had made a place in my heart not as a translator but as an intelligent and sensitive writer. Our roles had however been chalked out for us even before I went to Delhi and we could never rid ourselves of them. We were to be adversaries and that is what we ended up becoming.

Nonetheless, I was deeply remorseful when Manto suddenly left Delhi. Krishan had been transferred to Lucknow. Rashid had seen to it that Akhtar-ul-Iman was served notice. Chadha, Meeraji and Raja Mehdi Ali Khan spent all their time wheedling and cajoling Rashid. Rashid perceived me as Krishan's ally and was always on the lookout to harass me. Manto's absence had turned out to be rather arduous for me. It is true that there were constant skirmishes that often deteriorated into personal wrangling when Manto was there, but what is also true is that the presence of good writers provided the stimulation to write well too. Besides that, I also felt a peculiar intimacy with Manto. After Manto's departure for Bombay, I lifted the blockade that I had perforce imposed upon myself about not praising Manto's stories. 'Boo' was published about a year or a year-and-a-half after he went to Bombay and led to an explosion. Chaudhary Nazeer asked my opinion about the story and I praised it highly. I was not much concerned about the content of 'Boo'. What I admired was the technique with which Manto had broached and worked upon a highly sensitive theme. The alertness and restraint with which Manto had written the story did not just deserve appreciation, it was also worthy of being emulated. I had read the story to several of my friends, including Yashpal, the well-known Hindi short-story writer. I recommended that every Hindi writer must read 'Boo' to understand better the technique of short-story writing. Bedi's 'Lajwanti' is the only story that I feel may be seen as being at par with 'Boo'. Besides that, there is no other story in Urdu literature that I can think of as being even close to it. 'Lajwanti' is exceptional not just because of its form but because of its content too.

Anyhow, I seem to recall that I had written a letter to

Chaudhary Nazeer in which I had referred to 'Boo' and he in turn had discussed it with Manto. In fact, I discovered that he had sent its summary to Manto, who mentioned it to me once I was in Bombay. Perhaps it was after finding out about this letter that Manto's attitude towards me softened a bit. This is probably the reason why Manto proposed my name when Nitin Bose, the director, came to Filmistan to make a film and they began to look for a new dialogue writer.

But there was another reason too. I was somewhat instinctively conscious of it but it was in Bombay that it became substantiated. I would have happily lived under the misconception that Manto nursed no hard feelings about me and that his earlier antipathy had thawed, had he not, while discussing the events that had occurred in Delhi under the influence of alcohol, mentioned the script of *Awara* that I had rehashed. But the truth is that Manto had never forgotten the incident. About a year earlier, his standing was not very strong in Filmistan. It would have greatly perturbed Manto had I had come to Bombay at that time and formed a clique with either Shahid or Santoshi. Both Shahid and Santoshi had already left Filmistan and Manto had become the apple of Mukherjee's eye before he decided to call me to Bombay. Friends told me that Manto would shred my dialogues to tatters and that though I would get a good salary, my life would become hell. I immediately understood that he had planned a way to avenge the way in which I had minced his play. It was not possible for me to withdraw at that stage since I had already agreed and the information that I was going to join the film industry had already been widely disseminated in Delhi. I therefore decided not to go back; however, I also prepared a well-thought-out action plan for the duration of my stay at Filmistan.

I did not put my signature on the contract until I managed to get a chair, a table and a separate room for myself. This was my first safety measure to rule out chances of quarrels with Manto. I also ensured that only I would write dialogues for Nitin Bose and do the dialogue direction.

My first film was *Mazdoor* and the second one was *Safar* which was directed by Bibhuti Mitra. I wrote dialogues for both films and in this way, my first year and a half in Filmistan passed quite comfortably. Manto was of course quite out of sorts when he discovered that I had successfully sidestepped the trap he had laid for me. I knew my own disposition well enough and so planned the whole thing to avoid any new confrontation or quarrel.

But despite all my caution, Manto was eventually successful in harming me. My first film *Mazdoor* did not do well at the box office but my dialogues were acknowledged as being one of the best that year, 1945, and I was even awarded a certificate for it. My second film *Safar* was a hit and naturally my reputation and credit perked up. It was at that time that Ashok Kumar expressed his desire to produce another film and Mukherjee too agreed to work with him. Each of Manto's two films *Shikari* and *Chal Chal Re Naujawan* had taken two years each to be completed but had still turned out unsuccessful. So, Ashok Kumar approached me and asked me to write a story. I narrated two or three plots to him. Ashok Kumar selected one and asked me to write its outline. I, however, told him that I would write only on the condition that I be paid two thousand rupees for it. I did get a salary of six hundred and seventy five rupees at that time but my view was that I had been employed as a dialogue writer and not as a story writer. I would charge two thousand for writing a story while dialogue writing would be a part of my job. Though Ashok Kumar and Mukherjee were brothers-in-law, their relationship was quite a strained one. Ashok Kumar asked me to talk to Mukherjee. I refused since I knew that Mukherjee was not very happy with me. He then told me that he would talk to Seth Chunni Lal and I should write down the outline in the meantime.

When Manto found out that Ashok Kumar had asked me to write a story and I had demanded two thousand rupees, he joined forces with Vacha. Vacha was known to serve the best alcohol. He took Ashok Kumar to his flat and did not allow him to leave until it was settled that Manto would write the story for a new film and that the mahurat for it would take place the very next day.

Since there was no ready story and the mahurat of *Aath Din* did happen the next day, the film ran into a lot of rough weather. That of course is an entirely different story. Manto had complete information that I had asked to be paid separately for writing the story and had agreed to do so after being assured of the payment. (It is of course also true that when the film was midway, Manto too started demanding that he be paid for the story and successfully managed to wrangle some money.) What I really felt bad about was that Manto had conspired to get me kicked out and especially at a time when I had already finished writing the outline of the story and was waiting for Ashok Kumar to have a look at it. The mahurat of *Aath Din* took place and since Mukherjee was not very happy with me I had little choice but to eat humble pie.

But within a few days, I worked out a strategy for revenge. It was decided that Dattaram Pai, the editor of Filmistan studio, would direct *Aath Din*. Though it was Ashok who was the director for all practical purposes, Dattaram Pai was an extremely capable editor and his word carried great weight. I joined hands with Pai and bagged the comic role of Pandit Tota Ram in *Aath Din*. The role was a minor one, limited to a scene or two when the film first took off, but I played the part so well, and that too without any retakes, that Ashok decided to extend it through the whole film. I was the one who wrote the dialogues for Pandit Tota Ram since the character was to speak in Hindi. If Manto wrote one line as Pandit Tota Ram's dialogue, I increased it to four; if he wrote one scene for him, I extended it to two. I am fond of stage acting and do not consider acting in films worthwhile but I still continued to play that comic role only to trouble Manto. And he became really vexed with all this. One day the situation deteriorated so much that we came to blows.

This time around, Manto and I left Filmistan together. Vacha and Ashok were Manto's friends and he went with them to Bombay Talkies which Ashok had bought over after separating from Mukherjee. Manto, however, failed to deliver even a single story there. I met Ashok Kumar on my way back from Panchgani. I asked him, 'Why did Manto leave?'

He told me that Manto had written a story but they selected 'Mahal', a story by Kamal Amrohi. Manto left without saying a word. This despite being told that the next film would be made on his story.

There was a clear split between Vacha the sound recordist who was Manto's friend and Vacha the owner of Bombay Talkies. Moreover, Manto had become surrounded by the same people who had left Filmistan because of him. So when he found that the road ahead had become blocked, he just walked down the side alley and left for Pakistan. It is true that both Vacha and Ashok had received a few letters about having Muslims in key positions; but the studio could not have been destroyed and everybody working there left jobless. Moreover, all this did not have any effect on either Shahid Latif or Nazeer Ajmeri. The real reason why Manto became so dispirited was that Nazeer Ajmeri's story was the one which was selected first and then Kamal Amrohi's story was the next to be chosen. Manto decided to leave Bombay the day he found out about the selection of Kamal Amrohi's story.

There was a very big difference between Manto turning his back on hostile situations and Bari-saheb doing so. There was an element of cowardice in Bari-saheb but in Manto's case it was his strong ego that became the reason for his backing out. And it is within his ego that the secret of Manto's greatness is concealed. Manto was not averse to flattering others. I have seen him sit close to Mukherjee and reel out Ghalib's couplets just to cajole him. (Though reciting Ghalib to Mukherjee was like singing to the deaf. This of course in no way takes anything away from Mukherjee's genius. He was incomparable in his own field, but appreciating Ghalib went beyond his abilities. As far as he was concerned, even a minor poet from Bengal was better that Ghalib.) I have seen Manto narrate vulgar jokes in get-togethers with Vacha and Ashok. I have also seen him sit amongst illiterate actors and music directors and jabber rubbish with great gusto. (Manto called it 'rubbish' while the others described it as 'humour'.) None of these things that he indulged in hurt his ego because, first and foremost, he considered all others to be inferior to him; and secondly, even if these people thought of Manto as erratic or a drunkard, they considered him to be a dialogue writer of the highest order. The meeting at All India Radio where Rashid, the Programme Assistant from Lucknow and I criticized Manto's play, and Ashok's decision at the studio of Bombay Talkies to select not his story but those by Nazeer Ajmeri and Kamal Amrohi, were incidents that seriously wounded his ego. After that it became very difficult for him to continue staying there. A thick-skinned opportunist would have stayed on but this kind of humiliation was something that Manto's ego was incapable of tolerating. And since Manto did not possess the ability to hit back after being hit, he fled the battlefield on both occasions, and each time he had to undergo severe hardships. He almost came close to kicking the bucket the second time but his ego still did not allow him to strike a compromise and avoid distress.

It was important for Manto to be the cynosure in parties or meetings both formal and informal. If any other person happened to become the centre of attention, Manto would quietly slip out without as much as saying a word to anyone. While it is true that I had witnessed this facet of Manto's ego right at the start of my job at Filmistan, there is one specific incident that I can never forget.

The year was 1945 or '46. I can't recall what month it was. A famous actor from America or England was visiting Bombay. Just before this, I happened to have seen a film in which this actor was shown participating in a motorcycle race. His antics during the race were so very funny that the viewer was left in splits. This actor visited a couple of studios in Bombay. Rai Bahadur Chunni Lal invited him to Filmistan too. That evening S. Mukherjee, Ashok, Vacha, Chitalkar, Burman and Nepali gathered in the open canteen.* That actor was a little delayed since he had to first visit the Film Producers Association. The senior Mr Mukherjee decided to leave but the others continued to sit there and chat. Manto sat with the bosses and in Shyam's words, 'continued to fritter away his witticisms on them'. I was sitting with Nepali, Burman and some others. Finally, the actor arrived with his wife. He looked exactly as he did in the film. He had a long face and it seemed as though his jaws had been held from both sides and pressed together. His wife was very beautiful. It was evident that the craving for wealth and fame had brought the beauty

---

*C. Ramchandra, actor, music director and singer, sang under the name Chitalkar. Burman was Sachin Dev Burman, music director and singer. And Nepali was the nom de plume of the poet and lyricist Gopal Singh Nepali.

and the beast together. Anyhow, Rai Bahadur Chunni Lal
and Mukherjee were the first to walk in, a little ahead of
him. The canteen had one large table with several smaller
ones scattered around. The big table was for the bosses and
the other people were sitting at the smaller ones. I sat with
Nepali at a small table. Manto, along with Ashok and Vacha,
continued to sit at the big table. A large number of people had
accompanied the actor. Some friends of Rai Bahadur were also
there. Ashok and Gyan Mukherjee were of course amongst the
bosses. Mukherjee gestured to Vacha and Manto suggesting
that they sit at one of the smaller tables. Vacha got up to sit
with Chitalkar at a small table. He tried to persuade Manto to
sit with him but Manto refused. He quietly slipped out in the
ongoing confusion about seating guests. I was watching the
show that was playing out in front of my eyes. When he passed
me on his way out, I asked, 'Why?'

'Let's go.'

'Why?'

'All this is nonsense.'

'Sit,' I said to him. 'We have waited for more than an hour
for this nonsense to happen. Let's just wait another half an
hour while it's going on.'

But Manto did not stop. He quietly slipped out of the
canteen.

Manto's sketch of Shyam* in the collection *Ganje Farishte*
reflects this facet of Manto's egotism. Shyam was visiting
Lahore and he had many fans who were keen to meet him.
Shyam was like a magnet attracting people and this was a
serious blow to Manto's ego. Manto writes:

'Shyam told me, "Stay with me." I was, however, deeply

---

*Sunder Shyam Chadda, a prominent leading man of the time and a great
friend of Manto's.

disturbed by his mental restiveness. I promised to meet him at the Faletti Hotel that night and left.'

But whatever I have seen and understood of Manto leads me to believe that it was nothing but his ego that made him walk away from his old friend who had wished him to stay. I had seen him go through the same turmoil and caginess on the arrival of the American actor. Manto suddenly became sad when Mukherjee gestured to him to leave the table. After that it became impossible for him to continue. Manto did meet Shyam at the Faletti Hotel but the outcome of this visit was no different from the earlier one and Manto left the place in a much more aggrieved state. When he was with Shyam in Bombay, it was not Shyam but Manto who was the centre of attention. He managed to attract the actors and directors towards himself due to his skillfulness, his jokes and his sense of humour. However, in Lahore, the crowd was not constituted of artists but ordinary people, all of whom knew Shyam. And if some among them did know of Manto, it was clear that the heat of the moment had wiped him out of their minds. I know very well how this would have aggrieved Manto who considered himself superior to everybody else.

Manto was a master at mercilessly cutting down others to size but had no talent for going through a similar slaying himself. He cracked jokes about others but had no ability to put up with them if he became the target. He was extremely sensitive and touchy. And despite being an exceptional writer with deep psychological insight, he did not seem to realize that others too could be sensitive and touchy. I used to sometimes ponder this issue but I then realized that this was a common human weakness. Tolstoy was blinded by lust several times but persistently criticized it in his short stories and novels. Balzac unmasked innumerable truths in his short stories and novels but could never understand in real life that wealth must not be squandered away on childish things; that one should neither build castles in the air nor borrow money thoughtlessly. I understand these things quite well today but in those days I was not aware of this fact of life despite crediting myself as being someone who had figured out the truth about the world.

When I went to Delhi I discovered that one of Manto's stories, 'Tarakki Pasand', had become a major subject of discussion. It was because the story was constructed around the characters of Devendra Satyarthi and Rajinder Singh Bedi. Since Bedi was very close to me I read through the story as soon as I found some free time. The incident at the core of the story was something I knew about because Bedi had told me of it. Satyarthi suffered from the literary disease of reading out his stories to others. He once stayed with his family in Bedi's house and began inflicting his stories on Bedi every morning and every evening.

Bedi was a clerk in the post-office at that time and lived in Lahore cantonment. He hardly had any space in his two-roomed house and it was difficult to find any privacy with Satyarthi's continuous presence. Satyarthi would be all set to read out his story when Bedi reached home exhausted after a full day's work. To make matters worse, not only would Satyarthi read out his story, he would also seek Bedi's opinion. Not stopping there, he would ask Bedi to tweak and revise his story as well. All this would also seek on till late in the night. When he got up in the morning, Bedi had to listen to the revised version. Satyarthi stayed there for a month and Bedi, during this time, hardly got time to even talk to his children. This is the main plot of Manto's story 'Tarakki Pasand', except for the fact that he has made the ending somewhat dramatic by describing how Parmarthi (Satyarthi's fictional name in 'Tarakki Pasand') becomes a pest and gobbles up every second of his host's time to such an extent that the poor man finds no place but the bathroom to be amorous with his wife.

The story is good. It is spicy as well. I found it interesting too, but felt bad that Manto had captured in writing that incident of Bedi's life which he had himself narrated. I think Bedi was the only one who had any right to put it on paper, or Manto should have sought Bedi's permission before writing the story, but the writer in Manto did not have the patience for this. He wrote impulsively as soon as any idea came to his mind. He did not even bother to consider the fact that writing about personal events carried the danger of destroying friendships and raising barriers between friends.

However, this did not happen to Satyarthi and Bedi. On the contrary, they formed a joint front against Manto and the two got together to write a story in which they took the lid off Manto's private life and failings in much the same vein in which he had ridiculed Bedi and Satyarthi's conduct, physical attributes and private life. The story was published in Satyarthi's name and he was the one who did actually write it. The story is titled 'Naye Devta'. Bedi had of course read through it and his creative contribution resulted in excellent characterization.

The writers of 'Naye Devta' have derided Manto's behaviour, habits, selfishness, inebriation, egotism, caprice, perversion, his writing about sex, and many other flaws in such a poised manner that he was badly stung. Later, as was his habit, Manto himself began to spread ideas about how mean and quirky he was.

The publication of 'Naye Devta' led to a hullabaloo in the literary circles of Lahore and Delhi. Manto did not think twice before humiliating even his closest friends. He also did not consider anybody to be as good as himself and so this incident gave his friends and companions an opportunity to get back at him. Whenever friends got together, they would manage, through some or the other means, to raise either the topic of the story, Satyarthi or Bedi, and tease Manto. Manto would be very annoyed at the mere mention of the story. I recall an incident connected to this.

It was lunchtime and people had gathered in Bedi's room after finishing their meals. There was some chitchat. Bedi, his head hanging low, was sitting on his chair and listening to everybody. Manto was seated on the chair just opposite. He had pulled up his feet and was sitting on the chair with his arms wrapped around his folded knees. Rashid, Quddus and many other Programme Assistants were standing around Manto. Hafiz Javed had spread out a durrie on the floor and, sitting with his back to the wall, was quietly listening to the conversation going on around him. I had arrived a bit late and, since there was no space in the room, I had seated myself on the chest of records that stood in the corner of the room. The chest was quite high and I sat with my legs dangling. Just then somebody mentioned Satyarthi, describing him as a substandard short-story writer. The person was immediately challenged by someone who said, 'But he has done wonders with "Naye Devta".'

'Wah! Well done!' Krishan suddenly responded to the comment, raising his head and his right hand.

But as soon as he said this, his eyes met Manto's who was suddenly on the alert at the mention of Satyarthi's name. Krishan's raised hand gradually came down and he lowered his eyes once again.

Not to be stopped, somebody added, 'Oh! You think that Satyarthi really has the gall to write such a story? It was Bedi who actually wrote it.'

'No, it's not Bedi's writing. It's definitely written by Satyarthi. Bedi has just embellished it and made it sharper. We've heard that Faiz contributed too.'

Hearing this, Manto brought his feet down. His large eyes

widened further and looked like they would leap out of his face. All other voices were drowned in the rough abrasiveness of his when he said, 'Not just Bedi and Faiz, even Taseer has contributed to it. So have Tabassum, Sant Singh Seekhu and Mohan Singh.'

And then he added in English, 'Manto is an institution.'

I am not sure what came over me at that point but I did not allow Manto to finish, 'People really do cherish misconceptions about themselves. That Shyam Lal Kapoor, the editor of the magazine *Guru Ghantal*, he too believed himself to be an institution.'

The mention of Shyam's name was followed by loud laughter but it was silenced before I could finish what I had begun to say. Manto got up, crazed with anger, and hurled the choicest abuses at me.

On any other occasion, I would have planted a tight slap on Manto's face in response but one needs flair to joke as much as one needs it to quarrel. The person who gets aggravated by jokes and abuses, or hits out in response, is the one who is truly vanquished. People guffawed even more loudly at Manto's abuses. Krishan did not. He held Manto's hand and said, 'What are you doing?'

Manto restrained himself immediately. He held my hand and said softly in English, 'Don't mind it!'

At that time I would not have raised my hand against Manto even if he had abused me further. However when Manto abused me once again, I got ready to beat him up. There would have been bloodshed if he had not stopped himself.

This happened when we were in Filmistan. *Aath Din* was being shot and I was playing the comic role of Pandit Tota Ram. Most of the shooting for the film was done at night and Manto was not in the habit of coming to the sets during night shoots. However, he started attending after I shrewdly managed to get the role and began changing the dialogues he had written. He disliked night visits to the sets because that was his 'drinking time', but he started coming because he was apprehensive that I would end up distorting his dialogues.

I nursed a grudge against him for the way in which he had harmed me in connection with the story for Ashok Kumar and was determined to give him a hard time too. It is, however, my practice to hardly ever quarrel in a way that makes me appear to be in the wrong. I always try to ensure that the onus falls on the other. On this occasion too, I provoked Manto to such an extent that he lost control and abused me. Those who heard him naturally came to the conclusion that the fault lay with Manto.

On set, I had to get the hero married. I was sitting on the ceremonial seat with my torso naked and a dhoti tied around my waist. Wrapped around my neck was a long scarf with the name of Lord Ram printed on it. The pandit's turban rested on my head. The scene included a quarrel between me as the pandit and the hero's mother (played by Leela Misra), and a short dialogue that required me to deliver the following words: 'So, what do you think I am doing here? Merely killing time! Merely angling around!'

Ashok Kumar was directing the scene. Manto had had his drink and was quietly sitting on the side watching. A mischievous idea crossed my mind and I suddenly said, 'I cannot deliver this dialogue.'

'Why?' Ashok asked.

'"Killing time" is a really violent phrase. A pandit sitting in the ceremonial seat, a scholar of the Vedas, a follower of dharma, can never utter a phrase like this.'

'But it is just a popular idiom,' Manto said, peeved.

'There are many idioms that decent people never utter. In the same vein, a pandit who is about to perform a ceremony will never utter a violent idiom.'

'But the gist of the idiom has nothing to do with violence.'

'Killing? Angling? Angling the fish? Killing it? What does all this mean? Its gist may be whatever but a pandit can never, ever utter it.'

'People from Bengal don't just fish but also eat it.'

'But Tota Ram is not from Bengal and neither is the film about Bengalis.'

'You are talking rubbish.' Manto was annoyed. 'You have no choice but to deliver the dialogue.'

'I cannot utter these words. I am a Brahmin sitting on a holy, ceremonial seat.'

'I too am a Brahmin,' Manto thundered.

'Your ancestors may have been Brahmins. What you are doing right now is merely killing time. Angling! Fishing!'

And then Manto lost control and flung out an abuse.

I can't help smiling when I think of how absurd my objection was. The truth is that even that day I was smiling internally, though on the outside I had remained utterly serious while emphasizing the point that no devout pandit would sit on the holy seat and utter those words. The objection was completely insubstantial but anybody who is familiar with the film-world knows that making such objections is common. Despite the objection being totally insubstantial, an issue such as 'should a Brahmin utter or not utter a dialogue like this' becomes imbued with immense consequence. The people from the film-world are very insecure and even the most determined atheist here has a mahurat. Ashok and Vacha began to see the point of what I was saying. My position was further fortified after Manto abused me. Since I was not joking and had made up my mind to take up cudgels against him, I said, 'Look here Manto, I am not a wrestler but I also know that neither are you. If you utter a single word anymore, I will physically throw you out of the studio.'

The incident took on a colour that made Ashok extremely anxious. The shooting stopped. He was worried that if both of us refused to budge, the shoot would come to a standstill, resulting in the loss of four thousand rupees. He took Manto along and went out of the studio. A little while later, after we returned to the set, Manto pressed my hand and expressed regret.

After that, he did not sit there and went home. He never again came to the set during night shoots. I revised not just dialogues but complete scenes. Manto, however, never confronted me after that day.

Manto's favourite hobby was to utter abuses. His routine talk was peppered with ordinary, commonplace abuses but he cherished a desire to hurl a couple of really obscene ones at Krishan. Krishan, however, never allowed a situation to reach that point. Manto, of course, wanted to abuse me too. I have related two such occasions already. He abused me on another occasion again. The tension between us had somewhat diminished in those days. (Mukherjee had invited Santoshi back once more in order to harm both Ashok and Manto. He had also selected one of his songs for *Aath Din*.) I didn't know much about this but Manto disapproved of Santoshi's visits since he had asked me to write songs for him. We were walking from the music room to the office when Manto, while going up the steps, abused me in a low voice.

There was a time when my language too was sprinkled with abuses. My much-respected father was an expert at exploring and discovering new and innovative invectives. Even otherwise, Jalandhar is a region that is highly productive in churning out these new ground-breaking word. When friends meet, they welcome each other with those hefty words. I too was no different. (Today, that seems like a dream, and even though my wife still considers me rather uncultured, the fact is that there is a complete contrast between the Ashk from Jalandhar and the Ashk from Allahabad.)

I wish there existed a camaraderie between Manto and me; we could have abused each other with ease. The abuse he heaped on me while going up the office steps had no element of warm informality or friendship. It carried within it the unseen sentiment of condescension and denigration. I realized that if I tolerated the abuse in silence, I would become the victim of many such abuses, and the absence of an easy comradeship would make it impossible for me to abuse him in response.

I immediately reacted. 'Look here Manto, if you are from Amritsar then don't forget that I am from Jalandhar. You will be completely razed to the ground if I begin to abuse you. Don't ever dare abuse me again.'

Manto never again abused me after that day. His immeasurable frustration was expressed in his desire to perform my kapaal kriya but he could dare abuse me no more.

Why did a constant tension exist between Manto and me? Why did we keep quarrelling with each other? I have deliberated a great deal on this and have come to the conclusion that the two of us were placed on the opposing sides of the chessboard of life and were left with no option but to relentlessly clash. Our fight continued even when we just happened to merely sit with each other. We were like pawns attacking the opponent's move to checkmate and defeat him.

It is not true that we did not try to come together but our egos and extreme caution became a major barrier between us. Whenever I attempted to work out a reconcilement, Manto refused to patch up and remained obdurate.

Once it so happened that evening had come, the lamps were lighted, and I was sitting at my table writing either a play or a story. Kaushalya was in the kitchen preparing dinner. Suddenly, I heard somebody call me from outside in a harsh, sharp voice, 'Ashk'.

'Manto!' I thought and my heart missed a beat because I had gone to his house (9, Hasan Building, Kashmere Gate, Delhi) three or four times but he had never come to my house in the last year and a half. This despite the fact that the distance between our houses was not more than half a mile. My house was not the only one that Manto had not visited. He had never visited Kishan Chander's, which was very close to mine, either.

I did not respond immediately. Neither did I get up to open the door. I knew that it was Manto's voice but I found it hard to believe that it could really be him.

'Ashk,' the same harsh, sharp, somewhat irritated voice came again.

I got up and opened the door. Manto, Safia-bhabhi and a fair young man with beautiful eyes and sharp features entered the room.

Manto made the introductions.

'This is Masood Parvaiz (I have forgotten whether Manto said that he was his nephew or friend.) He wanted to meet you and so I brought him here.'

I had two small rooms besides another anteroom and a kitchen. On one side of the sitting room was a table and chair to work on and a durrie and a thick sheet was spread out on the other side. I pointed towards it and said, 'Sit, sit.'

I then called out to Kaushalya and said, 'Come and see. Manto and Safia-bhabhi are here.'

Manto and Parvaiz sat down and Safia-bhabhi went into the kitchen. I tried to strike up a conversation until Safia-bhabhi and Kaushalya joined us.

I remember nothing about this meeting except that Masood Parvaiz had very attractive features and beautiful eyes.

I glanced at him many times through the corner of my eyes. I was convinced that one day he would become a famous film star. (He was employed in some film company at that time or perhaps was trying to get into one).

Manto kept talking of this and superficially touching upon one or the other topic. I, however, remained frigid and distanced and made no attempt to get actively involved in the conversation. I did not even bother to ask Parvaiz about which writings of mine he had read, when he had come to Delhi, what he did and how long he would stay? (CHECK) I did not give any personal touch to our talk. I allowed Manto to do all the talking. In fact, after Kaushalya joined us, I left them to carry on with the conversation and pretended to work.

Why did I behave in this manner? Whenever I try to think about this, I find it difficult to believe that Parvaiz wanted to meet me and Manto had abandoned his evening drinking-session to get him over to me. I can accept the fact that Safia-bhabhi may have wanted to meet Kaushalya. She was fond of Kaushlaya and Kaushalya too had a lot of regard for both Manto and Safia-bhabhi but Manto mentioned nothing about any of this. I did not believe that the excuse he had offered for coming to my house was true. And then, the manner in which Manto came to my house, the way in which he had called out to me, the posture in which he sat, the style in which he spoke, all of it was done in a manner that unmistakably communicated that he had done me a great favour by coming to my house and that I should remain eternally obliged to him for doing so. He managed to quite casually communicate to me that he had not visited Krishan's house in the last one-and-a-half years. It was the manner in which he had done all this that offended me.

I am not sure what Manto felt about this meeting but as far as I am concerned, I found it difficult to forget the poor taste in which it had happened. I am quite a vagabond and Manto is a, of course, a vagabond par excellence. But if we happen to be in the same spot, something tugs hard at the strings of our egotism in a way that they immediately get highly strained. I distinctly remember wondering why I was sitting at the table pretending to write instead of sitting on the durrie with Manto, Masood, Safia-bhabhi and Kaushalya. Why was I not participating in the conversation going on between them? They had come to my house and I should not have been so petty. But I could not warm up to the visit; I could see through Manto's real intention, which he had camouflaged under some kind of superiority complex. I certainly felt a fleeting sense of pity for having somewhat dethroned Manto from his zenith but at the same time, this also gave me a great deal of pleasure.

Manto never again came to my house either in Delhi or Bombay. He preferred to leave Delhi and go away rather than climbing down any further.

A month and a half after the birth of my son in Bombay in 1945, Manto suddenly came to me and said, 'Safia has come. She wants to meet Kaushalya. Take her along with you.'

I was writing the dialogues for *Mazdoor* at the time and though there was no occasion for any competition between Manto and me, he used to be clearly irritated while talking to me. Manto came down with Safia-bhabhi when the car from Filmistan arrived. He walked up to the porch of the office to see her off. After she sat in the car, I told Manto, 'You too come along,' though I knew he would not.

'No, you go.' Manto frowned. Then he turned and went away without even waiting for the car to start.

I have already said that our roles had been predefined for us and we had little option but to enact them. It was not just a matter of our nonchalance, egotism or stubbornness; the state of affairs was such that friends had presumed we were opposed to each other and assessed all our actions in that light. It may or may not have been our intention to needle each other but friends always construed everything as being such. I recall a small incident.

During his days at All India Radio, Manto usually dressed in a khadi kurta-pajama but sometimes he also wore suits. Manto had probably been paid for a story for some film, or perhaps for no specific reason, he had got a very good suit stitched for himself with cloth that cost around ten or eleven rupees per metre (which was considered a very high price at the time). It was during that time that Kaushalya had quit her job and received a consolidated amount of three hundred rupees as her Provident Fund along with a year's salary. Kaushalya got a good suit and a sherwani stitched for me from the money she had received. I wore the suit to office. During the meeting, Manto and I incidentally sat to Krishan's right.

Krishan asked me, 'So then, what's the cost of the cloth?'

'Twelve rupees a metre,' I replied.

Krishan looked at Manto. He smiled mischievously and said, 'He will not spare you from a challenge in any field.'

The meeting started before Manto got the opportunity to say anything acidic or nasty.

Krishan, in an essay on Manto, has mentioned typewriters and has greatly dramatized the incident. It is not true that Manto had two typewriters and that I had bought three. The fact is that Manto had an Urdu typewriter and I bought two typewriters, one each for Urdu and Hindi. In doing this, I did not intend to compete with Manto but the event was represented exactly as such by friends and they also quoted it to heckle Manto.

I had seen Manto using his typewriter and had liked the idea. I began to feel that I too should buy one. The other reason lay in the admiration with which Krishan and other friends looked at Manto when they saw him typing out plays. They were truly impressed and praised Manto for this. Manto too was proud of the fact that he had the ability to directly type out anything on any topic. He would often ask Krishan, 'Tell me Krishan, on what topic should the play be written today?

However, sometimes the topic could be decided by a radio artist too. Once Ghulam Mohammad said, 'Manto-saheb, write a drama on Randhir.'

And Manto's fingers immediately settled on the keys of the typewriter and started generating words on paper.

786—then the title, *Randhir Pahelwan*, Randhir the Wrestler. After that—the sound of herding the cattle, the jingling of ankle bells etc.—Along with this were heard the words, 'May you get bitten by a snake—May you break your limbs'—now the song... Let the song start—and in the background the mooing of cattle and tinkling of bells can be heard.

Then, another day somebody said, 'Manto-saheb, write a drama about kabootari, the hen pigeon'

And Manto immediately started typing.

The crowing of the cock—the sound of footsteps of stony stairs—again, the crowing of the cock. The sound of two girls humming a song, as if they were whispering a prayer under their breaths—this humming goes on or a few minutes, then the aarti starts—aarti gets over—(silence)—the holy bell rings again—(silence)—it rings the second time—sound of footsteps on stony stairs (to communicate that the two girls are walking out of the temple).

These long dashes and breaks are a very common feature in Manto's plays and are evidence that he used to continuously think while writing. After he started writing, he would stop after completing a paragraph or two and light a cigarette. He would pull up his feet on the chair, sit for a while and then start writing once again. Manto had once spelled out a formula to me. He said it is best to pen down a couplet or a song if one can think of nothing much. Keep working out the next dialogue in the meantime and if you are still not able to do anything, then just write poetry in prose.

I had already written some successful plays such as *Lakshmi ka Swagat, Huquooq ka Muhafiz, Paapi, Samjhauta* and *Chatha Beta* before I joined the All India Radio. I think plays that have the possibility of being staged are the ones that can fall in the category of good plays. It is a fact that plays written for the radio have immense potential and, even today, the number of people who listen to plays on radio is much higher than those who go to see them on the stage. This gap was much wider ten years ago, but after Independence people have become much more knowledgeable about theatre. Plays are being staged with a lot of enthusiasm in schools, colleges and the amateur stage. Earlier, there were hardly any performances and those which were staged occasionally were more often than not translations from the original in English. I have been fond of the stage since childhood and I have been trying my best to revive it. I have attempted to write plays that could be staged easily without much expense. Moreover, it has always been my effort that original Hindustani plays and not ones translated from English, must be made available to people who wish to stage them. The accuracy of my assessment may be judged from the fact that today my plays are read and acted all over the country, from Kashmir to Trivandrum and from Punjab to Bengal. The sale of collections of my plays is much more than those of my short stories and novels.

Manto's radio plays did not impress me. It is true that Manto has experimented successfully with new techniques and has managed to fully exploit the potential of the radio.

However, after seeing and listening to his plays, I have arrived at the conclusion that plays for the stage can be redesigned for radio after minor alterations and people who listen to the radio would find such plays no less interesting than any other radio plays.

Though Manto's plays did not make an impact on me, it is true that I did nurse the desire to directly type out one or two plays on the typewriter and show Krishan that it was not difficult to either type or write a radio feature in this way. And then one day, I mentioned the idea of buying a typewriter in front of Manto. He had bought his typewriter on installments and knew the agent well. The agent came at once to the office. I filled up the contract on which Manto signed as a witness. Manto wanted that, like him, I should also buy the typewriter on installments. I too had signed the contract for installments but then realized that I would eventually end up paying three hundred and twenty-five rupees for a typewriter that cost two hundred and twenty-three rupees. I felt that the interest being charged for such a small amount was too high and so, when the agent came to collect the installment, I paid him the full amount. This resulted in the sowing of another seed of hatred in the hearts of my friends. Manto, Krishna, Rashid... all of them were dead against saving money. They squandered money as soon as they got it. It did not matter whether it was earned or borrowed. Manto did not like the fact that I could pay two hundred and fifty rupees at once even when the typewriter was available on installments. Actually, I too did not hoard money but after the death of my first wife I had been badly humiliated for a measly sum of sixty rupees that I had borrowed from a relative. After that, I decided to never borrow money from anyone and to get into the habit of saving even under difficult circumstances. I had fifteen hundred rupees when I started my job at All India

Radio. I clearly remember how friends would tease me about the fact that Manto typed out his plays. In the same vein, they began to tease Manto about me paying the full amount at once. I did not have much problem learning to type in Hindi since I already knew how to type in English. So, I practised for about a month and then directly typed out a feature and handed it over to Krishan. When our friends found out about this they began ragging Manto and said, 'Look here bhai, your monopoly has ended.'

Anyhow, I soon bought an Urdu typewriter too and started going to office with both the typewriters. Friends began to mock Manto again. I remember the day when Manto and I had left office together. Manto was carrying the typewriter in his right hand and a leather bag in his left. I carried the two typewriters in both hands. Manto was heckled so badly by friends that evening that he got exasperated and said, 'I am going to sell off this damn typewriter and start writing by hand.'

But Manto never wrote his plays by hand and neither did he sell off his typewriter (even though Krishan Chander has so written). Manto continued to type as long as he was at All India Radio in Delhi. When I went to Bombay at his invitation, I found that the typewriter was still with him even though he had not used it for a year.

Images of large pieces of leather and a brush float across my mind when I think of that typewriter; for these were the two things that Manto kept along with it. Every morning when he came to office and kept his typewriter on the table, the first thing he did was to clean the keyboard with the brush. He then used the leather pieces to further buff the keys till they began to shine. After that, he would bring out the file with his papers from his beautiful bag and settle down to type.

Manto was always very clean and tidy. It is only proper that Devendra Satyarthi in his story 'Naye Devta' has named him Nafasat Hasan. While it is true that Manto did sit and drink in grubby hotels and restaurants, his love for cleanliness was reflected in everything inside his home. He did not hesitate to clean up the house if his wife happened to go out. Once, when I had just joined my job, I had gone to his house at 9, Hasan Building, Nicholson Road, Delhi. When I reached, I saw him sweeping the room with a broom in his hand. His khadi kurta-pajama was covered with dust. He widened his large eyes still further and gestured to me to go sit in the living room. I have often wondered what was so special about those large eyes— which almost jumped out of Manto's face—that I have never been able to forget them!

Manto came in after having a wash and changing his clothes. Krishan probably wanted the script of a new play. Manto pulled out some very beautiful files with glittering brass clips from inside a drawer. Actually, Manto used to cut the files we got from the radio station into two and use them as two different folders. He used to place the script inside these two covers and clip them in the middle, upar neeche aur darmiyan. I may or may not have been impressed by Manto in any other way but I was deeply impressed with his refined taste and methodical style. I loved this way of storing one's scripts and the first thing I did after reaching home was to go the market and buy a hundred clips. I then clipped my scripts with glittering brass clips too.

I don't have much idea about the amount Manto charged for his stories or about the royalty he received. When he was in need of money, he would hand over his story, play or collection to a publisher at any cost, however small. As far as I know, he had given over the copyright of about twenty or twenty-one stories to a publisher for just three hundred rupees. What was however true, is that he was against giving his stories to a publisher without receiving payment. Quite on the contrary, Krishan did not care about payment. I am not sure about what he does now but in those days, he would give away his stories without taking any money (not merely the stories, he had even handed over *Tilism-e-khayal*, his collection of stories, without taking any advance). And since he did not demand any payment for his stories, the publishers of magazines often published his photograph as well as comments in his praise. Krishan had a unique way of asking for payment. He made no demands at the time of giving the story but at some later stage, he would ask for some amount under the pretext of some urgent need and thus also gave the publisher an opportunity to feel that he had obliged him. I functioned in a way that was different from both Manto and Krishan. I have never given a story free of charge. I never bothered about the story being published in the beginning or the end of collections, but as far as possible, I tried to obtain full payment. Obviously, whether it was Chaudhary Nazeer, Maulana Salahuddin, or Shahid-saheb, nobody was happy with me. Anyway, the one thing that was common between Manto and me was that he used to take the payment (small or big amount) at the time of handing over the story, and so did I.

I remember an interesting incident regarding this that occurred in Delhi. There was a gentleman named Agha-Sarkhush in Delhi. His father was a well-known poet and he used to bring out a magazine, probably called *Chamanistan*, in his memory. Agha-Sarkhush once came to the office. He had all the abjectness and the dithering of parasitic publishers looking for a free lunch. Sarkhush entered the room after seeking permission and stammered and faltered as he introduced himself. I recognized him immediately. I had seen him on some earlier occasions: entering Krishan's room like a thief and whispering into his ear.

However, I offered him a chair even though he refused to sit. He kept standing and told me that he wanted to bring out a special issue of *Chamanistan* in memory of his father, the famous poet Agha-Shair-Qazalbash. He also informed me that Krishan had promised to contribute a story and requested me to do the same.

I told him that I would not give him a story without advance payment but since he had been working for the benefit of society, I could offer him one if he managed to first convince Manto to do so.

Sarkhush said, 'I have still not talked to Manto but I do hope that he will be willing to contribute.'

'That's fine,' I said, 'if he agrees, then I will too.'

He quietly took his leave and went away. He took one route and I took another to go down the stairs. When I reached Manto's room, I found that he was typing out a play.

I had not yet finished telling Manto about my conversation with Sarkhush when he entered the room with a great deal of hesitation and began to talk about the purpose of his visit.

'How much will you pay me?' Manto asked. 'I will write the story today itself.'

Agha-saheb grinned, revealing a full set of teeth.

'I am bringing out this issue in memory of my late father, the famous poet from Delhi...'

Manto, however, did not allow him to finish. 'Look here gentleman, you are bringing out a special issue in memory of your father. I too need some money to offer flowers at my father's grave. Since I cannot bring out a special issue in his memory, I must at least plant a few fruit trees there.'

Manto widened his eyes and looked at him in a manner that made it impossible for him to stay there even for a moment longer.

I walked out of the room with him but he could not gather enough courage to ask me for a story.

It is not true that Manto and I quarrelled all the time. We also had many opportunities to come closer to each other. Yes, it is true that we quarrelled all the time when we were in Delhi; but what is also true that I stayed in Manto's house for about eight or ten days when he had called me to join as a dialogue writer in Filmistan. Later, I made sure that Manto and I didn't work for the same unit. Even then, the two of us often sat together, recited couplets for Mukherjee, told him jokes, and listened together to all the tittle-tattle of Raja Mehdi Ali Khan. While I never read out anything of what I wrote to Manto, he did read out two or three of his stories to me. In fact, he wrote the story 'Swaraj ke Liye' right in front of me. He stopped writing the story midway, and when he did finish it after a gap of two or three months, he read it out to me afresh.

Manto used to live in a somewhat old flat on Clare Road in Bombay. The flat was on the second storey. A big room served both as the drawing and dining room. There was another smaller room with a partition. There was a bed on one side of the partition, and the kitchen on the other. Most people in Bombay did not use a stove and cooked on a wood-fire brazier instead.

There was hardly any scope for beautification in the bedroom though the bed and the dressing table were indeed very beautiful. The drawing room, however, was well decorated with a sofa set, table and chairs. In one corner was the dining table with chairs around it. A cupboard with Manto's clothes and shoes stood in another corner. On the right side, next to the wall, was a table with some things kept on it in perfect order.

Manto had come to the railway station to receive me. The

Frontier Mail stopped at Bombay Central. Manto was already there, standing in front of the second-class coach. As soon as I got off the train, Manto asked me to walk beside him. Kaushalya had to go off to Admiral House and she asked him to call for a pick-up for her. Manto was slightly irritated, but he organized it. Kaushalya went off to Admiral House and I went with Manto to Clare Road. I never again went back to Delhi. I stayed with Manto for the first eight or ten days and after that with a relative on Kendal Road.

My first memories of those days in Bombay are of the mosquitoes, the noise outside Manto's flat and Manto getting up at four in the morning to fill up and store water.

Manto prepared my bed in the big room on the first night. People generally don't use beds or charpoys in Bombay. They mostly sleep either on the floor or on folding beds. Manto too had spread out a folding bed for me. It was December yet it was hot inside the room. I did not have any idea about the climate of Bombay. It was bitterly cold at that time in Delhi and I had brought heavy bedding with me. A new place, a warm blanket, a folding bed, and to top it all the mosquitoes— I could not sleep till late in the night. And when I did drift off, some strange sounds began to come from the room inside. My slumber was disturbed and I kept wondering about the commotion. Was something troubling either Manto or bhabhi? I even got up once and walked up to the door but then turned back. The noise continued for about an hour or so. I was so troubled that when Manto spread out my bed the next night, I told him, 'Listen yaar, I find it difficult to sleep inside. Put the bed in the balcony.'

And Manto spread out the bed in the balcony.

But I could still not sleep. Inside I was restless because of the heat and on the balcony because of the noise. Manto's flat was close to the road and the buses and cars went rumbling around till midnight; the clamour started all over again early in the morning. I am a light sleeper and even the fluttering of paper is enough to disrupt my sleep. I woke up several times and whenever I opened my eyes I saw a bus, a tram, or a car piercing the dark. However, I somehow slid into sleep. When I woke up next I found that the night was in its last phase. There was a nip in the breeze. Noise, like the earlier night, soon started from the room inside once again. I started wondering about the source of the noise. Was somebody inside in some trouble? But if there had been any problem it would certainly have become apparent from Manto's or bhabhi's expressions. I therefore gave up my intention of getting up to find out the reason behind the noise. I kept lying down in silence but I could not go back to sleep as long as the noise continued. I had just about drifted off when the first tram rattled away from somewhere close by, conveying to the inhabitants of Clare Road news of the dawn of another day. After that it was impossible for me to go back to sleep. When I got up in the morning I felt as if I had been hammered good and hard.

During breakfast I asked Manto, 'What happened in the morning? Were you awake?'

Manto responded with a heavy abuse and said, 'We get water only early in the morning. We are on the upper floor so there is not even a drop of water here by the time we get up. That is why I get up at four in the morning and store all the water we need through the day.'

I got accustomed to the rattle of trams and buses during my stay there but I continued to be shaken out of sleep at least once when Manto filled up the water at four in the morning.

Of those seven days, the memory that is still fresh in my mind is that of the cuisine in Manto's house. I don't remember the cutlery as being exceptional but what I will never forget are the pure ghee parathas and curry that Safia-bhabhi used to cook. Manto was a very light eater. His appetite had probably been killed by excessive drinking. But whether it was in the studio or at home, the food cooked in his house was sumptuous. Though I did not have a weak stomach in those days, I had begun to suspect that I had some problem with my digestion. I used to take special care not to over-eat but despite this I am absolutely convinced that I always ended up doing exactly that.

My third unforgettable memory of those days is that Manto hardly ever mentioned literature at home. I am not sure whether others too had the same experience but as far as I am concerned, I never saw Manto discussing anything about his stories or plays with Safia-bhabhi. However, it will not be correct to say that Manto was generally quiet when he was home. He used to be at complete ease, talking of many different things, cracking jokes and narrating incidents effortlessly. His jokes were spiced with sarcasm and his tales spun off into various others. None of these, however, were even remotely connected with literature and I would wonder how someone who talked of such mundane stuff could be the creator of stories like 'Naya Kanoon' and 'Hatak'. It is a well-known fact that Chekhov used to talk of all kinds of things under the sun but became evasive as soon as there was any mention of his writings. Manto too used to camouflage his writing and creativity under the garb of humour, like the ocean that experiences mighty storms in its depths but hides them so effectively that what is visible on the surface is nothing more than the gentle motion of tender waves. Manto too concealed his compassion and love for humanity under illogical, disorderly conversations, crude jokes, abuses, and drinking. I have often felt a deep dislike for Manto for personal reasons but I have always been fascinated and attracted to him because of his writings.

Manto took great pride in the technique with which he developed his stories. Krishan has written: Manto stitches the costume of his stories with extreme care. One does not find even a small crease. There isn't a single careless stitch. The hemming is perfect and after all this is done, it is ironed in the most perfect way. Manto's stories are tidy and cluttered, and the language polished yet simple.

But it was not because of technique that I liked Manto's stories. There was a time when I used to love Maupassant's stories but, as my literary taste matured, I began to notice a great deal of artificiality in his technique. After I read about twenty of his stories at one go, I found this artificiality recurring repeatedly in the climax of his stories and it became difficult for me to accept this ungrudgingly. It was after that that I started reading Chekhov and felt that his stories made a much deeper impression than those of writers like Maupassant, Maugham and O'Henry despite lacking their technical brilliance. One can fully read through Chekhov's stories without becoming aware that one is reading fiction. I do not know if Manto was influenced by Chekhov but he was certainly influenced by Gorky, Maugham, and through him, Maupassant. His love for the downtrodden and his progressive perspective can be traced back to Gorky. His brilliant technique may be due to the influence of Maugham and Maupassant. But if Manto remains alive in people's memories, it will not be because of the distinctive technique, of which he was so proud, and which Krishan talks of. Technique, in fact, detracts from his stories. I really like his stories 'Hatak', 'Swaraj ke Liye' and 'Nangi Aawaze'. The standpoint of these three stories is progressive and all three are replete with Manto's boundless love for humanity. Nonetheless, there is a sense of artificiality in the climax of all three stories.

Let us talk of 'Hatak'. The story is not exceptional because its climax is amazing like that of Maupassant's 'Necklace'. Take away the last line from 'Necklace' and the whole story will come tumbling down like a house of cards. This, however, is not true of 'Hatak'. Sugandhi is completely stunned when the seth rejects her with a depreciating 'Unh!' and speeds away in his car. The woman Sugandhi living within the prostitute Sugandhi has remained uninvolved in the whole transaction until that point. But she too is stunned and insulted by the rejection. And it is at this point that the story should have been concluded.

However, the story goes on and we find that Sugandhi comes back home and loses her temper the moment she spots Madhav. Manto takes four pages to describe Sugandhi's anger at this point, which I feel is excessive and disproportionate. It would have been enough for Sugandhi to merely utter one harsh sentence, an abuse, or an insult like 'Unh!' She could have thrown Madhav out of the room, spat on his face and closed the door, leaving him as stunned as she had been at the seth's rejection. Then the climax of the story would have been like that of Maugham or Maupassant. But Manto is neither Maugham nor Maupassant. He likes his climax to be dramatic and so Sugandhi starts pulling down pictures from the wall and throwing them down in the bazaar one by one (though in real life the first picture thrown from the second storey would have fallen on somebody's head and finished off the whole thing).

Sugandhi did not know that Madhav was sitting in her room. She would have worked out some scheme in advance if she had. To begin with, she would have enquired about his case, thrown out his picture, then she would have ridiculed him, and finally thrown him out. However, it was not Sugandhi but Manto who had planned out everything in his mind, just like he had done in 'Khushiya'. Sugandhi merely kept doing what the writer wanted her to do. When anger touches its peak in real life, it is not expressed in a well-defined or structured way.

One needs time and a cool head to develop, extend and plan a response.

Nonetheless, despite this limitation, there is no doubt that 'Hatak' is an excellent story and it is because of the content of the story that it becomes so. About two or three years ago, during the meeting of the Progressive Writers' Association at Allahabad, the critic Mumtaz Hussain declared that 'Hatak' is not a progressive story. When 'Hatak' was published for the first time, it was considered a major landmark in the realm of progressive stories. How could something that was considered progressive at a point of time be transformed into conformist at another? It defied all logic and I could not understand it despite Mumtaz Hussain's explanations.

When Sugandhi turns back to go home, she ponders over her rejection and thinks, 'He did not like my face—so what if he didn't?—I too don't like the faces of so many men—that man, the one who came that moonless night, he was so ugly—did I not make a fuss? Was I not disgusted when he slept with me? All that is fine but the fact is you are not the one who rebuffed him...you are not the one who rejected him.'

Clearly, she had not rejected him because she could not have afforded to do so. However filthy the man, she had no alternative but to sell her body to him. It was for this reason that she was not upset with either herself or Ram Lal but with the seth (and this anger is the one that the writer feels. The writer believes Sugandhi and Ram Lal are victims of capitalism and their pain and agony agitate him deeply. He expresses all his deep-seated anger against that seth because he considers him as a symbol of tradition).

This paragraph is what transforms 'Hatak' into a grave human tragedy. The progressive aspect of 'Hatak' will remain pertinent till the social system that makes a woman go through this hatak, this humiliation, of having no choice but to sell her body even to the filthiest man for a beggarly sum of money exists. And this will continue to be the same despite the fatwas issued by the immature critics of progressive writing. Just in case the system undergoes a change, 'Hatak' will gain historical status and will be read by future generations as a chronicle of barbarism and cruelty.

The major strength of 'Swaraj ke Liye' also lies in the fact of it being a satire against the unnatural social ideals and falsehoods imposed on human beings. One by one, Manto has peeled off the layers of hypocrisy and exposed this falsehood in a very creative manner. However, the climax of this story, too, is ineffective. The point that needed to be established here was that Shahzad Ghulam Ali had been performing a natural act in an unnatural manner. As a reaction to this unnatural indulgence, he made a firm decision to never sell products made of rubber. This would have the served the purpose of illuminating what Manto was hinting at. But Manto refuses to stop here. Manto had made Sugandhi mad in the end. In the same way, he makes Shahzad Ghulam Ali crazy, even though he was evolving as a perfectly normal character through the story. And Manto finishes the story in the following way:

'Ghulam Ali was about to add something more to what he was saying when his servant entered. He was carrying a child, probably Ghulam Ali's second son, in his arms. The child was holding a beautiful balloon in his hand. Ghulam Ali jumped at it like a mad man. There was an explosion like the bursting of a cracker. The balloon burst and all that was left hanging in the child's hand were small pieces of rubber and thread. Ghulam Ali pulled the pieces of rubber from his hand and threw them away as if they were loathsome.'

This climax turns the story into a disgusting one. Manto had already drawn the reader's attention to the fact of Ghulam Ali hating a specific rubber object by mentioning that he had decided to never sell rubber objects. That he jumps at the balloon as soon as he sees it is what turns him into a crazy man. If Manto wanted to communicate the fact in such an overt fashion, then there was no need for the earlier suggestion. The introduction of the second allusion makes the story somewhat nonsensical and transforms Ghulam Ali into an insane individual.

Nonetheless, despite this flaw, the story continues to retain a distinctive position among Manto's stories. Manto has not merely expressed fundamental concepts but has also portrayed the authentic political condition of the time in such a manner that one feels like showering infinite praise on him. It cannot be established if Shahzad Ghulam Ali was a real person, but just a few days before Manto started writing, the newspapers had reported that Gandhiji had got a couple married at his ashram and, after the wedding ceremony, announced that the couple was to stay together as friends till India became independent. I don't remember what Manto said after reading this news, but I do recall that he had smiled sarcastically and showered some of his choicest abuses at the idiocy of the couple. A few days later, he had begun to write the story.

One of Manto's earlier stories, 'Paanch Din', also dealt with the same theme. In 'Paanch Din', a professor who claims to treat his girl students as his daughters tells them:

'I am a lie, a colossal lie. My whole life has been spent lying to myself and working at transforming the lies into truth. Oh! It is such a painful, unnatural and inhuman act. I slaughtered one single desire but little did I realize that I would have to commit a series of murders after this first one. I believed that blocking a tiny pore could not be of much consequence but I did not know then that it would mean shutting all the other doors of my body too.'

Manto has written about the same theme more explicitly

in 'Swaraj ke Liye'. Mahatma Gandhi has written in his
autobiography about how he was performing the husband's
job in his newly wedded wife's room when his father was ill
and confined to bed. What is quite surprising is that despite
experiencing this fact, he thought it proper to obstruct this
natural expression in others. One of his sons was in love with
his friend's daughter. When Gandhiji found out about this, he
announced that he would allow his son to marry his beloved
only if he was able to sustain his love for her for five years. And
he then sent off his son to some far-off place to carry on with
his struggle for India's independence.

A man and a woman in Gandhiji's ashram fell in love with
each other and went to seek his blessings. He imposed the
same five-year incarceration on these two as well, declaring
that he would himself get them married if they remained firm
after sacrificing their emotions in the yajna of the freedom
struggle for five years.

His son kept his resolve for five years and Gandhiji granted
him permission to marry his beloved. The other devotee could
not bear to live through the internment and eloped with his
lover.

Manto did not know of these incidents; I am quite certain
he would have written a few more sarcastic stories like 'Swaraj
ke Liye' if he had. As far as I know him, in the first case,
he would have written about Mahatma Gandhi himself, or
represented him as a sanyasi or a spiritual guru. He would
have then shown how the man continued to love the woman
in the five-year trial period imposed by the guru. This happens
because love is nurtured under the shadow of unquenched
desires. So, when the man gets married in the sixth year, his
earlier spiritual perspective is replaced by a corporal, physical
one. The result is that he begins to detest his lover. As far as
the second instance is concerned, he would probably not have

written a story about it. He may have just described the whole thing as it occurred. He would have allowed the two ashram inmates to elope since it is in keeping with the law of nature.

It is difficult to understand why Mahatma Gandhi endorsed such sadism. He remembered his own youth very vividly, why then did he choose to disregard the youthful passions of others? But, then, he was probably a master in understanding the psyche of the masses. He also knew how to win over the hearts of the public in Hindustan. But Manto was no politician and was deeply tormented when he witnessed the repression and killing of natural emotions in human beings. His irritation is expressed when, in 'Swaraj ke Liye', he puts the following words in Shahzad Ghulam Ali's mouth:

'The world has had so many reformers but people have forgotten their teachings. What has remained behind is the cross, holy threads, bangles, beards, and the hair in armpits. We have more expertise and experience than the people who lived here a thousand years ago. I just can't understand why the reformers have not kept in mind that they have been distorting human beings. Many a time I feel that I must shriek, "For God's sake, just allow the human being to live as one. It is true that you have already managed to distort human beings but at least now have pity on them. You are trying to transform them into gods but the poor creatures have actually lost even their human qualities. At best, from among thousands of people, a couple may be able to successfully kill their sensual passions. Moreover, what purpose will be served if everybody burns their sexuality to ashes?"'

And Manto's story becomes great as soon as he highlights fundamental human emotions.

The climax of 'Nangi Aawazen' is also no different from those of 'Hatak' and 'Swaraj ke Liye'. Much like 'Hatak', 'Nangi Aawazen' too focuses on human tragedy. The refugees have to sleep on a big, long terrace. They try to attain some privacy by screening off their beds from others by erecting partitions of jute mats. Manto's story describes the torture that unmarried young men go through when they are surrounded by married couples. Bholu in 'Nangi Aawazen' is sensitive like Khushiya. If he had not been a sensitive young man, Bholu would have had no hesitation in sleeping with his newly wed wife. (It is quite clear that Manto has infused his own sensitivity into Bholu, much like he does with Khushiya.) The story actually ends at the point when Bholu's bhabhi is not able to understand the pain he is living through and tells her husband that Bholu is sexually impotent. The story becomes a consummate tragedy right at this point.

After such a climax, Maupassant would have considered it sinful to write even a word more. But Manto is not Maupassant and he cannot control his anger. He had earlier portrayed Sugandhi and Shahzad Ghulam Ali as being deranged. Now, in this story, he goes a step further and makes Bholu go completely mad. Bholu tears off the mat screens when he is gripped by extreme anger. But the story does not finish here. It moves further to show how Bholu is hit on the head by Kallan's bamboo pole, causing an injury that makes Bholu utterly mad. Manto concludes the story with the following words: 'He now roams through the bazaars completely naked, without a shred of cloth on him. Whenever his eyes fall on a hanging mat, he pulls it down and tears it into pieces.'

Nonetheless, despite this weakness—like his other story 'Shareefan'—one never forgets the agony expressed in 'Nangi Aawazen'. Manto is angry, furious, seething with rage, when he finds human beings, gifted with a bounty of emotions by nature, left with no option but to live like insensate brutes. And when Manto gets incensed, he loses all control and sense of proportion. He becomes eccentric when he is the grip of uncontrollable anger and even goes to the extent of disregarding the art of story writing. It is this fury that one finds reflected in the endings of 'Hatak', 'Swaraj ke Liye' and 'Nangi Aawazen' that are so similar to each other. But then, it is probably because they are infused with this anger that these stories also become imbued with an agony that has made them unforgettable.

However, declaring that anger always managed to erase technique out of Manto's mind would not be correct. Both his anger as well as his agony are intact in 'Shareefan' and so is his technique. The rioting and barbarism that went on in Punjab left one bewildered. Anybody who witnessed it was forced to ask, 'How could this have happened? How could civilized people, who had been fond of each other, who had loved each other, who lived and ate together, suddenly become so ruthless and cold-blooded that they went to the extent of raping the same women whom they had considered their mothers and sisters?'

Manto has provided an answer to these baffling issues in his story 'Shareefan' where the last line brands us like a heated metal rod, leaving an indelible mark on our hearts and minds.

I have always been fond of Manto's stories and have always empathized with his rage and frustration. However, I have never been able to go along with him as far as his perspective about human beings in general was concerned. Manto passed critical comments about the Buddha, Christ and Mahatma Gandhi, and I may have even approved of some of them, but I don't feel obliged to make similar comments. Manto was not wrong in representing the whole range of human emotions, including our bestiality, our hollow humanity and perversion. The problem arises when he selectively approves of some of these perversions, and refuses to accept any restraint on innate human emotions under the assumption that human beings can retain their humanity only when they are allowed complete freedom. Manto's stories like 'Mummy' and 'Padhiye Kalma' are evidence of this conviction. I feel that the innate emotions of human beings at present are identical with those of their early ancestors! Humans beings are essentially monsters and reveal their true colours when the constraints of culture and civilization loosen their grip over them. It is then that their innate qualities are unveiled and they reveal themselves as entirely selfish, self-absorbed, egotistical, malicious, greedy, irascible and sensual! It is by repressing these instinctual emotions that one gradually evolves into a human. What we recognize today as humanity, as opposed to barbarism, is something that we, who are essentially barbaric, have acquired after a great deal of effort over ages. Over the years countless mystics, philosophers, writers and poets have played a crucial role in this process of evolution. Overcoming their own innate impulses, these people contemplated, deliberated and expounded means through which the monster was transformed into a human being. Manto was a lover of humanity and so he was deeply distressed when he saw human beings behaving wickedly. The real issue, however, is not the wicked behaviour of people but the reasons that impel them to behave in a wicked manner. Therefore, Manto should have used his discretion to decide who he should get angry with. He was never able to figure out who his pen must target.

Ali Sardar Jafri has closely analyzed Manto's anger in his preface to *Chugad*, a collection of Manto's short stories and writes: 'The characters fleshed out by Manto may have been human beings at some point in time, or may have had the potential of becoming humans, but our society, established on the foundation of plunder and pillage, has turned them all into beasts. These are a very special variety of beasts, who despite having the facade of human beings, are not actually humans. This frustrates Manto and he then pauses to peep into their souls and is amazed when he discovers that the hearts that throb in there are still human... But this same society has brought forth many commendable people too, who are struggling to seek out their lost humanity, to acquire it once again. They look like humans, their souls are human and so are their hearts! They have managed to win back their treasured humanity through long struggle but Manto is blind to them and this becomes the cause of what may be termed "literary terrorism" that he often succumbs to. If he would have had his way, he would have given way to political terrorism too.'

Manto in the preface to the collection *Manto ke Afsane* writes: 'When my heart is rid of the fear of the pistol in my hand going off on its own, that is when I shall wander around, brandishing it. And after identifying my real enemy, I will either empty all the bullets into him or riddle my own body with them. When one of my detractors will criticize my act and declare, "He was mad," my soul will acknowledge it as a very precious award and wear it prominently like a treasured medal.'

But Manto didn't seem to realize that the strongest adversaries of humans are humans themselves, whose monstrous desires have taken the shape of market and capitalism. These innate passions of individuals persistently keep knocking within them, impatient to emerge out into the world. Human beings need to constantly struggle like their ancestors did. The enemy cannot be decimated merely by pumping bullets into the body of a single individual. This battle has been going on since the inception of the world and will continue till its end. Human beings will keep struggling and transforming system after system. Finally, they will either completely demolish their monstrous tendencies and be transformed into divine creatures, or completely annihilate themselves. But till one or the other thing happens, it is certain that they will continue to endeavour to evolve into genuine human beings.

Sardar Jafri has also written: 'Manto fails to recognize his real adversary and shoots around blindly, and in the process, wounds nobody at all. Consequently, in the final analysis, his passion against social repression is converted into terrorizing human beings themselves, the same human beings whom Manto loves from the core of his heart.'

Nonetheless, many exceptional stories by Manto do express the zenith of his intimacy, reverence and complete empathy with the agony of human beings. After reading the above comment Manto responded by saying that, 'Sardar is a clown. He has absolutely no idea of the darkness in the human heart, something that I perceived a long time ago.'

I had accumulated fourteen thousand rupees over my two years in Filmistan. My plan was to utilize this money to start my own publishing houses in Hindi and Urdu. Both Manto and I had decided to leave Filmistan. One day I approached Manto and said, 'I want to publish twenty of your best stories in Hindi when I start my Hindi publishing press. What royalty will you take?'

'Forget about this royalty business,' Manto responded. 'Just give me five hundred rupees in cash and you can freely publish my stories till eternity.'

I would definitely have published Manto's stories, except that I fell seriously ill. The doctors declared that I had TB and as a result, instead of going to Lahore, I ended up in the Bel-Air clinic in Panchgani. Despite my attempts to fulfill the promise I made to Manto, it has not been possible for me to do so for the last five years. The stories have already been translated into Hindi. If I had known that Manto would bid goodbye to all friendship and all enmity in such a rush, I would have abandoned my own books and published a selection of his stories in Hindi.

Manto has written: 'None of the desires I had during my childhood and adolescence were ever fulfilled. Or let me put it like this: any fulfillment of my desires has been soaked in my tears and cloaked in my hiccups. For as long as I can recall, I have been an impetuous person who can be hurt very easily. If I wish to have something sweet and the wish is not fulfilled instantly, the sweet loses all its charm for me. It is because of this that I have constant bitterness in my throat; and unfortunately this itch has been accentuated further because of the fact that whoever I have loved, or given a place in my heart, has not just emotionally wounded me but has also taken undue advantage of my love.

'When I lost all hope and found that everyone I loved had betrayed me, I felt like a bee trapped in a desert that could see only sterile sand spread out to the horizon and not a single flower from which it could hope to suck some nectar. Despite this, I was not chastened and continued to love, and as usual, nobody thought it was worth anything. When this callousness crossed all limits, and I recalled the treachery and aloofness of my so-called friends, the memory created a tumult in my heart. This resulted in a serious conflict between various aspects of my personality. The emotional, immortal, and external sides of my personality waged a war with each other, which is still ongoing. My external personality, that which others saw, demanded that I hold the people around me accountable, lose all concern for them, cleanse my heart of all love for them, and turn it into a piece of flint. But the emotional aspects of my personality gave an entirely different colour to these painful episodes, leaving me with little option besides feeling proud of the fact that I had made the right choice in life. All I had desired was to love and to continue to

love, since love is the causal principle of all creation. I am not
very sure at which unfortunate moment this conflict struck
root, but now it has become an unalienable part of me. It
doesn't matter whether it is day or night but whenever I have
a moment of leisure, I find that my physical and emotional
selves take up arms and confront each other. Anybody talking
to me during these moments will find my tone and attitude
very strange. There is an irrepressible bitterness in my throat.
I sincerely try not to sound bitter and I am sometimes even
successful; but in these moments, if somebody informs me of
any undesirable incident, or if I experience something contrary
to my disposition, I become entirely helpless. And my tongue
cannot help but articulate exactly what goes on in my mind
and heart. It becomes impossible for me to assess the sarcasm
and bitterness of my words in these moments. I have always
remained conscious of my integrity and I am fully aware that
I can never hurt anybody. If I have ever offended or caused
any pain to my friends and acquaintances, then it must be
understood that the reason does not lie in me but in that
special moment which makes me crazy.'

I came across the above lines while reading Manto's story 'Ek
Khat' and felt a pang of regret for not having met Manto when
his apparent, worldly personality was still dormant and he
hadn't yet experienced the betrayal and coldness of his friends.
However, Manto is not the only one who nursed a grievance
about betrayal by friends; I too have the same complaint.
When I read the lines quoted above, I felt that Manto was not
just writing about himself but about me too, except that I have
not been tortured by my apparent personality in the same way.
I, too, have been deeply pained by the betrayal and neglect
of old friends. But even when I suffered deeply, my tone was
never bitter. Through my reading and my experiences with my
father and life in general, I have developed an approach and

understanding that friendship and love are completely one-sided. If I consider somebody my friend, if intimacy with him gives me pleasure, then it is my responsibility to maintain this friendship and intimacy. It is when I begin to wish that he too must love me in the same way, and when this wish remains unfulfilled, that pain strikes root. This has caused me much pain in the past but I am now beyond it. I continue to preserve my friend's love in my heart but have stopped expressing it. One cannot live without loving, so I choose another friend and try to sustain my friendship with him. I feel I am like a flower brimming with nectar and fragrance. If the flower becomes fond of a bee, it tries to attract it with its fragrance. It gives the flower great joy to offer all its fragrance to the bee. But when the bee goes away, the flower treasures the memory of the bee in its heart and then invites another. There are times when the flower feels very lonesome and sad but this feeling of loneliness is blown away by the memory of the pleasure that the offering of the nectar and fragrance had brought him. Manto wrote the above lines with complete emotional sincerity and since I have seen Manto from very close quarters, I cannot deny the truth they express. It is my misfortune that I met Manto at a stage when his apparent personality had already made his tongue fiery and his attitude stubborn.

Manto is right when he says that he did not hurt anybody on purpose. It is because of this that he expressed deep regret after losing his temper and abusing me twice. On both occasions, I had felt that Manto and I could have been good friends if we had not met so late in life. We certainly would have been very good friends had we met in early youth.

We did not hear much about Manto after he left Bombay. I once received a letter from him from Lahore. It was written on the letterhead of Maktaba Jadeed, the publishing house, and stated that he, along with Mohammad Hasan Aksari, was going to bring out a magazine and I must send one of my stories for it. I was quite ill in those days. I had come to Allahabad based on the support promised by some friends, who completely abandoned me after I arrived. I was under severe mental and physical stress. I still gave my word. I never found out whether the magazine was finally published or not. At least I never saw any issue and I am absolutely sure that I would have written a story for it had I seen a couple of issues.

Except for this letter, I had no correspondence with Manto after my days in the Bombay film industry. Of course, whenever a new story by Manto was published it became a topic of discussion at home. Kaushalya and I would discuss it for a few days and then the mundane demands of life would divert our attention from it.

And then, all of a sudden this January, we heard Manto was no more. We could not believe it when we first heard of it. The news was broken to me by my friend and neighbour Pandit Bhairav Prasad. He was a big admirer of Manto. He edited the widely circulated Hindi magazine *Maya* for ten years and had just joined as the editor of *Kahani*. He published many translations of Manto's stories in *Maya* and had, only a few days earlier, published 'Toba Tek Singh' in a special short-story issue of *Kahani*. The story has won a permanent place for Manto in the hearts of Hindi-language readers.

I did not believe Bhairav. He confirmed the news, saying that it had been published in *Amrit Patrika* and that there had also been a radio broadcast about it. I rang up Gopal Das, the Assistant Station Director at the radio station. Unfortunately, his daughter was critically ill and so he had no idea about it. I then rang up Muneer-saheb at the studio. I was certain that he would have accurate information but there was still time for the transmission to begin and Muneer-saheb had not reached the studio yet. I could not rest in peace. I rang him up again in the evening. He not only corroborated the news but also said that a half-hour-long programme had been broadcasted by Pakistan radio.

After this, I went home and told Kaushalya that the news was true. Her eyes filled up with uncontrollable tears. In those days Krishna Sobti, the well-known Hindi writer, was a guest with us. I did not wish to eat but I sat at the dinner table for the sake of children and the guests. Dinner ended but I continued to talk to them about Manto for a very long time.

The two people in Allahabad who knew Manto were Mahmood Ahmed Hunar* and me. Some people had heard his name and some others had read his stories. Anyhow, Mahmood Ahmed Hunar and Bhairav Prasad Gupt decided to organize a memorial meeting to mark Manto's sudden death.

Though there is some trouble among the Progressive writers because of some lapses in the past, they often manage to get together and organize programmes in Allahabad that are attended by a fairly large number of people. The conventions held on writers like Ali Sardar Jafri, Ahtesham Husain and Rajinder Singh Bedi have been quite well-attended but the meeting held after Manto's death was so absurd that its bitter memory will always stay with me.

To begin with, it was decided that the meeting would be organized by either Firaq-saheb or me. I am not sure how, but soon it was announced that the meeting was being organized by a publisher from Chowk who brought out many magazines that published detective stories. Lately, for about a year, he had also begun publishing a magazine of detective stories in Urdu. He was hardly educated, but he had made enough money and now desired to cultivate some writers as his friends. One of

---

*Editor of the magazine *Shahkar* published from Allahabad.

the ways in which he fulfilled this desire was by often inviting writers to a coffee house, and placing a hundred-rupee note from his pocket on the plate when the bill arrived. Hunar-saheb was probably working in his publishing house at the time and so it was decided that the memorial meeting too would be held there. Unfortunately, the sky was overcast with clouds since morning that day and it started raining from about ten or eleven o'clock. It was a cold January day. The rain accentuated the cold and by the time evening approached, it had become bitingly cold. Trying to protect ourselves under umbrellas and raincoats, Kaushalya, Krishna Sobti, Kumari Vaishi Seth and I sat on rickshaws and reached the venue. Two young short-story writers in Hindi, Kamleshwar and Dushyant, accompanied us on their bicycles and were completely drenched by the time they reached.

Both the office and the home of the publisher were on the second storey. Some straw and bamboo mats had been hung like curtains to mark out the office. The cold wind pierced through the mats. I had to escort three women and so got a little delayed but I was comforted a little when I found that people had still not turned up for the meeting. The only person who had arrived before us was Mujeeb, the editor of *Naya Hind*. He too went away when he realized that people would arrive late due to the rain.

We walked through the tables scattered around in the office and entered another big room. A part of the room was covered with bookshelves that went right up to the ceiling. The rest of the floor was covered with a carpet. There were some sofas, their backrests blackened with use and dirt. There was a round table in the centre. On the table on the right was a radio which the publishers seemed very keen to play. Each and every item in the room seemed to loudly announce and establish overuse and bad taste but it was cold outside and the room was warm.

We sat down and kept casually talking of this and that. This went on for another half an hour but, when no other writer arrived, and the rain fell harder, we decided to start the meeting. My name was proposed as the chair. It was a serious occasion yet I could not help but smile at the bizarre situation. What could we have said at this meeting which we had not discussed at home? Besides the host and his son, seven out of eight people had come from my house.

The meeting finally began. Hunar started reading 'Jeb-e-kafan', the last article in Manto's collection *Yazeed* in which Manto has written about his literary pursuits in Pakistan and about the overall aesthetic and literary condition there. He writes, 'For a long period of time, I refused to accept the mayhem after the Partition as being final. I continue to feel the same today as well but somewhere down the line I began to recognize and accept the monstrous fact.

'I have plunged deep into the ocean of blood that has been streaming from human bodies wounded by human hands. I have dived deep into this bloody sea that surrounds me and have emerged with some pearls in my hand; pearls of the sweat of repentance, of the toil and effort that was spent in spilling the blood of brothers, of the tears of frustration overflowing from the eyes of some for having failed to kill their humanity.'

Hunar's voice was ringing in my ears but my eyes were visualizing the many glittering pearls from *Siyah Hashiye*. A Progressive critic had sneered at this, saying, 'From the pockets of corpses that Manto describes in his collection *Siyah Hashiye*, he has managed to collect stuff like the rings from their fingers and the leftover butts of smoked cigarettes.'

I can well imagine how pained Manto would have been on reading such a comment. It is clear that the critic had completely failed to appreciate the pain that tormented his mind and heart. The anecdotes in *Siyah Hashiye* have sprung out of this pain and agony. There is no doubt that many of the pearls spread across *Siyah Hashiye* are devoid of the usual sparkle. They are not suffused with the ductility of tears. There exists a kind of exasperation engendered from suspicion and distrust. Nonetheless, stories such as 'Haivaniyat', 'Joota', 'Kasr-e-nafsi' and 'Safai-Pasandi' are evidence of Manto's frustration, anger, empathy and goodwill. Besides this, the sarcasm in stories such as 'Karamat', 'Munasib Karyavai' and 'Sadke Uske' is also permanently etched in our minds.

Hunar was still reading. 'I am an ordinary human being. I was infuriated...and in this angry frame of mind, I had prepared lethal muck that would have stuck permanently to the faces of my so-called critics. I, however, began to feel that it would not be proper for me to do so. There is no doubt that it is human to retaliate, seek an eye for an eye, but the essence of human wisdom lies in the ability to maintain silence, and that of sedateness in the ability to endure.'

I recalled how Manto had abused Rashid* after he had edited a joke and how he had writhed and squirmed at my criticism. Then, he was any ordinary human being, seeking an eye for an eye, but his experiences in life had turned him into a sober and patient man. This glimpse of Manto was new for me. I wish I had met him at this time.

After the reading ended, I once again repeated what I often talked about: the time we spent together at All India Radio and in the film industry. Almost everybody who was there had heard me talk about it at some or other time. Kaushalya had heard the stories many times over, yet her eyes were brimming with tears. When I looked at her after I finished, I found that her eyes were still full and her nose seemed to have become a little longer. I am certain that if there had been no issue with

*Nazar Muhammad Rashed, known better by the name Noon Meem Rashid, was a prominent Urdu poet from Pakistan.

the visa, and if Lahore had not been as far as it was, and if Kaushalya could have had her way, then she would definitely have gone to Lahore to be with Safia-bhabhi. That was the only thing she wished to do at that point.

It was quite late and I got up to leave. The host walked towards me with a cup in one hand and a plate with some sweets in the other. Right behind him stood his beloved son and other employees with tea and plates with sweets. He kept one of the plates in front of me and bared his teeth.

'I don't feel like it,' I told him.

He picked up a cup of tea and walked towards Kaushalya. She sprang up from her seat in a rage. He eyes were already red and now they had begun to glow with anger, 'Is this an occasion on which one should offer tea?' she asked and started walking out.

The host was not a man who would give up easily. 'It's the first time you have come to my office. You must at least have a bite. Hee, hee, hee,' he sniggered.

I could not help but imagine how Manto would have torn this man apart and razed him to the ground in a situation like this. I, however, only patted his shoulder and said, 'We will have our fill when we come again for some other meeting.'

And then, all of us came back home. It continued to rain for long in such heavy torrents that it seemed like the clouds had planned to empty themselves out that day; as if this was their last chance to bring down rain.

One morning, about four or five days after the meeting, I saw an issue of *Aaina* dated 31 January lying on my table. I was turning its pages when my eyes fell on a piece of writing that was surrounded by a black border. It turned out to be an article: 'Saadat Hasan Manto: Empty Bottle and a Brimming Heart'. I read the article at one go. Krishan's deep emotions and affection were clearly visible in the article. I would have liked it even more if its conclusion had not been as fanciful as it was but it had become almost a habit with Krishan to do this. Krishan has an extremely powerful imagination and this often leads to the fusion of fact and fiction in his writing. Despite this, I really liked Krishan's piece and said to Kaushalya, 'Krishan has written a really good article on Manto.'

Kaushalya was sitting in the sun with Krishna Sobti. She asked me to read out the article to her.

I went inside and got the issue of *Aaina*. I sat on the edge of the wooden frame of the charpoy and started reading. I had finished almost half of it when I reached the following lines, 'Manto died at forty-two. There was still a lot that he had to talk about. It was only recently that life's harsh experiences, the callousness of society, contradictions between social control and life force had made him write a story like "Toba Tek Singh". We feel grief not because of Manto's death. Death is an inevitable fact of life. We feel the grief for those unborn creative pieces that could have been penned only by Manto...'

Just then, I felt some kind of a rasping in my throat and it became difficult for me to read on. Actually, this hoarseness began at the point where Krishan wrote, 'All India Radio is still there. So is the bar of the Maidens hotel, and the Urdu bazaar as well; that is because Manto was actually an ordinary man. He was a poor writer. He was neither a minister nor an important politician for whom flags are flown at half-mast. He was an oppressed writer of an oppressed tongue.'

I had, however, managed to rein in that hoarseness with great difficulty and tried to continue reading the rest of the article but by the time I reached the above point it became impossible for me to go on. I still somehow continued. 'There are many outstanding short-story writers in Urdu but Manto will never be born again and there will be no one who will have the courage to take his place. This is a fact that I know very well and so do Rajinder Singh Bedi, Ismat Chughtai, Khwaja Ahmed Abbas and Upendranath Ashk...'

Tears fell uncontrollably down my face. I continued to read a little more in the same condition.

'All of us, his competitors, those who love him, those who quarrelled with him, those who were fond of him, those who disliked him, those who loved him, friends, companions, feel the weight of the heavy girder of his death on our shoulders today when is he is not among us.'

Tears obstructed my vision. I threw down the magazine, went to my room and did not emerge until evening.

Today, I am amazed when I recall that day. I saw my father pass away but did not weep. I, of course, had no love for my father but I did not shed tears even when my mother died. But why did my eyes overflow with tears when I was reading that article about somebody I considered half-baked and impulsive? Manto was not my relative, nor was he my brother or a friend... but an enemy!

# The Foul-mouthed One

## Ali Sardar Jafri

WE HAVE LOST THE MOST FOUL-MOUTHED MEMBER OF our literary world and the void created by his absence fills us only with desolation and loneliness. He had the kind of foul mouth that could have been the envy even of people who have the chastest and most uncorrupt way with words. We know of many who are foul-mouthed. Our filthy and sullied society has spawned countless foul-mouthed people, like cacti and thorny bushes in a desert. But none of them have Manto's panache—he knew how to make those thorns flower. He took foul and offensive language to a height at which it transformed into literature and art. His readers feel angry and exasperated at times and then there are times when they just love him for what he writes. What, however, his reader cannot do is leave a story by him unfinished.

When a magazine arrives, Manto's writing is the first to be read. We are keen to find out who has been abused. Whose turn it is to be battered by him. Which hidden aspects of society has he unveiled. People are as eager to get their hands on a new book by Manto as they would be to see the beloved for whom they had been waiting, the one who arrives in their city without notice. People run towards it in droves.

And that same foul-mouthed one has now left us. A large number of people are lamenting and weeping. He will never again write a story. Never again will he publish a book. Never again will anyone be offended. Never again will any lawsuit be filed against him. Never again will such an intelligent madman go to a lunatic asylum. Never again will such an indomitable drinker set foot in any drinking hole. Never again will a person like him attend get-togethers where he will quarrel with friends even as he showers his love on them. All one now has are the memories this delightful conversationalist left behind.

Manto was like an extremely intelligent, adorable but irate child who had a grievance against his father, who was envious of his brothers, and who had broken all his toys in angry protest against some injustice. He had hesitated to put his arms around a mother who loved him and whom he too loved deeply because of a peculiar notion of pride and self-esteem. And now he seems to be showing everyone that he never had any love for those toys. In fact, he claims that he found them quite ugly and goes on to announce, 'These chairs are far more beautiful; the bed too is a toy I can play with. Look out! This sickly, eczemic dog is far more compassionate than you are; this lame cat is more beautiful.'

A smile would appear on his face when he realized that he had managed to make everyone stop everything that they were doing and watch his antics in amazement. This habit stayed with him even in adulthood and it seemed like he continued to wreak vengeance upon society by bombarding it with his foul language.

One sometimes comes across similar foul language in earlier writings. It is a distinctive feature of some other writers as well. But it was Manto who took it to impossible heights and exploited it to create immortal, incomparable characters in Urdu literature. Future generations will learn a great deal from Manto but Manto himself will never come back to us. They will learn from Manto what and how they should write as much as what they should not write about. Nonetheless, what is lamentable is that none of them will ever be as spiky, incisive, pungent, acidic—and as sweet at the same time—as Manto was.

Manto began his literary career by translating the Russian

and French writers, and the impact of their style and narrative
strategies is evident in his early writings. However, none of
the writers from this group—with the exception of Gorky—
managed to move beyond a realistic criticism of the bourgeoisie
age. It is this framework that shaped Manto's early creative and
intellectual phase.

Those were strange times indeed! Europe's decadent
capitalism was undergoing transformation on a large scale
and evolving into fascism. This also pushed many young rebels
towards subversion and anarchism that was being expressed
through forms like French Dadaism and Surrealism in the
realm of literature and art. The perceptions and rationalization
of these movements were rooted in the inability to identify
the real adversary and comprehend the historical evolution of
human existence. Besides this, in India of the time, the rotting
feudal administration was plastered over with the leprous
layers of foreign imperialism. This led to the rise of not only
the revolutionary struggle for Independence but also to the
rise of political terrorists and of romantic rebels in literature.

And thus the Russian Revolution, the Jallianwala Bagh
massacre, Bhagat Singh, Kropotkin, Victor Hugo, Gorky, and
Romanov's short story 'Without Cherry Blossoms' had become
the basis for Manto's mental and emotional creative realm
about twenty years earlier when I first met him in Aligarh.
Gorky's influence was clearly visible in the vagrant characters
that Manto created in his early writing. It is possible that
some other factors—that I am not aware of—may also have
influenced him. Manto brought together all these elements
and, after weaving them into the fabric of bitterness of his
personal life and injustice in social system, he shaped it into a
new and distinctive personality that came to be known as the
writer Saadat Hasan Manto.

His special and unique personality allowed him to

challenge anything and everything. He could not compromise with anything; he could not lower his head in defeat; he could not plead for anything; and he could even go to the extent of not demanding his dues. The intervening twenty years witnessed many new influences and circumstances that continued to impact the scene. Gorky, the revolution in Russia, Victor Hugo and Jallianwala Bagh gradually receded into the background and Bhagat Singh, Kropotkin and Romanov became increasingly prominent. Somerset Maugham was added to the list after 1940. It is possible to disagree with Bhagat Singh's preference for violent methods but we can never doubt his love for the country. In the same way, one may have serious literary and ideological differences with Manto but one has no option but to accept and acknowledge his sincerity, honesty, love for humanity, for the country, and strong sense of anti-imperialism. And then it is not difficult to understand that Manto could smash society to smithereens and scatter its remains far and wide. However, he could neither reconstruct it nor design a new costume to cover its nudity. He was an outstanding pioneer of social realism of our times and the commander-in-chief of his battalion of literary militants. It was his innate decency and love for humanity that constantly urged him towards literary militancy

After 1940, he constructed his own yardstick for judging the success of his stories: the more controversy and uproar his stories generated, the more successful they were. Once, in 1945 or 1946, he told me in Bombay, 'Sardar, it was no fun writing this story. Nobody has abused me and neither has any law suit been filed against it.'

Manto, unlike Rajinder Singh Bedi, could not penetrate the hearts of his sad, dejected characters and provide evidence of the sincerity of the human heart. Neither could he, like Ismat Chughtai, provide shelter to innocent sinners and cover them up with the purity of the cloth that covers Mother Mary. And of course he could not, like Krishan Chander, use his pen to bring together the agony of this simmering society to provide a glimpse of a more hopeful and beautiful future. Manto was more attracted to distortions of the psyche than to the pain of people. He got more pleasure in groping through the hearts of those who were sick than the healthy ones. His heroes are not just vagabonds. They are anti-socials and criminals that he picked up and flung at society—and broke into his bitter, sarcastic laughter after doing so. He believed that those who wore garments of faith were complete frauds and if he caught any glimpse of devotion or the fear of God in people, he would strip them naked.

Society was like a rotting onion in Manto's hands. He laughed even as he peeled off its layers with great skill and precision, and said 'Look here! This society of yours is nothing but a heap of stinking onions peels.'

Today the onion bulb is still there and so is its peel, creating the illusion that there is something hard and substantial at the core. But the fingers that peeled off the layers with such finesse are now lying cold in the grave, and every writer desires that his fingers become infused with the magic of Manto's, even if it is only for a day.

Manto's greatness lies in the manner in which he exposes society's naked body in front of its own eyes. He dug human corpses out of brothels, bazaars, drinking holes, the four walls of domesticity, and every dark corner of society, stood them out in a public place and proclaimed, 'Look here! These are the beasts that were once human!'

But Manto's tragedy lies in that he could not see the faces of those people whom he could have brought into the public eye and announced, 'Look here! These are the human beings who were once beasts!'

Manto was not able to grasp truth in its most holistic and authentic form. He merely looked at oppression in isolation, protested against it and then dropped it. These things can make us somewhat cruel and unkind, in the same way in which we become insensitive to poverty, cruelty and filth because we get accustomed to them and start tolerating them without much anxiety. We leave a dead body on the road and walk away; we watch a hungry man but continue to eat. Similarly, writers too become so used to repeatedly portraying repressed characters in their writing that, at times, even extreme cruelty and the most painful tragedy may fail to touch them.

It is because of this that Manto has written some shoddy stories along with some outstanding ones. If on the one hand he has written exceptional stories like 'Naya Kanoon', 'Tarakki Pasand', 'Kabristan', 'Mootri', 'Khol Do', 'Mozel' and 'Toba Tek Singh'; on the other, in the words of Sajjad Zahir*, he has also written such 'painful but irrelevant' stories like 'Boo' and 'Hatak', besides appalling but meaningless stories like 'Sarkande ke Peeche' in which he has described human flesh being cooked in a vessel. He would sometimes be so sensitive a person that he could perceive the throb of that child's heart who was sitting in a train and whose father was unable to play with him. At other times, Manto would become so heartless that he could not hold back from cracking jokes even at the expense of deeply tragic events like the riots of 1947. He got so caught up in the human world of actions and encounters that he got personally involved in them and, in the process, lost sight of their causes and their underlying motives. Such a writer can simultaneously become both gentle and merciless in his personal and domestic life too.

And then such a writer turns into an individual who is

*Sajjad Zahir was one of the founders of the All-India Progressive Writers' Movement in India.

dissociated from both friends and enemies. His self-centeredness does not allow him to go along with either the Progressives or the fundamentalists. So, Manto too was distanced from both these groups and had become accustomed to pronouncing his own verdicts. These verdicts took the shape of stories and were sometimes correct and beautiful but at other times wrong and ugly too.

From the perspective of art, Manto was unique and unparalleled. There was nobody like him. No other writer had the ability to create the impact that Manto could with the simplicity, dexterity and perspicacity of his language. Manto's sharp and astute characterization, his well-structured plots, the narrative of his stories, amazingly satirical, incisive and cutting style, and his poetic charm was unique to him. He could flesh out a character in a couple of words. He narrated his stories however he wanted and after reading his stories one does not get the impression that they had been written to be read. They appear to be ordinary yet exceptional at the same time, like a spring that bubbles down a mountain, or a tree that has grown freely without any impediment. The uniqueness of his stories has to be accepted without any qualms. And this is no mean achievement. In fact, this is the mark of an artist.

Manto was a sensitive man and so he twice ended up in a lunatic asylum. He was fearless and thus had to present himself in the court many times. He was persistent and stubborn and had interminable clashes with his opponents. He had a high sense of self-esteem and so he starved. His thirst was eternal and so he kept drinking. He could not whip up the passion to live on and so he died. But he was an artist and thus he continues to live on even after his death.

And now, finally, you would want to know why he was foul-mouthed. Because this society abused him, foul-mouthed him, like it has done to lakhs and crores of other people. Manto's foul-mouthing has not brought about much damage. In fact, its benefits far outweigh any harm it may have caused. Manto's 'foul-mouthed-ness' is that rare, incomparable and cherished wealth of our literature which we will treasure and keep alive; and sure enough it is that which will keep us alive too!

# The Compassionate Destroyer

Abu Saeed Qureshi

THE FIRST RIOT DURING THE FESTIVITIES OF INDEPENDENCE occured in Amritsar. I was in Lahore at the time and Saadat Hasan Manto was in Bombay. The slaves celebrated the joy of liberation by burning up homes to light up the neighbourhood. Half the city was reduced to rubble even before the decision about whether Amritsar would go to Pakistan or Hindustan was made public. When the first act of this Theatre of Gaiety ended, my wife told me, 'Go, get whatever you can retrieve.'

However, when I did reach Amritsar, my relative stopped me at Farid Chowk. The chowk was in a 'Muslim neighbourhood' and my house was in the 'Hindu neighbourhood'. I was told that it was extremely hazardous to go there. I was also told that I could be stopped and attacked on the way. And yes, of course I could go there, provided the lorry belonging to Muslim League turned up, but none appeared. I asked my relatives, 'Can I not go even up to Katra Jaimal Singh?'

In response, I was informed, 'You can go up till the shop that belongs to Shahabe, the milkman.'

Beyond that was territory which the Hindus ruled. I assured them that I would stay on this side of Shahabe's dairy and not go beyond it. Katra Jaimal Singh looked like a replica of Berlin after the Second World War. A huge mass of rubble and debris had come up right in front of Kucha Vakeelan, just a little beyond Shahabe's shop. Manto's house was on that street. On my right, just at the opening of the street, stood a huge pile of rubble like a dense iron curtain separating my past from my present. It was impossible for me to look through it. But fortunately, my friend was still alive and my heart whispered to me, 'There's hope of seeing your friend as long as he is alive somewhere in this world.'

I turned away from that heap of bricks and stones that blocked Kucha Vakeelan, looked at my companions and said, 'Let's go.'

But today, after that large mass of rubble has been removed, my friend has departed from this world.

Kucha Vakeelan was where the Manto clan lived. Saadat used to say: 'Manto means measuring scales in Kashmiri. Riches in the homes of our ancestors in Kashmir were weighed on scales and that is the reason we began to be known as Manto.' I never took the trouble of verifying Manto's statement. After all, we don't take our friends to courts and police stations for verification, just as a lover does not keep gauging his beloved's beauty against yardsticks provided in books. Had Leonardo examined Mona Lisa's lips closely with a magnifying glass, the world of painting would have been deprived of that beautiful and charming smile.

So Kucha Vakeelan was where the Manto clan lived. Right at the entrance of the lane stood the house of Masood Parvaiz's father, Khwaja Hafizullah. This was the first house one saw on the right as soon as one stepped into the lane. There was a small well outside the house. Just ahead of it was the bungalow of Khwaja Abdul Hameed, the deputy superintendent of police. There was a haveli in front of this house. Saadat's house was to the west of this haveli. One of its doors opened towards the south and the other towards the east. Saadat's room was on the right, close to the entrance at the east. This is the room that became the well-known Dar-ul-Ahmar of Manto's articles. Right next to the door were two wooden boxes. A cotton mattress covered with a thick Multani sheet was spread out over the boxes. In front of this, close to a window on the western side of the room, was a writing table. To its right was a small cupboard. The books that didn't fit into the cupboard lay on the table against the wall. Besides these were pens, an inkpot and pencils on the table. Further on the right was a fireplace with a ledge on which stood a statue of Bhagat Singh. On one side of the statue was a table lamp and on the other the receiver of an old-fashioned telephone. Manto had once gone through a severe ordeal trying to make a phone call from a public phone booth. He failed to make the call despite trying for a long time. He then broke off the receiver from the instrument and kept it in the pocket of his overcoat, muttering and grumbling, 'What a fraud!'

He has described himself as a fraud too; but if there is one thing that can be said about Manto, it is that he was far from a fraud. He was a very transparent person and there existed no gap between his internal and external selves. He was like the moonlight that used to light up the eastern side of his room.

I saw his room for the first time in 1931. In those days I was a student of science in the Hindu Sabha College and I spotted Manto on the verandah of the college. He was wearing a red striped bosky shirt and red bosky pajamas. His feet were shod in chappals. He wore a fashionable short coat over his shirt. He was clicking a photo of Prakash, my classmate. A mere glimpse of Prakash was enough to transform the Persian scholars of my college say 'Bkhal-e-hindvash-bakhsham-Samrkando Bukhara ra'* and they were prepared to crack open each other's skulls with hockey sticks for him. That was the first time I saw Manto.

'Who is he?' I asked a classmate.

'Tommy,' he answered.

I had heard Manto's name earlier but he had been nicknamed Tommy in his neighbourhood as well as in the college because he was very mischievous. Anyhow, this Tommy, who was

---

*A line by the Persian poet Hafiz: 'I can give up the cities of Samarkand and Bukhara in exchange for the mole on the face of this Hindustani boy.'

clearly trying to charm the 'angel', appeared somewhat strange to me. I could never have imagined that any sensible man would come to college in red bosky pajamas and a red striped shirt—in short, in a night suit. That being my opinion, I made no effort to find out more about him. The incident too slowly paled into insignificance.

Sometime later, my father passed away. I had gone to the photographer Ashiq Ali's studio to get my father's photograph enlarged. Ashiq Ali was a renowned photographer at that time. He had come back after a sojourn in the Bombay film world and had a range of superb cameras, the likes of which could not be found in studios of photographers even in big cities. Photographs from the film world decorated his showcase and looked magical as light and shadow played upon them. As far as Ashiq Ali was concerned, he believed it was the art of photography and not the business that was of greater consequence. The satisfaction of the customer was considered secondary and he was known to rip up photographs if they did not match his standards—even though the customer would have happily taken them. He did not hide his fondness for alcohol and drank openly while, on the sly, his servant would polish off the spirit used for developing photographs. Ashiq Ali had processed two or three photographs of my father but had torn them up saying, 'Wasn't up to the mark, my friend.'

He needed more time to reach the ideal and I had to regularly visit his studio to check if that had happened. It was on one of these visits that I met Tommy and asked, 'So then, did Prakash's photograph come out good?'

'Did you really think there was film in the camera? Well, there wasn't,' he answered.

This first meeting gradually developed into a good friendship. He was ready to die for Marlene Dietrich's legs and I used to sigh over Garbo's beauty. Manto had crossed that

bridge upon which I then stood four years earlier. He was born
in May 1912 and I in May 1916. We shared the passion with
which we loved the two film-stars and this common fervour
drew us two penniless lovers close to each other.

I am deeply obliged to Greta Garbo and Marlene Dietrich
who were responsible for initiating my friendship with Manto.
Their photographs were the magnet that pulled me to Kucha
Vakeelan for the first time. The distance between Hollywood
and Amritsar was navigated in the blink of an eye.

Many colourful film magazines were stacked up next to
Manto's study table. He spread out his entire treasure in front
of me and said, 'Take whichever photograph you like.'

We got some photographs framed as well. The use of binding
paper in framing had just begun for the first time then. Like
his inventive photography, it was Ashiq Ali who first started
using this new binding paper in Amritsar. Our deep interest
in this paper was a living advertisement for it. You can imagine
for yourself the legs of Hollywood actresses under coats with
decorated borders. The love-affair was, however, beginning
to become too expensive for us and so we decided to do the
binding ourselves. The costs, however, were still too high and
then Manto had the brainwave that we could use pastel paper
instead—our experiment turned out to be hugely successful.

I never got the opportunity to meet Saadat's father. He had
already passed away when I met him. A large photograph of his
father hung on the wall opposite to the one with photographs
of Bhagat Singh, Marlene Dietrich and Joan Crawford. The
photograph showed Saadat's father in a bandhgala, a Kashmiri
turban, a beard, and with large eyes. We always had the feeling
that he was constantly watching us, his expression touched with
severe disapproval. It was probably to hide from these angry,
razor-sharp eyes that Saadat had once run away to Bombay
after being certain that he would fail in his Matric exam.
Manto used to often say, 'Mianji was a strict disciplinarian.'

Saadat's sister once narrated the following incident to me: Saadat was petrified of Mianji. Once he was flying a kite on the terrace when Mianji suddenly appeared. Saadat did not think twice and jumped on to the terrace of the next house. He was injured of course but he tolerated the pain without a whimper.

Manto neither sought nor accepted support of any kind. He intensely disliked anyone who begged for mercy. He kept flying kites and jumping off terraces all his life. He sometimes landed on other people's heads too; they in turn became aggravated, hurled abuses, and cried out for legal assistance. Manto, however, continued to insist, 'I too have a right to fly kites. The sky is no one's private property and belongs to all. Anybody who tries to trip me up must know that I will jump back and land on their heads. I must warn people who may have plans of cutting off my kite's cord that they will certainly not be spared. I will crack their skulls with bricks.' Manto was wounded many times when society played with him but not once was an appeal for mercy heard from him.

His father was a munsif at the court. He had married twice. Saadat, his mother and his sister, Nasira Iqbal, inherited nothing except bitter memories after his death. Manto's writing is infused with this bitterness that comes to us with the suddenness of a quinine tablet among a handful of sweet toffees. The intensity of this bitterness may be gauged by the difficult times Manto lived through, especially in the years before his death. Society is expected to shield and protect human beings. In fact, it is considered to be a person's guardian, a second father even, but this same society failed to do justice to Manto. The custodians of morality kept taking him to court throughout his life for writing about sex, which for them was filthy and obscene. It never occurred to them that if the relationship between man and woman is offensive, then Adam must be considered the first man to experience it. Anyway, no one can argue that sex is in any way connected with pleasure in Manto's writings. Manto never tried to vend sweets and toffees. Neither was any cocaine stocked in his shop. Only quinine was available. Manto soaked up the bitterness around him. He lived with this taste of bitterness in his mouth and it was in an attempt to neutralize this that he poured more and more of it down his throat.

He was drinking heavily and was often in a state of intoxication in the last two years of his life. His liver was badly damaged. He came very close to dying at the end of 1953 and the doctors declared it a miracle that he had managed to survive. They also warned him that a year or two was all he had if he did not give 'it' up. Manto, however, could not be stopped. He picked up the bottle again and, this time, drank straight from it. He did not even feel the need for a glass. It seemed like he was in a rush to arrive at a destination where there were neither rocky cliffs nor those who trade in stones.

His condition suddenly deteriorated on the morning of 18 January 1955. He vomited blood and was taken to hospital in an ambulance. The ambulance, however, brought him back home before it reached the hospital. Manto had reached his final destination.

In May 1953, I went to meet him on my way from Karachi to Peshawar. He did not recognize me immediately and was a bit startled to see me. The expression in his eyes made it quite clear that, mentally, he was somewhere far away from his physical surroundings.

Manto's sister told him, 'Saadat, Saeed is here.'

His face suddenly lit up and his eyes—that had been blankly staring into space—travelled to my face.

'Come, come, Khwaja,' he said.

My eyes involuntarily fell on his glass. He too caught on to what had crossed my mind and, without giving me the chance to express anything, he said, 'It's fine, my friend, it's fine! Don't start off with your preaching.'

His large, unblinking eyes were accusing me: 'So, you too have become a preacher! It was to avoid the wretched preacher that I sought refuge in alcohol. I had expected better treatment from someone like you.'

There was immeasurable beauty in his large, restless eyes. There was a time when he had developed a deep interest in collecting different varieties of speech from Punjab. He used to often talk about it to his friends and say that all poetry was fraud when compared to the creativity in these speech varieties. He used to often quote the following couplet to many of his friends:

*Gora rang te sharbati aakhiyan*
*Khand vich kaid keetiyan.*

Eyes full of nectar in a fair face
Are imprisoned in sweetness

His own eyes were not very different and seemed to be brimming with nectar. The difference, however, lay in the fact that instead of being surrounded by khand, his eyes were veiled behind a screen of cigarette smoke and looked like two lakes surrounded by mist with who knows how many ships of joys, desires and tears submerged in their watery depths. From the moment these eyes looked upon the world, they had been searching for the love and care of which Manto had been deprived in his childhood. So deep was this void that even the sincerity of his friends and the appreciation of his admirers failed to fill it up.

All through his life Manto used his pen to rip through society's garments and unveil deceit and hypocrisy. One such garment that he tore apart was that of religion. There are many Rasputins living all around us in our country. Even the devil cannot match these charlatans with their long beards, glowing visages, spotless turbans, untainted long gowns, and the talent to plan out their future swindles. The believers are so badly trapped in their web of deceit that there seems to be no hope of their liberation. These people claim to satisfy all the unfulfilled desires of the heart; they claim to convert ash into gold. The dust of their feet is believed to be the cure for incurable diseases. Their employment exchanges procure jobs for the jobless. They gift springs to the childless. They rid virgins of evil spirits. The old man in Manto's story 'Saheb-e-Karamat' is one such character. He deceives a poor and simple peasant by intoxicating first his wife and then his daughter to cool down the fire of his lust. Maulvi-saheb, the old man, leaves behind his beard and scarf under the pillow when he goes out in the morning. Such crimes, concealed under the garb of religion, frequently occur all around us.

This is Manto's characteristic style. Crimes committed under the guise of religion continue to routinely occur all around us but newspapers choose not to highlight them. The vision of a writer, however, is so keen that it delves deep under the pretence of civility and culture to scrutinize that which lies hidden under their folds. The hollow, outward spectacle is something that neither impresses nor convinces the writer.

Manto wields his pen to dramatically scrape off the many different kinds of beards growing on society's face. He rips these beards off and hands them back to society, declaring loud and clear, 'Here, keep to yourself all this make-up that hides your true colours.'

Many Saheb-e-Karamats lie hidden underneath these layers of make-up but at times they come out from these shadows and reveal themselves. These layers of deception conceal many other monsters too who are masters at duping beautiful, young girls and then abandoning them in busy market places. These girls are eager to return but by then the doors of paradise are locked to them forever.

Manto has demolished the effigies of many outdated traditions and created many new paradigms with his own flesh and blood. He has then put these models on empty shelves, on exhibit for the entire human race.

I see a reflection of Adam and Eve in the characters of Gopinath and Mummy. Their offence is the same as the one committed by Adam and Eve and through them Manto reminds us that their transgression can be traced back to the original transgression of Adam and Eve.

In Manto's religion, a human remains human despite his sins. In his scheme of things, sins are a creation of God too. In the words of the poet Iqbal, humans retain God-like qualities even though they are constituted of earth. And for his epitaph, he writes: Saadat Hasan Manto lies buried here/In his heart are interred all the secret techniques of writing/It is as if he lies under tons of earth, wondering who, between him and Khuda, is the better writer. Can we not grant him the luxury of even this hyperbole?

He was Kashmiri, and like those women who pick coal from train tracks, he would collect the burning embers of love and compassion from the fiery temples of crime and sin to fill up his kangri. This he would do so that those souls, freezing under the onslaught of rituals and restrictions, could warm themselves at his kangri. These are the embers which remain concealed in his characters: in Siraj's indifference, in Bismillah's sad eyes and in Sharda's cigarette case. Their invisible heat warms that oven in 'Sadak ke Kinare' on which food is prepared for uninvited guests. He walks about, concealing this warmth-giving kangri in the bulge at his waist.

Manto was himself a victim of that great freeze. Like Prometheus, he stole fire from the gods. It was for this crime that he was lashed to a rock, and vultures tore at him in punishment. To feel deeply, and to understand everything, is the biggest crime, and Manto's fireplace is alight with this crime. But what is the statue of Bhagat Singh doing on top of that fireplace? Creation and destruction perhaps go hand in hand.

Manto's creativity was first sparked by translations. As far as I can remember, the first long story he translated was about a ghost whose hand had been cut off. This was the first and last experience and translation of its kind. Bari-saheb was a student of History and Economics. He had no great affinity for fiction, yet he knew enough to guide his disciples on what was good and what bad. And thus the works of Victor Hugo, Lord Lytton, Gorky, Chekhov, Pushkin, Gogol, Dostoevsky, Oscar Wilde and Maupassant made an appearance in Dar-ul-Ahmer, Manto's room. For Bari-saheb, Victor Hugo was the greatest novelist in the world. We got his books from far and wide and read them like they had been recommended in our syllabus. Bari-saheb wanted *Les Miserables* translated but its thickness was too daunting. However, *The Last Days of the Condemned* was translated as *Sarguzasht-e-Aseer*. This book is a vociferous statement against the death penalty—the condemned man's younger son protests all forms of injustice. The translation of Oscar Wilde's *Vera* is also a memory of that time.

Manto has discussed *Vera* in detail in his sketch of Bari-saheb. The book was related to the extremists and anarchists of Russia who possessed all kinds of weapons. In the Amritsar of that time, anyone who wanted to buy even an airgun was likely to be blown away by a cannon. But when posters challenging the rulers began to make their appearance on the walls of the city, which stated that czars were being overthrown in Russia, investigations of these disciples of Bhagat Singh, who wanted to recreate these Muscovite dramas in the lanes of Amritsar and herald the end of the British monarchy, began in Kucha Vakeelan. But the white-collar folk of the area turned away these investigators, saying, 'Go away mian, mind your business. These are our own children.' And thus was trouble averted. I often think that had the police followed its usual strict course of action in this matter, Manto possessed all the qualities which would make him another Bhagat Singh. His story 'Tamasha' reflects many of these qualities. In 'Tamasha', the uproar caused by the Marshall Law in Amritsar has been looked from the point of view of a child—the hero of that story is Manto himself. He was about seven at that time. The cruelty of the law had prevented this child from growing up normally. And, at that stage, he could have hardly turned to his relatives, indifferent as they were to him. He harboured a dislike for beaten paths too and his hatred for the selfishness of leaders only grew. He was hungry for sincerity, hardly a quality to be found in them. He screamed, 'Save Hindustan from its leaders.'

> Save Hindustan from those leaders who are vitiating its atmosphere. These so-called leaders keep a small money-box with them in which they pick citizens' pockets to collect wealth. You can smell the stench of betrayal and corruption in their every breath. Weighed down by huge garlands, these so-called leaders bring out massive processions, give long speeches at crossroads, and build roads for themselves which lead to luxury. They collect donations, but have they ever presented a Bill to combat unemployment? These people, whose souls are lame, whose brains are crippled, whose tongue is paralyzed and whose limbs are useless, how will they lead the nation? Hindustan doesn't need many leaders, it needs just one who embodies the qualities of Caliph Umar, and

who carries in his breast the soldierly qualities of Ataturk. (Published 1942)

From the date of publication, it is clear that this piece was written much before Independence and represents the first phase of Manto's life. But having read it, it doesn't seem necessary to point out what his attitude towards politics and political leaders was. He made his views clear in yet another article:

> I have no interest in politics. I include leaders and quacks in the same category. Politics and quackery are both professions. I have as much interest in politics as Gandhiji has in cinema. Gandhiji doesn't watch cinema, I don't read newspapers. We are both wrong. Gandhiji should watch films and I should read newspapers.

In a humorous manner, Manto has attempted to show that people in politics people lack a sense of balance and a sense of humour. Gandhiji and films are merely symbols. Saadat, in his Mantoesque way, has brought to the fore one reality by means of another. To bring out contradiction is the chief technique of satire and Manto excelled at it.

> It was that very same Bombay where the Congress, by imposing prohibition, rendered thousands of toddy-tappers unemployed. That same Bombay, urusul bilad, that bride among cities, one part of whose veil was silk and the other coarse jute. That same Bombay where, at the feet of tall skyscrapers, thousands sleep on footpaths.
> The Muslim League is the masjid, the Congress the temple. The Congress wants self-rule and so does the Muslim League but the two cannot work together. Their blood comes together only in gutters and cesspools.

In this situation, his abhorrence to politics was but natural. He thus reached Bombay from Amristar. The drama troupe,

Moscow ka Mandwa, had disbanded soon after they put up their advertisements. The scenery, curtains, all the paraphernalia, were locked up in the director's house and was eventually bought up by a bookseller from Lahore at dirt-cheap rates. Then, book publishing was a show business like any other— wrestling, cattle fairs, contracts to sell intoxicants, the flesh trade. And that book, *Vera*, was an actual drama for which a licence was required. This licence wasn't received and the producer fled—Bari-saheb had vanished. He didn't even know the climax of the play. He had forgotten that the author of *The Picture of Dorian Gray* was as far away from extremism as Gandhiji was from cinema. In the climax, Vera, Oscar Wilde's heroine, plunges that very dagger into her chest which she had brought to stab the czarevitch with. She was in love with the prince. Love triumphed, duty could only keep looking on slack-jawed.

But the uproar hadn't yet ended. The 'children' weren't done with their games. The producer, Bari-saheb, reappeared after vanishing for fifteen days. He was now in the garb of the editor and publisher of a weekly, *Khalq*. We were ordered to start work immediately so that there was no delay in publication. Manto's story, 'Tamasha' was published in the first issue. I too wrote a very revolutionary article, 'Mazdoor' in which capitalists had been criticized roundly. I wrote under a pseudonym, Adam. Manto too did not take a byline at all out of fear. Bari-saheb wrote an article on Marx and Hegel in his typical oratorical style which I will probably not understand even today. Yet, he was our pir-murshid, whose spiritual guidance distinguished us amongst our contemporaries. And because of this, even our professors (among who were luminaries like Faiz Ahmed Faiz and Sahebzada Mahmood-uz-Zafar) began to view us with respect. In such a situation, there was hardly anything at all Bari-saheb would say which was useless or meaningless. People may or may not have understood his essay, one consequence of its publication was that the police was alerted. But *Khalq* ran into financial problems soon after the first issue was published and Bari-saheb's dreams of ushering revolution in journalism were also shattered.

Bari-saheb would make big plans, dip them into cups of tea and drink them up. He would dreams strange dreams. He would say that it is important to go to jail if one is to sharpen the sentiment of revolution. Saadat would tell him, 'You're talking nonsense Bari-saheb. You won't last even two days in there.' However, this dream had reached the level of insanity. 'That day isn't far when you visit me in jail. In jail! You'll see.' He wanted to keep a diary. Pink paper of very good quality was procured and given to a bookbinder so that he could make one, bound in black leather. A picture of an iron-barred door was pasted to the first page very neatly. A calligrapher was engaged to write, in beautiful hand, the following words on the picture: 'Jail Window'.

The communist writer Bari was an extremely unrealistic man. His disciples didn't have even a fraction of the devotion Bari had for Marx and Engels. Marx's materialism was too heavy a burden on their tender souls. Their individuality could not make peace with collectivism. Manto's ego would not allow him to accept the God which the crowd, the collective, accepted. But his own godhood was yet still a distant dream.

# My Friend, My Foe

## Ismat Chughtai

I WAS SOMEWHAT NERVOUS AS I CLIMBED UP THE WOODEN stairs of Adelphi Chambers. I felt like one does just before stepping inside an examination hall. I was anyway rather ill at ease when meeting unfamiliar people, and as if that was not enough, the 'unfamiliar' in this case was Manto—whom I was going to meet for the first time. My nervousness slowly increased and reached the fringes of terror. I was panic-stricken and told Shahid, 'Let's go back. Manto may not be home.'

But Shahid poured cold water over my plans. 'He never goes out in the evenings because that is his time to drink.'

Now just imagine. This was like routing the vanquished! Was it not bad enough that, to begin with, this was Manto! And now to make it worse, this was going to be a Manto who would be drinking! But I strengthened my resolve. What was the big deal, anyway? He certainly couldn't gobble me up! Let his tongue be thorny if it was. I was not some fragile bubble that would deflate with a mere puff. We climbed up the dusty and creaking staircase. The door of the flat was half-open. There was a sofa-set in the corner of what appeared to be the drawing room. On the other side was a clean, white bed. Near the window was a long overladen table with a large chair in front of it. On the chair, sitting on his haunches, was a thin, wiry man, with an ant-like emaciated face.

'Do come, come in,' Manto said pleasantly, and stood up. He was wearing a khaddar kurta pajama and a Jawahar-cut jacket.

Manto always sat on the chair with his knees folded, which made him look small in size. But when he stretched himself out, he looked rather tall. And whenever Manto slithered out of his sitting position and stood up on his feet, he gave the impression of being full of venom.

'Oh! I had imagined you would be someone terribly dark, thin and feeble. Half-dead, in fact,' he said with a toothy smile.

'And I had imagined you would be a roaring Punjabi with a loud voice,' I responded.

I had decided that he should be paid back with his own coin. He must not be allowed to dominate.

And the very next moment we started arguing with all our might. It seemed as though we had done grievous damage to ourselves by not being acquainted with each other earlier and now needed to compensate for the loss. At times, the exchange of words became somewhat tangled and knotted but since there was still some reserve between us, I left it for the next meeting. For many hours after that, our jaws continuously chopped and sliced hordes of words and sentences about many different issues. I soon discovered that like me, Manto too was in the habit of not waiting for the other person to finish. He would start his retort without listening to the full response. And with this, whatever little formality remained disappeared. In quick succession, dialogue transformed into argument, argument into proper dispute and, on the strength of having known each other only for a few hours, we called each other— in rather literary language—stupid, crazy, and the architects of flawed arguments.

The combat went on, but I also detached myself a little and looked closely. Behind those thick glasses were eyes with large and dark pupils that seemed to be leaping out. Quite spontaneously, the image of a peacock feather floated through my mind. Now, what have eyes got to do with a peacock feather? I could never solve the puzzle but whenever I looked at those eyes, the image of a peacock feather would flash through my mind. It was perhaps the arrogance and the impertinence, along with congeniality, in those eyes which brought the image to my mind. My heart would miss a beat whenever I would look into them! I felt I had surely seen those eyes somewhere, seen them at close quarters. Guffawing, smiling solemnly, and showering barbs of sarcasm. Frail limbs stiffening as if they were approaching death. Manto had a headful of hair, sunken, pale cheeks, and yellowed, crooked teeth. Suddenly, Manto broke into a choking cough. I was alarmed. It was a cough I was familiar with; I had heard it in my childhood and was deeply vexed.

I have forgotten what it was exactly but, in response to something, I said, 'This is completely incorrect.'

And we broke into a proper fight.

'You are just arguing for the sake of argument.'

'This is foolishness.'

'It's cheating, Ismat-bahen.'

'Why are you calling me your sister?' I asked in a tetchy voice.

'Just by the way. I usually don't address women as sisters. In fact, I don't even address my own sister as sister.'

'Then, are you saying it just to tease me?'

'Not at all! How did you arrive at this conclusion?'

'Because my brothers always taunted me, teased me, beat me up, or got me beaten up.'

Manto laughed loudly. 'Then rest assured that I will always call you my sister.'

'In that case, you must also always remember that my brothers don't have a very favourable opinion about me...This cough that you have, why don't you get treated?'

'Treated! The doctors are asses. Three years ago, they had declared that I would die within a year. That I have TB. It's obvious that I have proven their prediction false by not dying.

And now I consider doctors nothing but fools. Magic healers and hypnotists are much more intelligent than these doctors.'

'Before you, there was another elderly gentleman who used to claim the same thing.'

'Which elderly person?'

'My brother Azeem Baig. He is now resting under the earth.'

Soon we were arguing about Azeem Baig's art. Shahid and I had come for a short visit, but we got so engrossed in conversation that before we realized it was eleven o'clock in the night. Shahid, who had been observing our skirmishes from the sidelines, was wretched with hunger. It would be one by the time we reached Malad and so we decided to eat at Manto's. Manto asked me to fetch spoons and plates from the cupboard and went out to get rotis from a hotel.

'Just take the pickle from that jar.'

Manto hurriedly put the food on the table and sat on his haunches on the chair. The table, which till some time ago was an arena of literary activity, quickly transformed itself to serve as a dining table. Ignoring all etiquettes of serving others before beginning, we started right away, as though we had been eating together for years.

Heated discussion accompanied the food. After meandering a little, Manto kept coming back to 'Lihaaf', tearing it to pieces. That short story had become a real pain for me at the time. I tried my best to ignore him but he stubbornly refused to give in and shredded it completely. He felt really let down when I told him that I regretted writing 'Lihaaf'. He harangued me and called me myopic and a coward. I was not willing to accept the story as my masterpiece but Manto insisted that I do. Soon, all restraint was thrown to the winds and we went beyond 'Lihaaf' to argue frankly about many other things. And I was surprised to see the ease with which Manto could say the most rude and vulgar things. He said them with such bravado, spontaneity and innocence that one did not feel odd at hearing them. Or perhaps he did not allow the space for others to ponder over what he said. One felt amused rather than disgusted or angry with his words.

He mentioned Safia once again, just before we were to leave. Manto had remembered Safia many times through the evening.

'Safia is a really good girl.'

'Safia cooks saalan really well.'

'You will be really happy to meet her.'

'Why don't you call her if you miss her so much?' I asked him.

'So, you think that I can't sleep without her?' He was beginning to show his true colours.

'One can fall asleep even with a noose around one's neck.' I evaded the issue.

He laughed.

'You really love Safia, don't you?' I asked him in a confidential tone.

'Love!' He shrieked as though I had abused him. 'I don't love her at all.' He made a bitter face and rolled his big, black pupils. 'I am not a believer in love.'

'Oh! So, haven't you fallen in love with anyone?' I asked, faking wonder.

'No.'

'Have you also never had mumps? Or pox? Surely you must have had whooping cough.'

He laughed. 'What do you mean by love? Love is something that is really immeasurable and limitless. We have love for our mother, sister and daughter...and also for our wife. We love our shoes and chappals too. One of my friends deeply loves the bitch he owns. Yes, I loved my son.' He jerked himself up higher in the chair at the mention of his son. 'Khuda ki kasam, he was this tiny but moved about. He had a big body. When he crawled around on his knees, he used to scratch out mud from cracks in the floor and eat it. He really listened to me, he obeyed me.'

Like many other fathers, Manto too had begun to convince us about the distinctiveness of his son.

'Believe me, he was barely about six or seven days old when I began making him sleep in my bed. I massaged his body and bathed him myself. He was not even three months old when he started giggling loudly. Safia needed to do nothing at all. All she did was feed him. She would sleep like a log through the night. I used to quietly give him milk from the feeding-bottle and she would not even find out about it. One should disinfect the feeding-bottle with eau-de-cologne or spirit before feeding children, otherwise they break out into a rash.'

He was speaking very seriously, and I kept looking at him and wondered, 'What kind of a man is he, this specialist in bringing up children?'

'But he died,' Manto said, faking an expression of joy on his face. 'It's good that he died. He had made me his ayah. I would have been washing his nappies had he been alive today. I would have become completely worthless. It would not have been possible for me to have done anything else. It's true, Ismat-bahen, I loved him.'

Just as we were leaving, he said again, 'Safia is going to come soon. You will be really happy to meet her.'

And truly, I was overjoyed when I met Safia. Within minutes we became so fond of each other that we almost hugged and started whispering secretively, talking about things that only women say to each other. Things that are not meant for the ears of men.

Manto became jealous when he saw Safia and me intimately whispering to each other and started tossing jibes at us. He stuck his ear to the other side of the wooden wall and overheard some of our whispered talks. Like a naughty child, he said, 'Tauba! Tauba! I could never have imagined the kind of filthy things women talk about.'

Safia's ears became red with embarrassment.

He began to tease us. 'And I did not expect this at all from you, Ismat-bahen; that you would talk like uncultured, uneducated women who gossip with neighbours. When did you get married? How was the wedding night? When and how was the baby born? Tauba!'

I stopped him in his tracks.

'This is really the limit, Manto-saheb. I did not think you would be so narrow-minded. You call this filthy? What is filthy about this? The birth of a child is the most beautiful moment in this world. And these whisperings form an important part of our training school. Do you think I was taught in college how to give birth to a baby? Like you, the aging professors there turn their noses up and say, "Tauba! Tauba!" It is from women in the neighbourhood that we have learnt the most important secrets of life.'

'Safia lacks all refinement. She knows nothing about literature. She rejects everything as obscene. She is seriously upset with your writing. Don't you get tired of talking to her for hours about how much turmeric should be added to korma, or to dahi-bade?'

'Oh Manto-saheb, whoever adds turmeric to korma!' Safia was shocked.

And Manto began to quarrel. He vehemently insisted that turmeric must be used in all kinds of cooking and it was sheer tyranny and injustice if it wasn't.

'I had a Rajput friend who drank a mixture of ghee and turmeric before exercising. He was an expert wrestler.'

But we were equally insistent that his friend had been actually consuming sludge, not ghee and turmeric. Under no condition were we ready to accept that turmeric was used in cooking korma. Manto eventually had to concede defeat.

If Manto and I decided to meet for five minutes, the meeting would invariably stretch out into a full programme of five hours. Any discussion with Manto was like honing the mind to achieve a razor's edge. It was as if cobwebs and layers of accumulated dust were being swept away. And off and on, these discussions became so lengthy and raucous that they seemed like a messy tangle of cords and strings. Actually, our ability to think and comprehend used to just fade away! The two of us persistently carried on with discussion, continued to argue and ensnare each other, often reaching the breaking point of goodwill. I possessed the talent of camouflaging my defeat well but Manto would be reduced almost to the point of tears. His eyes would seem to tauten and fan out like peacock feathers. His nostrils would quiver, his face would look embittered and, when he got exasperated, he would call out to Shahid to champion his cause. After that, the literary or philosophical battle would be transformed into a completely personal and prosaic one.

Manto would walk away in a huff. It would then be Shahid's turn to quarrel with me, 'Why do you talk so rudely to my friends? Today Manto left angry. Now he will never enter our home again and, as far as I am concerned, I no longer have the courage to visit him. He is such a blunt man and capable of saying something brusque, which could put an end to my relationship with him.'

I too sometimes felt that I was often quite abrasive with Manto. This increased the likelihood of Manto becoming offended with me and, consequently, wrecking my relationship with Safia, which had by then become stronger than that with him. Manto's idea of self-respect was so inflated that it often came across as arrogance. He loved to impress his friends and he would get really infuriated if he was mocked in front of those who held him in high esteem. He believed that the two of us belonged to the same camp, and could thus argue with each other as much as we wanted, but we must avoid attacking each other in front of others. And he considered most people he knew intellectually inferior to him.

However, if I had an argument with him in the morning, and then quite by coincidence met him in the evening, he would greet me with great warmth; as though nothing unseemly had ever occurred between us. He would continue to talk with the same intimacy. Then for some time we would be over-courteous and not challenge each other. But I would soon be fed up with this hypocritical façade, the fireworks on each side would be ignited and would explode with the intensity of bullets.

People would often watch us do battle with great pleasure. Having no option, we would get together again when we realized that—we argued for our own pleasure, not to become a spectacle and provide a cockfight to others to gawk at. Manto's opinion was that we may have any number of arguments, even highly obnoxious ones, in the privacy of our homes but we must present a joint front in gatherings and get-togethers. Our joint front must be strong enough to make others lick the dust. But I often forgot my allegiance to this front and more often than not, the front buzzed like an angry beehive.

I could never understand if Manto lost control after drinking or if he drank because he was not in control. I never saw any unsteadiness in his walk, nor did I find him faltering in his conversation. I failed to perceive any difference in his behaviour—except that when he had had a bit too much, he tried very hard to convince others that he was completely in his senses. He exasperated others in his attempt to establish that he was not drunk.

'Believe me, Ismat-bahen, I am not drunk at all. I can give up drinking today. I can give up drinking the day I decide to. You can bet with me.'

'I will not bet with you because I know that you are bound to lose. You cannot quit drinking...and you are drunk right now.'

Manto tried to convince me in many different ways that he could give up drinking at that very moment; he would offer all kinds of evidence to establish it. It was just a matter of my taking up his bet. I got so fed up with this that one day I accepted. And Manto lost. I did win but my victory brought me no reward—we had not decided on an amount. After this, whenever Manto was under the influence of alcohol, he stubbornly insisted on a bet and refused to let me go till it was done. The only way in which I could shake him off was to accept—which I did because he would leave me with no choice.

Manto was often in the habit of praising himself and, if I were around, he would include me in this circle of praise. At those moments, he considered nobody besides the two of us as writers of any worth. He used to be especially critical of Krishan Chander and Devendra Satyarthi. He would blow up if one praised them even a little. I used to often tell him that since he was not a critic, there was no need to take his opinion seriously. Which would be followed by Manto heaping abuses on critics. In a way, he considered the very existence of critics lethal for literary creativity.

He would breathe fire. 'All they say is sheer nonsense. Just continue to do the exact opposite of what they say. The people who raise objections are the ones who read my stories on the sly. They seek proxy gratification instead of extracting a message from them. And if that was not enough, they feel guilty for the gratuitous pleasure they enjoy and begin to attack the stories.'

He sometimes got so disturbed that I would have to try to pacify him, saying, 'You should not respond to them since you know what they write and say is rubbish. You should ignore critics if you feel they are worthless. But what you must not do is condemn and reject public opinion.'

He, however, would continue with his grumbling.

One day he came to me with a solemn expression on his face and said, 'We will file a lawsuit.'

'Who do you mean?' I asked.

'Us,' he said, 'us meaning you and I. This damn fellow has published a collection of both your stories and mine, along with a statement saying they are so obscene that the nation needs to be protected from them. Now, does this wretched fellow not owe an explanation for doing the opposite of what he professes? On the one hand, he is propagating the stories by publishing the collection and, on the other, he has ensured that he makes money from them. How could he publish our stories without our permission? I am sending him a legal notice asking for compensation.'

But he probably soon forgot about it all.

While it is true that Manto did boast about himself, but more than that he loved to praise his friends sky high to me. I have never been able to comprehend the immense fascination he had for Rafiq Ghaznavi. Whenever Manto mentioned his name, he always used the choicest of words like lafanga and badmash to describe him. He would often tell me how Rafiq Ghaznavi had married four sisters one after the other, and how there was no tawaif in Lahore who had not licked his boots.

He talked about Rafiq in exactly the same way in which

boys talk of their elder brothers. He described every minute detail of his romantic exploits. One day he suggested that I meet him.

'Why should I meet him? You have said so many times that he is a lafanga,' I asked Manto.

'Oh! But that's exactly why I want you to meet him. Who on earth is responsible for your misconception that a lafanga and badmash is a bad man? Rafiq is truly a gentleman!'

'Manto-saheb!' I said, 'Lafanga, decent, badmash! I just can't understand what kind of a man he is after all! I am probably not as intelligent and experienced as you think I am.'

'You are merely pretending.' Manto was clearly upset. 'And that's why I want you to meet Rafiq. He is a very interesting man and no woman can resist falling in love with him.'

'I too am a woman,' I said, pretending to be anxious, and Manto got very irritated.

'I consider you to be my sister.'

'Your sister could be a woman too.'

Manto guffawed, 'Could be! Well said!' But he remained unmoved, 'You will have to meet him. At least give it a try.'

'I have already seen him at the station but you had poisoned my mind so completely that I ran away, afraid of falling in love with that worthless fellow.'

However, it was only after meeting Rafiq that I realized how perceptive Manto was. Despite having all vices of the world, Rafiq possessed all the qualities of a sophisticated man. He had the potential to be an extraordinary knave, but at the same time he could be very honest and decent. I didn't bother with understanding the how and why of it; that was Manto's specialty.

Manto had the ability to closely go through all that has been discarded and thrown into the garbage and single out and collect pearls from it. It was his hobby to dig through mounds of rubbish with his nails because he had lost faith in those people who claim to cleanse and beautify the world. He lacked faith in their intellectual abilities as well as their judgment. He saw through the dark secrets hidden away in the hearts of so-called respectable and chaste women and contrasted them with the purity of the tawaifs living in brothels. A character like the Ghaatan, rotting in muck and sweat, was more fragrant for him than bejewelled young, glamorous women soaked in perfume. While it is true that 'Boo' is overburdened by images of the flesh and the body, if one looks closely, one can also espy the soul inside the body. The souls of people from the privileged classes appear to be the solid, undissolved pieces that float on the surface of spoiled milk while the souls of the repressed, far-removed from artificiality, seem unadulterated and pure in comparison. If the story cannot be seen as reflecting the issue of class differences, it is also not possible to see it as merely connected to physicality or flesh. The idea of class difference was a dominant one in Manto's mind. When he brought down and shattered the idol worshipped by the world, Manto felt that he had done something truly courageous.

He would narrate the escapades of his ruffian friends with immense pride. One day, I said to needle him, 'Your friends are liars. The truth is that they neither know thousands of tawaifs nor have they ever molested any woman.'

Manto tried to convince me how they really had indulged in all those misdemeanours, and other worse things.

'All lies,' I said, disconcerting him.

'Why, why can't you believe it? Anybody who wants to can go to the flesh market.'

'But these people don't have the guts to enter the rooms of the tawaifs. The most that they are capable of is to go there, listen to the tawaifs sing, and come back.'

'I too have been to the kothas of the tawaifs.'

'To listen to the singing, of course,' I teased him.

'Not at all! To get full service for my money, and I always made sure I got my money's worth.'

'I don't believe it,' I continued to insist.

'And why not?'

He got up and walked up to sit on his haunches right opposite me on the carpet.

'That's just what I feel. You just want to impress me.'

'Khuda kasam. Believe me, I did go.'

'You don't believe in God. Don't unnecessarily drag Him into all this.'

'I swear by my dead child. I went not once but...'

'What harm can you bring to the dead child by swearing falsely?'

And Manto knotted up his limbs to sit more tightly, determined to not to give up till he convinced me what a voracious visitor of brothels he was. He made Safia give evidence of this. I won that round with Safia in barely two minutes. I proposed that Manto may have told her about his visit to the tawaif but, for all one knew, even if he had gone there, he had probably turned back after greeting her.

Safia turned quiet and said, 'Now I have no way of knowing whether he just offered his wishes and turned back or...' She was caught in a dilemma.

Manto got very excited and ended up drinking a lot very quickly. He then started quarrelling and insisting that he would not let the matter come to an end till I accepted him as a frequenter of brothels. I was equally adamant that nothing in the world, however catastrophic, would make me accept that.

Manto was of course drunk. Besides that, his inherent sarcastic temperament made matters worse. He would have scratched my face black and blue if he had his way.

Safia, with a pathetic expression on her face, said, 'Just agree with him, bahen.'

Shahid said, 'Come now, let's go home.'

Manto began to heckle Shahid and announced that he would not let us leave till I relented and agreed with him. That led to a great uproar.

Manto told Shahid in all seriousness, 'Let's go to a tawaif right away. If I fail to win you over, I will accept that it's not my mother's milk that runs through my body but that of a pig.'

I provoked him further, 'I know quite well that you will not even go anywhere close to one. You'll just go up to Byculla Bridge, walk around a bit and come back. And anyway, we will of course not believe you. What's the point?'

At that point it seemed like Manto was on fire. He somehow restrained his anger and asked, 'How then can one convince you?'

'Take us, I mean take Safia and me, along with you.'

'I will not go,' Safia was annoyed. 'You are the one who has gone crazy and so you are the one who should go.'

'Let's all go.' I winked at Safia and, soon, all four of us got ready to leave.

The two of us—Shahid and I—prepared to leave but Safia, only God knows how, managed to convince Manto not to go. The next time we met, Manto joked and laughed a lot about our earlier fracas and whispered to me, 'At least accept it now.'

'Never,' I responded.

I have no idea if Manto's writings about tawaifs had their source in his personal experience but what I do know is that they were rooted in his principles and beliefs. Even if he had visited a brothel, he would not have looked at the tawaif as a mere physical body. He would have seen through the façade and grasped the emotions of a woman who cherishes values despite being a creature of the foul gutter. Manto broke the established norms of what was right and wrong, proper and improper, and created his own standards for assessment. It is possible for a sense of dignity and self-respect to strike root in a character as irreparable and worthless as Khushiya. An evasive and undependable character like Gopinath can raise himself above the gods who may bow down to him. Apparently respectable volunteers can turn out to be villains. And one who rapes a corpse can himself be transformed into a dead body.

Sometimes my quarrels with Manto would become so ugly that it would seem like our relationship would snap. Once he got so deeply disturbed by some issue that his eyes became bloodshot and, grinding his teeth, he said, 'I just need to use a few to fix you once and for all. I have not done it only because you are a woman.'

'Feel free to express yourself. Fulfill your heart's desires. You need not be so kind to me. Go on now, let me see the arrows lying unused in your quiver. Reveal them!'

'You will be embarrassed.'

'Khuda kasam, I won't.'

'Then you are not a woman.'

'So, according to you it is absolutely essential for a woman to appear to be embarrassed whether or not she feels so. It's a pity, Manto-saheb, that you too have different standards for men and women. I had thought you far superior to other men in this respect,' I added to provoke him.

'Not at all. I do not differentiate between men and women.'

'Then go ahead and say what you think would embarrass me.'

'No, I am no longer angry.' He laughed.

'Fine. Say it because we are friends then. What explosive thing were you going to say?'

'Nothing... I can't remember it now. It would not have been anything unusual. I probably would have uttered some vulgar abuse.'

'Is that all?' I said, disappointed.

'Or, I may have given you a tight slap,' he said shamefacedly.

'It would not have made much difference to me. You have no idea the kind of abuses my ears have heard. And I have been slapped really hard many times. It's the first time that you have offered me the privilege of being a woman. My brothers would have slapped me many times over by now.'

And so we patched up and became friends.

One day, troubled by the heat in my office, I thought of going to Manto's house, resting there for a while before returning to Malad. The door, as usual, was open. When I entered, I saw Safia lying down with a distressed and angry expression on her face. Manto had a broom in his hand and was hitting it around the bed. He had covered his nose with the edge of his kurta, which he held in one hand, and was wielding the broom with the other.

'What are you doing?' I asked, peeping under the table.

'Playing cricket,' Manto said, rolling his peacock-feather eyes.

'What should I do now? I thought that I would rest here for a while but it looks you two are not on talking terms,' I said, threatening to leave.

'Oh!' Safia immediately sprang up. 'Come, please come.'

'What was the quarrel about?' I asked.

'Nothing at all. I just happened to say that cooking, cleaning and running the house are not a man's job. That's it. He began to argue with me just like he argues with you. He started saying, "Why not? I can sweep the floor right away." The more I tried to stop him, the more he fought with me and said, "If that's what you feel then let's get a divorce,'" Safia said with a tearful expression on her face.

I broke into a fake cough to stop Manto's sweeping and said, 'Early in the morning the municipality sweeper pretended to sweep the courtyard and stuffed my throat with dust. Now you can satisfy your whims too. I am close to dying from the heat.'

Manto quickly dropped the broom and went out to a hotel to get ice. Safia went into the kitchen to fry spices for seasoning the daal. Manto brought ice in a towel and banged the towel hard against the wall to break the ice into pieces. He then put it in a plate in front of me and sat on his haunches.

'So then, say something,' he said, in his customary way.

The smell of the seasoning made me sick. 'Oh! Is Safia burning a corpse?' I asked, covering my nose.

Manto was startled. He rolled his big eyes and looked at me from top to bottom. All at once, he jumped up and rushed into the kitchen. He poured water into the pot sitting on the fire even as Safia kept screaming.

He came back, sat on the chair somewhat hesitantly, and broke into a smile. I just kept looking at him like an idiot.

Safia entered grumbling and severely scolded him. He then said very shyly, 'You are carrying a baby,' as though it was he and not I who was carrying the baby.

I immediately caught on that Safia must have felt sick at the smell of seasoning when she had been pregnant.

'Manto-saheb, for God's sake, don't talk like a midwife.' I was irritated.

He laughed loudly. 'Arre wah! What's wrong with that? You must be craving something sour. I will go get unripe mangoes.' He went downstairs and soon came back clutching some in the front of his kurta like a child. He peeled the mangoes and, sprinkling salt and pepper on them with extreme care, offered them to me. He then sat on his haunches and kept smiling as he looked at me intently.

'Safia! O Safia!' he yelled.

Safia entered the room, surrounded by smoke and wiping her eyes with the edge of her saree.

'You idiot, she is pregnant,' he said, holding Safia around her waist.

'Uff! There's a limit to being lewd. No wonder people call you an obscene writer.'

Manto became more vivacious when I rebuked him and began to counsel me like an elderly, experienced woman.

'You won't get stretch marks if you massage your stomach with olive oil.'

'The baby will be fair and childbirth will be easy if you eat coconut.'

'Don't chew ice during your pregnancy. It dries up the blood vessels. Isn't that so, Safia?'

'Oho Manto-saheb, what all you end up saying!' Safia was irritated but could do nothing beyond saying that.

Safia was very anxious about my condition when my daughter Seema was born. When Manto saw my daughter, the memories of his son were refreshed and he kept telling me how mischievous his son was. Safia too was moved.

Manto's eldest daughter was born within a year. I found out about it only after I returned from Poona. I immediately went to see Manto and discovered that he had shifted house. I had to ferret around for a while to locate his new house and, when I finally entered, I found the child's nappies hanging on a clothesline in the drawing room. The new house was very small and claustrophobic. Manto had decided to leave because he felt that the floor of the old house was very dirty. He was also worried that a splinter would injure the child when she started crawling, or she could develop a taste for mud by sampling dust from the floor. Nakhat could comfortably play on the clean floor of the new house. It didn't seem to matter much to him that Nakhat was only a few weeks old at the time.

'I have an aversion to children,' Manto used to say with utmost seriousness. 'I am really scared of them because they are pests and can take complete possession of me. I keep thinking of them all the time and can't concentrate on anything.' He would philosophize even as he washed the feeding-bottle.

Manto was very fond of my niece Meenu. He used to talk to her about dolls and toy cooking-pots for hours. Whenever she would demand tamarind from the tree outside, Manto would push a bamboo through the window and shake the branches till the fruit fell. He would then go downstairs and return clutching the front of his kurta full of tamarind. He used to get her to sit on the pot and one could hear him say 'shhee... shhee' to help with her toilet training. He accused children because he loved them and was completely vulnerable in their presence.

One day, when we were living in Malad, there was a sudden knock on the door at midnight. We discovered a breathless Safia standing outside.

'What happened?' I asked.

'I told him that one should not go to anybody's house in this condition but he of course refused to listen.'

And Manto entered along with Nandaji and Khurshid Anwar.

'Who is Safia to stop us from entering the house?'

The three men barged in holding a bottle and glasses. Shahid greeted and welcomed the party. It was concluded that they all were very hungry. The hotels had closed down and the last local train had left, so they announced that they would cook for themselves if they could just get the ingredients. All they wanted was lentils and flour.

Safia was not comfortable with the idea of men cooking but they were in no mood to listen to her. They attacked the kitchen and Manto started kneading the dough. Nandaji grabbed hold of the angithi and Khurshid Anwar was given the task of peeling potatoes. Of course, it was an entirely different matter that he was much keener on eating the potatoes raw than peeling them. The bottle too made its entry into the kitchen. All of them sat there on the floor and continued to cook and eat the parathas—often half-cooked. In quite a methodical manner, Manto first kneaded the dough, rolled out parathas and promptly made some mint chutney. After eating, they would have slept right there in the kitchen had they not been dragged out to the verandah.

This kind of life was what Manto was most fond of. He wanted a suitable income, drink, laughter, banter and no anxieties. Everything was a joke for him.

Around that time, the Lahore government filed a case against Manto and me. It seemed as if a long-standing desire of Manto's had been fulfilled. Lahore provided the opportunity for great revelry and enjoyment. Many get-togethers were organized and the visit became an excuse for a pilgrimage to the city. We went together to shop for shoes that were famous for their zari. The shoes looked lovely on Manto's feet, which were delicate and fair, like lotus flowers.

'My feet are really ugly,' I said. 'I will not buy such beautiful shoes.'

'And I get embarrassed that mine are like a woman's.'

Still, both of us ended up buying many pairs of shoes.

'Your feet are so beautiful,' I told him.

'Rubbish! Let's exchange our feet.'

'I swear by God! I have no objection.'

We had unending arguments about love though they all remained inconclusive.

He always said, 'What is love? I love my zari shoes. Rafiq is in love with all his five wives.'

'I mean the kind of love that a young man feels for a young nubile girl.'

'Yes, I understand,' Manto once said. It seemed like he was clearing the mist from some hoary past and talking to himself, 'There was a shepherd girl in Kashmir.'

'Hmm! And then?' I hummed, punctuating his narrative like one listening to a lengthy tale.

'Then nothing.' He immediately became defensive.

'You talk to me about vulgar things all the time but why are you suddenly so shy today?'

'Shy? You think I'm an idiot to feel shy?' Manto said, looking truly coy. It was after a great deal of coaxing that he told me the following.

'She used to raise the stick in her hand to direct her animals. A small part of her wrist would be exposed whenever she did this. I was somewhat unwell in those days. Every day, I would take a blanket and go lie down on the hill. I would hold my breath and wait for the moment when she would raise her arm and her sleeve would slide down and offer me a glimpse of her fair wrist.'

'Wrist?' I asked in amazement.

'Yes... No other part of her body, except the wrist, was visible. She wore loose clothes that concealed all the contours of her body but, with every movement of her body, my eyes leapt to catch a mere glimpse of her wrist.'

'What happened next?'

'One day I was lying down on my blanket when she came to sit at a little distance from me. She was trying to hide something close to her chest. I told her, "Show me what it is." Her face turned crimson with bashfulness. "Nothing," she said. But I became stubborn and told her, "I won't let you go till you show me what it is." She was almost reduced to tears but I did not relent. And it was after a great deal of persuasion that she opened her fist and stretched out her palm in front me, shyly burying her face between her knees.'

'What did she have on her palm?' I asked eagerly.

'A small lump of misri. It lay there on her pink palm, glittering like a tiny chunk of ice.'

'What did you do after that?'

'I just kept looking.' He was lost once again in his reverie.

'What happened next?'

'She got up and ran away. She then stopped at a short distance, turned back and came to me once again. She left the lump of misri on my lap and disappeared. It kept lying in my shirt pocket for quite a long time. Later, I kept it in my drawer where the ants devoured it in a few days.'

'And that girl...?'

'Which girl...' He was startled.

'The same girl who handed you that lump of misri.'

'I never saw her again.'

'What kind of a dull romance was that?' Disappointment brought an edge of irritation to my voice. 'I had hoped for a blazing, scorching love story from you.'

'It was certainly not squishy,' Manto lost his cool.

'Completely worthless, third-rate, pathetic love! What a pity! Coming back with a lump of misri—What an achievement!'

'So what should I have done? Slept with her? And left behind a bastard in her lap just to recall and brag about my masculinity?' He was furious.

'You are right. A lump of misri should not be crunched and munched. It is something that should be slowly sucked.'

This was that same Manto—the obscene writer; the one with the filthy mind; the one who wrote 'Boo', the same one who wrote 'Thanda Gosht'!

It is difficult to infer if Chaundvi Begum in the film *Mirza Ghalib* was Ghalib's beloved or not, but there is no doubt that the girl in Manto's thoughts was his beloved. He could have waited endlessly just to catch a glimpse of her wrist all his life. This contradiction was expressed in many ways in a number of stories that Manto wrote. On the one hand, he wrote 'Naya Kanoon' and 'Boo' on the other. He would wreck himself to pieces to write these stories. People possess a propensity to remember the 'obscene writer' but quite easily forget the storyteller. Whether this is done deliberately or it happens incidentally is irrelevant.

Riots had broken out in the country. After Partition, people shifted their homes from one locality to another. At that time, Manto was more or less a permanent employee at Filmistan and seemed quite happy. Manto needed appreciation by others to sustain him and here he received a great deal of it. Unfortunately, his film *Aath Din* flopped. And soon, for some reason, he left Filmistan and joined Ashok Kumar at Bombay Talkies. He was very fond of Ashok Kumar. We never found out what Mukherjee said that made Manto hostile to him.

'Nonsense! Mukherjee is a complete fraud,' he used to say bitterly.

After Manto joined Bombay Talkies, he managed to get me a job in the scenario department for a year and was thrilled about it.

'The two of us will write stories together. We will take the world by storm. You and I will write the story and Ashok Kumar will play the hero. Just wait and watch!'

One of Manto's stories was under consideration for production and Ashok Kumar liked it. Before that he had liked the story for *Majboor* but soon lost interest and began to show an interest in Manto's story instead. After I joined the studio, he read my story 'Ziddi' and this won his appreciation. Manto did not disapprove of what had happened. After that,

Ashok Kumar asked me to work on Manto's story and asked him to work on mine! The result was that Manto and I started finding faults with each other and our differences grew.

In the meantime, Kamal Amrohi turned up with the story of the film *Mahal*, which Ashok Kumar really liked and left our story in a lurch. The state of affairs would have been different had it been a matter only of our esteem. What was evident was the fact that our story was not being considered for the film and so we were not of any consequence. Sure enough, we were told not to be flustered since we would continue to receive our salaries according to our contracts but our stories were no longer being considered. As a result, all of Shahid's and my energies were channelized into getting a film made on the basis of 'Ziddi'. Soon, the production of *Ziddi* as a film in the 'B-grade' category began, without Ashok Kumar.

Manto's story, however, was held up. He kept sitting in his room all day and repeatedly modifying his story. He sometimes wrote the climax first and then came to the beginning. At other times, he started halfway to end at the beginning. And sometimes, he turned the mid-point into the climax. Despite these innumerable surgical procedures, Ashok Kumar did not approve of any version. Manto, however, continued to say, 'You don't know Ganguly. I know him well. He will definitely work on my story.'

'His role in your story is not a romantic one. He has to play the father and he will never agree to it.'

And then Manto and I would break into a quarrel but the language of our disagreement would remain literary. I was actually anxious about my own survival. And eventually the films *Ziddi* and *Mahal* were completed. Manto's story was abandoned. He had not expected this to happen and so he felt deeply insulted. He could put up with everything except being slighted.

At the same time, the situation in the country was getting worse by the day. Manto's wife and children were visiting Pakistan and they began to persuade him to come there. He tried to convince us too, saying that our future would be much brighter in Pakistan. We would get to occupy the bungalows of those who had left the country. There would be no challenge for us there and we would make easy progress. Manto was disheartened with my persistent refusal to leave India. Countless quarrels occurred between us even though a serious discussion regarding principles never took place.

This made me realize what a coward Manto was. He was willing to shield himself at any cost. In an attempt to safeguard his future, he had set his eyes on the property of those people who had been forced to flee their homes. I began to loathe him.

And then one day he just left for Pakistan without informing or meeting us. I felt deeply humiliated. After some time we received a letter from him saying that he was very happy. He had been given a very good house which was large, beautiful and expensively furnished. And he had once again asked us to come there.

*Ziddi* had been completed and we had started *Arzoo*. The bad times were at an end. We received two more letters from Manto. He asked us once again to come to Pakistan and had written about the possibility of a cinema hall being allotted to him. I was deeply distressed. I had no doubt about his affection earlier and now it was just being reconfirmed. But I tore his letters to pieces. I was upset that he had no regard for the principles I cherished. I did not stop him from going, why must he drag me along his path?

We heard once again about how happy Manto was.

His house had been taken away but the other house was good too.

Another daughter was born.

The years kept rolling past.

A third daughter was born.

And then we received a letter from Manto: 'Do something and call me back to Hindustan.'

We then got the news that a lawsuit had been filed against Manto and he had been imprisoned. We also heard that nobody tried to help Manto. Not a single protest or meeting was organized. On the contrary, some people felt it was good that he had been imprisoned. This will ensure that he is fixed once and for all, was the general feeling. There were no processions taken out, no resolutions passed.

After that, we heard that he had lost his mind and his friends had admitted him to a lunatic asylum.

And then, one day we received a letter from Manto. It was written in a completely alert state of mind and informed us that he was in good health. It then said that it would really be good if one of us could talk to Mukherjee and ask him to somehow bring Manto back. After this, there was no other news for a long span of time. I also got no response to my letter.

Then we heard that he had once again gone back to the lunatic asylum. I had begun to be somewhat afraid of receiving any news about Manto. I had lost the strength to inquire about him. Who knew what phase of life his next step would have taken him to? There was only a one-way road from the lunatic asylum.

It became difficult to endure hearing news about him from people who came from Pakistan. His drinking had gotten out of control. He was going around asking for money from anybody he came across, known or unknown. Publishers made him write articles on the spot. He polished off whatever advance he received.

In the last letter that I received from Manto, he had asked me to write an article on him. Quite thoughtlessly, my ill-omened tongue uttered, 'Now I will write an article on him only after his death.'

And now I am writing this piece after his death. Manto is not the only one who is dead. A great deal of what existed between Manto and me too has died, and an age has gone by since that death has taken place. What continues to live on within me is an ache but I can't put a finger on its cause. Is it regret for the fact that he is dead while I still live? Why is there a burden of on my heart as though I owed him something? I can't recall having been ever indebted to him. What do I owe him except the fact that he declared me his sister? But sisters often see their brothers die and can hardly do anything about it. People die and leave behind wounds that neither bleed nor ooze. They just keep silently smouldering.

Memories of Safia are coming back to me more than ever before. I yearn to be close to her, to embrace her and talk to her like we had talked at Adelphi Chambers years earlier. But those were chats about wedding nights and the delivery of the first child. This conversation would be about death. That is what scares me and my pen runs dry. Who knows what she went through in the last few years? I hardly have the heart to ask her, 'After the whole world had disowned Manto, did your love, like an immovable rock, still continue to support this tempestuous individual or did it too become limp with fatigue? Did the tremors of the last twelve or thirteen years crush you into conceding defeat or did you remain the same old Safia for your Manto-saheb? How did you respond to your relatives and sophisticated neighbours looking down upon him with disdain for defying social norms? How did you deal with the ruthless, unvoiced scandals that must have viciously encircled you? You must have felt so trapped. Did he breathe his last in your lap full of love or was his farewell that of a lonesome man isolated from his large family? Did the girls think of their father as mad, bankrupt and a drunkard? He did not give you anything besides deprivation and disappointment. I know so little of any of this. It is difficult to understand why there is not even a weak reflection of his life in his writings. He used to blame himself for the problems he encountered. He concealed his troubles as if they were his failings. He was proud of the fact that he could earn and squander away lakhs in an instance. That is why he found it difficult to believe that he could be driven to starvation and, so, he helplessly put his pen to paper and continued writing.

I hope that in the end you have not become frustrated with writers. They themselves struggle and pull the ones they cherish most into the quagmire as well... And then, one day, they abandon everybody and go away. But dear bahen, this is not just a characteristic of writers alone. Lakhs and crores of people in our country become victims of failure and disillusionment in this way. They may or may not be writers. They may be clerks but their lives and their deaths are no different from those of writers. The sensitive among them go mad and the thick-skinned ones spend their lives sobbing.

For some reason my heart keeps insisting that I have contributed to Manto's death in his prime. My clothes too are stained with the drops of blood that only my heart's eye can see. My world is the one that allowed him to die. Today, this world let him die, tomorrow it will be my turn. People will mourn. The liability of my children will weigh them down like a heavy boulder. They will organize events, collect donations for them, but nobody will attend due to their busy schedules. Time will move on. The load on people's chests will gradually become lighter and they will put all this behind them.

# Our Last Meeting

## Naresh Kumar Shaad

IT WAS AN AFTERNOON IN 1954.

When I reached Lakshmi Mansions with my poet-friend Nisar Najibabadi, I suddenly realized that I had forgotten Manto's house number. Incidentally, Nisar too had no idea but we did not have to look for it for too long. The first person whom we asked for directions took us right up to his door.

We found a lady standing at the door. As soon as my eyes fell on her, I knew that she was Manto's wife, Safia. 'Is Manto-saheb at home?'

When Safia nodded in response, I said to her, 'Please tell him that a friend from Delhi has come to meet him.'

Safia went inside and a few moments later Manto made his appearance. He seemed to be extremely frail, tall, brimming with an agitation that seemed to seep out of the pores of his skin from head to toe. He was wearing golden embroidered shoes, a white shalwar and carried his spectacles in his hand. He welcomed us in.

Manto-saheb lifted his legs up, folded them and settled down on a small couch. He then began to gather the sheets of paper scattered on the table. I glanced at him and was gripped by the thought that all the nerves of his body were throbbing and pulsating like mercury. His large eyes, however, looked like they did not belong to his body and had been externally stuck on a physical frame of flesh and blood.

After he had put the papers in order, Manto-saheb, while putting the lid of the typewriter over it, said to me, 'I have not left this room for the last three days. I have been working without a break. I have written letters to Uncle Sam, a sketch of Diwan Singh Maftoon, and was typing out a drama when you came.'

'Typing?' The word suddenly slipped out of my mouth.

'Yes, I was thinking and typing at the same time. And yes! I forgot to mention that a friend of mine has written a long, detailed English article on my stories. In fact, he has even translated it. And, yes! Yes, Naresh! Listen! You too must write a poem or two about me. These days, at my request, many of my friends are writing something or the other about me. I am personally not very fond of poetry but I also want my poet-friends to express what they feel about me. I am putting together everything that has ever been written about me in prose or poetry. And yes, my friends! You have not said anything about what you would like to have. Would you like a drink or something?'

I found Manto's large eyes turned towards me. He was looking at me through his thick glasses.

'No, no. Many thanks,' I responded.

'All right, that's fine. So then, what was it? What was I saying? Oh, yes! I am collecting opinions of all kinds that my friends have expressed about me and am celebrating my jubilee next month. What do you think about the idea? Look here, I am not in a position to spend too much but of course, I will organize tea. I hope you will stay on till the occasion. Oh come along! Stay back. What's the big deal? I will of course not be weighed against diamonds and pearls like Agha Khan but my friends deserve to be weighed against pens at my jubilee.'

'And those, of course, must be only Parker pens.' Nisar smiled.

'Yes, that's the way it should be,' Manto said, picking up the pen from his table. 'I am very fond of Parker. Oh! You people are not even smoking. This poor little box of cigarettes is gazing expectantly at you.'

Manto pushed the box of cigarettes towards me and said, 'Look at God's unkindness! Even Gold Flake cigarettes are being sold on the black market in Pakistan. These heartless black-marketeers don't even bother to see that these are merely Gold Flake cigarettes and not the Black and White ones.'

Just then, Safia entered the room and a pall of solemnity fell across Manto's face all at once. 'Safia, meet Naresh Kumar Shaad,' he said. 'He is an Urdu poet and has come from Delhi.'

'Yes, yes. He did tell me that he has come from Delhi,' Safia said with a melancholic smile and sat on the couch next to Manto.

I am not sure what happened to Manto but he then bombarded me with a volley of questions.

'Oh Naresh! You have still not told me anything about Delhi. About the people there. About your Progressive writers. About Krishan Chander. About Sardar Bahadur Ali Jafri. Yes, my dear friend! There are a whole lot of very interesting people there. What do you think, Safia? Naresh, have you been to Bombay recently? I swear by God, what an amazing city! Bombay! Urusul bilad—the bride of all cities! I miss Bombay every minute of my life here in Lahore. I have become a living memorial of Bombay here. Have you read *Ganje Farishte*, my sketches of the film personalities in Bombay? What do you think about it? And yes, another thing! What is the condition of writers in India? Recently, Yusuf, the owner of *Shah-rah** was here... What is your opinion about him? What kind of a person is he? I have heard that Partition has given birth to many new publishers, and that the bastards are hysterically publishing my books right and left without paying me anything. What do they think? Don't these stories have a writer? I will have to go there myself. Safia! You just wait and see! I will go to India

---

*The monthly periodical which was a mouthpiece for Progressive writers and which was once edited by Sahir Ludhianvi.

and settle with each and every publisher myself. Saadat Hasan Manto is not a man who will let even a paisa slip by him. I will see to it that those frauds pay me every single paisa of the royalty they owe me! Oh yes! I now remember. What is the name of that magazine? Arya... Arya something. No, no, it is not *Arya-gazette.* Yes! It is *Arya-vrat.* And, what is the name of its owner? It's slipping my mind. Oh! He is the one who had sent fifty rupees to me, and that too at a time when I was in desperate need of money. I had been admitted to hospital not long ago. That's the time I am talking about.... Life in the hospital is quite bizarre. I culled out some matter for stories from those strange surroundings.'

Safia got up and went silently to the other room. Manto too forgot about the conversation and looked preoccupied and lost for some time. He then got up and followed Safia inside.

And then, sitting there in 36, Lakshmi Mansions, I remembered Urdu Bazaar in Delhi, where Asrar-ul-haq-Majaz, too, in his state of semi-insanity, said absurd things to his acquaintances and friends for long periods of time.

'Manto-saheb went mad some time ago, didn't he?' I asked Nisar and without waiting for his response, asked my next question, 'Do you think he is somewhat drunk even now?'

'Now? At this time?' Nisar smiled and said softly, 'Not just at this time. These days we find that he is like this at all times. One doesn't know how Manto-saheb, in this condition...'

Nisar could not complete his sentence as Manto-saheb walked into the room. He sank into the couch and said, 'Naresh, you probably don't know that I cannot take payment for any of my articles. Neither can I claim any royalty for any of my books. I have given the rights for all my books to Safia. I cannot procure payment for any of my stories from any publisher or magazine till I produce an authority letter from her. Four collections of my stories are under publication currently. A collection of articles will also soon be ready. This collection has a very interesting title. Your heart will bubble with joy and excitement at the title of this collection. It is *Upar, Neeche aur Darmiyan.*'

'Assalam-alaikum.' The thunderous voice of a maulana with a long beard exploded and echoed around the room. This was followed by 'Assalam-alaikum Manto-saheb, assalam-alaikum' repeated many times over by the many small children who had entered the room along with him.

'What a bother!' Manto was irritated but then said, 'assalam-alaikum.' And putting his hand on the maulana's shoulder he added, 'Do come in. Please do come.'

'Fine then, Manto-saheb,' I said, 'allow me to take your leave now.'

'Where are you going, Naresh?' Manto-saheb almost screamed and then, introducing me to the maulana, he said, 'Miyan-saheb, this is my friend from India, Naresh. You should join us, Naresh,' he added. 'It will be good fun. What do you think, Miyan-saheb?'

And soon, Manto and Miyan-saheb, with all of us in tow, went to the park next to Lakshmi Mansions. A large number of children along with their parents had already assembled there. Manto-saheb was the chairman of the function. He took the chair and began to speak, 'I have been invited to this function today to distribute prizes among children who have excelled in sports, though I have no idea what kind of sports these children have participated in. However, before doing anything else, I want to announce that I wish to give two rupees from my side to a child...'

The children as well as their parents were taken aback and began to look at Manto-saheb in astonishment.

Manto-saheb started speaking once again. 'Look, Pakistan is an independent country. Children are a surety and a security deposit for the future. Every one of you must always be fearless and truthful. Therefore, I present an award of two rupees to the child who broke the glass pane of my window day before yesterday while playing gilli-danda.'

The solemnity of the crowd immediately dissolved and changed to merriment.

'Look, there is no need to be nervous or afraid. The child who broke the glass should just step forward, accept this prize, and then promise that he will not break any more glass panes with his gilli.'

Manto waited for a few minutes but when no child stepped forward to claim the prize he had instituted, quickly started distributing the other prizes among the children. We left the place after all this hullabaloo ended. Manto took me aside and asked, 'Do you have some money?'

'How much do you need?' I replied, pulling out my wallet.

'Not me, my friend, it is for the owner of the alcohol shop. About twenty or twenty-five rupees should be enough.'

'Yes, yes, of course.'

And then, Manto stopped an empty tonga going down the road. He went up to the front seat and sat with his feet up on it. He folded his knees and made himself comfortable in the same pose that he had struck on the couch in his room. Nisar and I sat in the rear. On the way I asked him, 'Manto-saheb, where will we drink?'

'At home, where else? All places for drinking have been sacrificed at the altar of Pakistan.'

'But, in your house...?' I hesitated a bit and then expressed my doubt, 'What if Safia-bhabhi minds it?'

'No, my friend. I have spent fifteen years with her. I understand her well. There's nothing like this.'

The alcohol shop was not very far. Manto took us to the shop as soon as the tonga came to a halt. The salesman was clearly on informal terms with Manto. He handed over the bottle and, just as we were stepping out, joked, 'Manto-saheb, I think it is high time. You must get a permit now.'

'Yes. You are right. Why don't you do this kind deed for me? Get a permit in my name and bury it with me in my grave so that this poor Saadat Hasan Manto's afterlife is not ruined. I did not feel the need for it in this life thanks to your benevolence but who knows, I may not be able to function without it under Allah's Islamic rule.'

The salesman laughed. 'You are absolutely matchless, Manto-saheb.'

And we soon reached Lakshmi Mansions with this absolutely matchless person. We found a gentleman already waiting for Manto. He quickly introduced him to us. The well-dressed young man was a college student, a scion of a wealthy family and one of Manto's great admirers. Manto sank into the couch and called out for his servant, who brought empty glasses. We got by with water instead of soda. That young man and Nisar were not regular drinkers. They stopped drinking after two pegs and lit cigarettes. I took very small drinks and sipped them at a snail's pace. The idea that I was a foreigner who did not possess the permit to drink had gripped my mind and clutched it firmly like a lizard clinging to a wall. Moreover, I was also conscious of the fact that I was a guest at the famous poet Qateel Shifai's house at Misri Shah. The place was quite far from Manto's place and I needed to go back there that night. Manto-saheb, however, was speedily gulping down the alcohol and relentlessly, and quite pointlessly, talking about different topics. Innumerable memories, varied thoughts and many other ideas seemed to simultaneously enter and create a tumult in his already restive mind. Nonetheless, what remained consistent all through this was the fact that all topics of discussion finally converged on Manto himself.

'Naresh, you do write prose too sometimes. I saw your "Surkh Hashiye" in *Beesvin Sadi*. You have mentioned my name too while discussing how "Surkh Hashiye" has been written in the style I used in "Siyah Hashiye". But my dear friend, you must write only couplets. I also came across a collection of your poems. The title slips my mind. Well, can't you recall it? It's the one with the cover that Firaq Gorakhpuri commented on. This Firaq is also a peculiar kind of man. He once sent me a letter which I could not respond to. So he wrote a second letter saying: Manto-saheb, why would somebody like you, who is the most obscene writer in the whole of Indo-Pak, bother to respond to my letter?

'And yes, you do know Adam, don't you? Be honest. Tell me, what do think of his ghazals? I am not too interested in poetry but I do have a couple of Adam's books. I was wondering why he uses the word sincerity so often in his ghazals. I hope it is not because he himself is completely deficient of it. Ahmed Nadeem Qasimi is a sterling and sincere man. Thank God Zaheer Kashmiri is not listening to me or he would have shredded Qasimi's sincerity to tiny shreds using the scissors of Marx and Hegel's philosophy. After that, he would have lectured us about national and international literary protests and completely destroyed the pleasures of our drinking.

'Now, do please enlighten me about what exactly these international literary movements are. They are all a big hoax! Actually, Saadat Hasan Manto is himself an international movement. You have read my stories, Nasir, haven't you? How many of my stories have you read? I think you must have read all of them. Well, if not all, you must have read many of them. Now tell me who your favourite writers in the world are. Who among Chekhov, Maupassant, Somerset Maugham, Gorky and Tolstoy do you prefer most? All right, let's add four more names. A selection of the best of my stories will be no less than the selection of the best stories by any of these writers. Don't you think I am right? Why aren't you saying anything?'

We were quite aware of Manto's temper and obstinacy and so we unanimously expressed our agreement with his opinion. Manto was gradually getting intoxicated and alcohol had started tightening its grip over his senses when, nonchalantly, he initiated the topic of Punjabi poetry.

'My friend, have you had a look at *Tiranjan*, the collection of Punjabi nazms by Ahmed Rahi? I have written my opinion about it in Punjabi right at the beginning of the book. Listen carefully. I am now going to present samples of some variants of the Punjabi language. The best of your poets cannot even begin to write like this. A mere utterance of any variety of Punjabi speech will easily outshine their lengthy collections of poetry.'

And a new door in Manto's amazing memory was suddenly thrown open and, one after another, the culture of Punjab and the many variants of the Punjabi language, deeply suffused with Punjabi traditions, began to emerge. Manto enlightened us with minute details regarding the background of many local speech variants. This increased not just our pleasure but also the splendour of the languages themselves. This would have gone on endlessly had Manto not realized that all the alcohol had been drunk. A look at his empty glass brought a kind of deadpan expression to his eyes too. The doors of his memory also locked up and he stopped almost mid-sentence, as though an automatic machine had suddenly stopped functioning.

I seized the moments of silence and said in a subdued voice, 'Manto-saheb, I have a long way to go. Do kindly allow me to leave.'

Manto yelled, 'No! You will not go anywhere. Not yet.'

He then turned towards the well-dressed young man and

said, 'You have your car with you, don't you? And enough petrol too? Come along, let's go to the Colonel's house.'

I once against tried to take leave in a muted voice but Manto-saheb ignored me completely. He walked out and pushed me inside the car. As soon as he got in, he started narrating an incident about an earlier car ride.

'One night, I was sitting in a car with Abdul Hameed Adam. Both of us were completely sozzled. On the way, the car lights suddenly stopped working. We came to a roundabout where a policeman signalled our car to a stop. However, the driver could not stop the car despite his best efforts and it was then that we discovered that the brakes were not functioning properly. The car finally came to a halt about ten or twelve yards away and I found that both the driver and Adam were very nervous and scared. The driver because he was sure he would be fined, and Adam because he would be caught for drinking without a licence. I got out of the car and swiftly walked up to the policeman. I did not give him the opportunity to utter even a single word. Instead, I asked him in an authoritative voice, "Oye! Where is your SP's bungalow?"

'The constable got scared at the mention of the SP. I understood that this was his Achilles' heel and so I continued in a threatening voice, "You are a constable and you don't even know where your SP's bungalow is? Even I know that it is somewhere around here."

'The constable's voice now became piteous, "Huzoor," he said, "I am new to this place. That is why I don't know where it is."

'I continued to rebuke him and then walked back. I got into the car and told the driver to drive away immediately.'

As soon as Manto finished his story I blurted, 'I hope the brakes of this car work!'

'Oh my goodness! What do I do with a man like you? You

have poured cold water on the whole story. And my dear friend Naresh Kumar Shaad, I swear by God, your name should have been Niraash Kumar Nashaad.'*

And all of us broke out in loud laughter.

The car was moving fast. It was 9.30 in the night. The roads were completely deserted. I happened to look outside the window and could feel my heart suddenly thudding louder and faster. The car was passing through the barracks of the Lahore cantonment. I lay a hand on my passport in my pocket and said in a tremulous voice, 'We've made a blunder, Manto-saheb!'

Manto was startled. 'What happened? All well, I hope.'

'You have brought me to Lahore cantonment,' I slowly forced the words out in a nervous voice. 'Right now I am drunk and I should not go to a new destination without informing the police in Lahore. And to make matters worse, this is the army area. I feel my heart will stop beating out of sheer fear.'

'It is for very valid reasons that your heart will stop beating,' Manto-saheb responded in a sympathetic tone. 'So then, what is your advice? What should we do?'

'I think we should go back.'

'But how will we get what we want?'

'You should have asked for more alcohol to be brought home. You could have drunk more at home. It is really risky to drink here. I cannot have even a drop of alcohol here.'

'Oh! Who the hell is saying that our purpose is to drink here?'

'So then what is your purpose?'

'To get you arrested and imprisoned in Lahore cantonment,' Manto said in a very grave voice.

---

*A play on words typical of Manto's style: Naresh (Emperor) Kumar Shaad (Happiness), becomes Niraash (Hopeless) Kumar Nashaad (Mirthlessness).

I could not laugh at his joke even though I tried. The entire atmosphere was so terrifying that I was gripped with the fear of Manto's joke becoming a reality. Finally, with God's grace, the car reached the Colonel's bungalow, but we discovered that he had gone off with his family to Rawalpindi to attend a wedding. Manto almost tore his hair out in frustration. He asked one or two servants in the house to get a bottle of rum from the army canteen but they refused. After spending a totally unproductive half an hour, we were left with no option but to return. Our mission remained unaccomplished and our desires unfulfilled.

The car kept moving and Manto-saheb kept sitting, looking lost and forlorn. The sparks of brilliant words in his impassioned mind had been extinguished. It was not only Manto's silence that left us tongue-tied and ill at ease, but also the painful awareness that the Colonel-saheb had gone away to Rawalpindi; that rum could not be procured from the army canteen; that all the shops had closed down; and that Manto's exhilaration was fading away.

Alcohol was like fuel for the weary flame of Manto's life but it was unavailable at that point in time. The car crossed the station but Manto remained silent. The car entered Misri Shah but Manto remained silent. The car finally stopped at Qateel Shifai's house.

I stepped out of the car and was just about to convey my regards and take leave when he too stepped out and walked along with me up to an electric pole a little distance away. He stopped there and said to me, 'Forgive me, Naresh, for being very petty. The proper thing would have been for me to invite you for a drink but I had no money. I had mentioned this to Safia too but... I deeply regret that, instead of extending the invitation to you, I ended up making you spend your money. I swear by God, Saadat Hasan Manto is a really mean chap.'

I had been more or less quiet since afternoon. Manto-saheb's words were imbued with the concentrated agony of his entire life. I felt my heart brimming over and I wanted to say something to comfort him but, just then, Manto-saheb looked at me with his large, passionate eyes. The eyes had absorbed the deadly poison of watching the world go by and seemed to know what remained unexpressed in my heart. 'We are fully aware of the agony that Manto is forced to live through because of his meanness,' his eyes seemed to say. 'We also know that you too understand it well. So what's the point of saying anything at all about it?'

Now when Manto is not in this world, the memory and darkness of that night in Lahore often returns to my mind in flashes rather than as an unbroken sequence. Manto-saheb's mottled and indistinct features keep emerging out of layers of darkness. His large, terrifying eyes keep keep staring at me and mocking this hypocritical, inhuman and immoral society, repeating over and over again: 'Saadat Hasan Manto is very mean! Really mean!'

# Manto in My Court

## Mehdi Ali Siddiqui

THE YEAR 1953 HAD JUST BEEN RUNG IN AND I WAS BUSY with work. The court was teeming with people when my reader came up to me and said, 'This gentleman here wants his case to be heard without delay.'

I lifted my head and looked up. I saw a man of average height and good looks. He looked somewhat unwell but more than that, he appeared harassed. The top buttons of his sherwani were open and he had a scarf wrapped around his neck. Addressing me in a voice that seemed to be broken and trapped in his throat, he said, 'I am Saadat Hasan Manto. I have come from Lahore. I am very ill. I confess to my crime. Kindly announce your judgment without any delay.'

One other person stood right behind Manto, as though it was he who had taken him into custody. He was the guarantor or somebody deputed by the guarantor; he must have assured the guarantor that he would get Manto absolved of all charges and ensure his freedom.

'Do please first take your seats,' I said.

'Ji,' Manto responded.

'Please do sit,' I repeated.

Manto looked distracted. He sat down on a bench behind the reader, looking preoccupied all the while. I picked up his file and started studying the case.

Manto was charged with writing and publishing 'Upar, Neeche aur Darmiyan'. I already had some knowledge about his case and had prepared myself for it.

I had never been completely disconnected from literary activities but my knowledge of Urdu short stories was limited.

I had decided to remedy this shortcoming and had therefore read a number of short stories in the preceding three or four months. I had read as many of Manto's articles, stories and critical essays as I could lay my hands on. I had read them all with great care and attention. I had diligently avoided reading that story for which he had been charged, as well as all the criticism that had followed the story. I did this to keep myself free of any prejudice. After having learnt of his writing and, through it, his personality, you can well imagine what I felt when Manto confessed his crime to shield himself.

I tried to look at Manto out of the corner of my eye but discovered that he had vanished from his seat.

He had gone out to the verandah and was walking around restlessly.

He soon walked in and said, 'Close my case, now.'

I said, 'Very well... But do please be seated.'

And I immediately started working on the legal formalities connected with the case.

Manto continued sitting but looked very uncomfortable and kept shifting on the bench.

I made an entry and wrote down his confession according to the rules. Everybody had anticipated that I would impose a hefty fine. When I did not do that, and instead told Manto, 'Manto-saheb, I will give my verdict tomorrow,' he looked very disappointed.

Manto started insisting that the judgment be pronounced immediately. In his opinion, not doing so would imply an undermining of the importance of his confession as well as compromise the stature of the magistrate. I, however, wanted to read the story first and reflect on it. I wanted to closely scrutinize it to see if it ought to be considered obscene or not from the legal point of view. Believe me, sincerity and attention to detail play a very important role in dispensing justice. Inflexible personal opinion and a blind, unthinking implementation of rules and regulations go against the basic spirit of justice and fair play. Nonetheless, this timeless convention is repeatedly sacrificed when petitions are filed in court.

Anyway, what eventually happened was that despite being reluctant to do so, Manto had no option but to wait.

At the session the following day, I wrote down my opinion in brief. Just like the previous day, Manto was there with his companion and was impatient to hear my judgment.

'Manto-saheb, how is your financial condition?'

'Very bad.'

'What is the date today?'

Somebody else responded, 'Twenty-fifth'.

'Manto-saheb, your fine is twenty-five rupees...'

To begin with, he did not grasp what I was saying and, turning to his friend, asked, 'Is he asking for the date or announcing his judgment?'

His guarantors were much more alert. They immediately went off to pay the fine and Manto started walking around in the verandah.

After some time Manto and his friends came to my room once again.

'Yes sir,' I said, 'what can I do for you?'

Manto's friend said, 'We have come to invite you.'

I immediately accepted their invitation. One finds no occasion for even a brief, formal exchange in the court. A casual discussion is of course out of question. Moreover, I too was keen to meet Manto informally because it was my firm belief that after Premchand, it was Manto who was the finest writer in Urdu.

The following day, I went to Zelin Coffee House straight from office. The coffee house was chock-a-block with people. I stood near the steps and Manto and his friends soon arrived.

Manto had been drinking but was in his full senses. He would sometimes pause during the conversation but the flow of the discussion remained unbroken. He sometimes addressed me directly and, at other times, he would turn to his friends and make critical comments about me. Nonetheless, every word he uttered was entirely sincere. There was no duplicity nor was there any hint of vacillation or confusion. All through the discussion, there was absolutely no attempt to impress or to create the notion of being impressed. There was no hesitation in criticizing the bad and commending the good.

Manto had constructed a standard norm for assessing the good and the bad. The norm he had established was free from every constraint and convention and it did not change with society. In short, that was the day when, for the first time in my life, I came across an outstanding artist who was ruthlessly truthful, completely forthright and free of deceit. This image of Manto is intact in my mind even today and will remain so as long as I live.

The discussion was long drawn out but extremely interesting.

He asked me, 'You don't drink?'

'No.'

'Are you a mullah?'

'No, I am a Muslim.'

He started laughing. His friend ordered a coffee for me.

I then discovered that these people had left an interesting discussion at a gathering to come and meet me at the coffee house. I apologized for the inconvenience and said, 'Actually, I am the one who should have invited you because I am the local person...'

Manto said, 'You seem to be an immigrant.'

'Still,' I replied, 'I am the one who lives in Karachi...'

He then asked, 'Why did you ask me to be seated during the session in the court? No other magistrate has ever treated me like this.'

'I don't consider discourtesy to be part of the protocol of court proceedings.'

He immediately broke into a smile and said to his friend, 'He seems to be a decent man.'

After some time, he said, 'I have not read your judgment. What have you written?'

I handed a copy of the judgment to him. He read through it very attentively, then turned to his friends and said, 'He is an educated man... Highly educated.'

He spoke as though I did not exist.

Then he turned to me and asked, 'So then, how much have you studied?'

I told him about my education and my degrees.

He laughed again and said, 'See, did I not tell you he is highly educated? And he writes English very well... Really well!'

He then asked, 'Ji, sir, why? Why did you punish me?'

It was then that I realized that Manto was a true artist. He had absolutely no idea that he had created something which was considered obscene by some. All he had done was written a story.

He told me that the story was based on a true incident. He also added that he had little control over the fact that the story was considered obscene since that is exactly what had happened in real life.

'Even today,' he said, 'society itself is obscene. All I do is represent its essence. It is entirely understandable that people with ugly faces vent their anger at the mirror.'

The fact is that he did not use even a single vulgar or obscene word during the entire conversation.

I was totally unprepared and could not have responded to him with the same ardour and frankness. In an attempt to sidestep the issue I said, 'Obscene words are not the only grounds.'

'Is there any other option?' Manto asked. 'Should the truth be hidden? You punish me for telling the truth.'

I did not consider it proper to give a direct and upfront response at that time but I do believe that there ought to be some difference between reality and its representation. If not, then the whole point of clothing our naked bodies becomes redundant. Why is it that people look for privacy for sex? Why are symbolism and connotation considered important attributes of literary aesthetics? A writer is a painter, not a photographer. Even photographers do not photograph the sexual act or the sexual parts of the body.

I evaded the issue again. 'I will discuss my reasons for punishing you some other time.'

'Give me your word.'

'I promise.'

I could not fulfill my promise in Manto's lifetime. I am doing that now.

The intention of law is not to obstruct literature from fulfilling its objectives and expectations. Law only requires that these objectives be beneficial for human beings. If the sole purpose of writing is not to benefit humankind but only to titillate and sexually excite, and the vocabulary and content are such that they will entangle the weak-willed in the mesh of sexual gratification and degeneration, the law will brand such writing as obscene.

There is mention of the sexual act and some of its other aspects in the story 'Upar, Neeche aur Darmiyan'. It includes details about the differences that exist in the sexual act across different classes of society. In the opinion of the law, this subject is not beneficial for society, despite it being factually correct. Law also recognizes the fact that instead of appreciating the beauty and nuances of differences that creep into the sexual acts of people from different classes, the majority of people would distort it so such an extent that it would degenerate into mere sexual gratification.

Surely one cannot find fault with this opinion, this apprehension of the law. It is possible; in fact I am certain, that writers will have serious differences of opinion with me on the issue. I can, however, not think of a better rationale for the legal yardstick to assess obscenity. Neither can I think of a better way to express the issue or to establish the relevance of this legal provision.

The truth is that I used to consider 'Upar, Neeche aur Darmiyan' obscene even from the literary perspective but that was not the time to go into details.

We sat there, in the coffee house, for a couple of hours. While it is true that Manto had made me promise something, it is also equally true that he too had made a promise to me. And like me, he did not find the time to fulfill that promise either.

This was my first and last meeting with Manto. After that, I received two or three letters he wrote to me from Lahore. I tried my best to do whatever he had asked to be done. It is also important to state that none of his letters carried any request for himself. He was an ideal friend who valued and cherished his friends and his letters were mainly concerning them. The last letter he wrote to me was on 17 January 1955, a day before he passed away, and I received it the day after his death.*

However, it is something else that is a very loved and special symbol of my brief but completely sincere and genuine attachment with Manto. He had begun to write a series of articles under the title 'Panchva Muqaddma' (The

---

*Respected Mehdi Ali Khan saheb,

I regret that I could not write to you for some time. Actually, I am quite seriously ill.

Fifth Lawsuit), about the events leading up to the lawsuit in connection with 'Upar, Neeche aur Darmiyan' in the journal *Naqoosh*. The first article was the only one that was published. It deals with some of the events that occurred till he reached the court. I am not sure if he was able to complete the other articles in the series. I am, however, quite certain that had he written the second article, he would have expressed some opinion about me. I had read the first installment and was waiting for the next one. The wait just kept getting prolonged.

It was around the end of 1954 that I found out that Manto had published a collection of short stories with the title *Upar, Neeche aur Darmiyan*. I was surprised as well as overjoyed when I was told that Manto had dedicated the collection to me. It is difficult to find more compelling evidence of the sincerity of his love and undemanding faith. I am more or less an obscure person and am pleased that my name will perhaps live on for some time in the world of literature.

---

I have been continuously requesting you for one thing or the other but that is only because your sincerity and love has touched me deeply and I do believe that you will not ignore my request.

The person carrying this letter, Rafiq Chowdhary-saheb, is a close friend of mine. It will be a personal obligation for me if you could listen and do the needful for him. He will give you all the details himself.

Can I be of some service to you?

I intend to come to Karachi for a few days. Hope to see you when I am there.

Yours sincerely

Saadat Hasan Manto

17 January 1955

# A Few Literary Encounters

## Shahid Ahmed Dehlvi

A SLENDER BODY, SHRIVELLED ARMS AND LEGS, OF average height, fair complexion, restless eyes, gold-rimmed spectacles, a cream-coloured suit with a screaming red tie.

A frail young man had come to see me. This was about twenty-four or twenty-five years ago. He was completely unceremonial, razor-sharp and amazingly articulate. The young man introduced himself to me, 'I am Manto. Saadat Hasan. You must have seen the special issue on Russian literature in *Humayun*. I now want to bring out a special issue on French literature in *Saqi*.'*

I was somewhat offended by his excessive informality at this first meeting. I decided to put him in place and so I asked, 'Do you know French?'

'No,' he said.

'So what is it that you are proposing to do?'

'I will translate the text from the English version and also edit this special number for you.'

'I edit my magazine myself,' I responded. 'And moreover, four special issues of *Saqi* have already been finalized. For the time being it won't be possible to publish any other special issue besides the ones that are already in the pipeline.'

When Manto saw that he could not get his way, he instantly changed the topic and, before leaving, he quite clearly impressed upon me that if I ever needed any article from him, I could ask him to send it to me on payment.

---

*\*Humayun* was a monthly published from Lahore. *Saqi* was published from Delhi and edited by Dehlvi.

That was the time when Manto did only translations. His book *Sarguzasht-e-Aseer* had just been published. Manto and I continued to correspond, though quite irregularly, and a few of his articles were published in *Saqi* as well. Yet this interaction did not evolve into a warm or friendly relationship. I always had the impression that this person was somewhat disoriented, a braggart and ill-mannered. To me, he seemed egotistic to a fault; though I also felt that his edges would smoothen out after he went through the vicissitudes of life.

I then got to know that he was a very staunch and rigid communist and that he had been asked to leave the Aligarh Muslim University on the grounds that he had tuberculosis. So he left Aligarh and went to his hometown Amritsar. His rebellious personality was a source of continuous distress to his family too and so he broke all connections with it. He continued his activities in Amritsar in the company of some like-minded friends. Their leader was Bari (Aleeg), the author of *Company ki Hukumat* (The Rule of the Company). All of them, however, were somewhat cautious and thus escaped being jailed or punished by the government. Later, Bari went away to Rangoon and Manto joined the newspaper *Mussavir* in Bombay.

Several years rolled by and Manto and I did meet a couple of times but the snag in the fabric of our relationship had still not repaired. I had no special rapport with him and my association with him was like the ones I had with any of the other writers. During the Second World War, he had joined All India Radio and when I met him for the first time after that, he said, 'From now on I will not take any payment from you.'

'Why?' I asked.

'I used to insist on it because I needed the money,' he responded.

There was a wonderful congregation of writers and poets at

All India Radio during the World War. Ahmed Shah Bokhari 'Patras' was the Controller. Chirag Hasan Hasrat and Dr Akhtar Husain Raipuri were in the News Department; Noon Meem Rashid, Ansar Naasri, Mehmood Nizami and Krishan Chander were in the Programme Department; Upendranath Ashk was the Hindi scriptwriter; and Manto and Meeraji were the Urdu scriptwriters. It was during this period that I found the opportunity to know Manto from very close quarters.

Manto had saved some money and bought two typewriters—one for English and the other for Urdu. He used to bring the Urdu typewriter to the station every day. It was quite normal for him to write two or three plays and features every day. He had almost totally stopped writing by hand. He would roll paper into the typewriter, punch the keys very rapidly, and then leave the office. Feature writing was considered to be exceptionally tough in those days but it was a walkover for Manto. The piece would be quickly typed out and then chucked with utter contempt: 'Here! Take your feature.'

Everybody used to be astonished by Manto's pace and what was even more extraordinary was that everything he wrote would be precise and accurate, leaving absolutely no scope to tinker around with even a little.

It was after Manto's arrival in Delhi that his era of short-story writing began. His stories were written in an entirely unique and innovative style. He needed no prompting to turn in a story every month for *Saqi*. It was during this time that Manto wrote 'Dhunwa', which was published in *Saqi*. After its publication, I was called by the Press Advisor to his office. He was an educated and cultured person and had been my classmate when I was pursuing a degree in English literature. He said to me, 'Look here, bhai, be a little cautious. These are bad times.'

I did not pay much attention to the conversation but did

mention it to Manto. As expected, and in keeping with his character, he was livid but after this he became a little more guarded when it came to *Saqi*.

However, the ulcer which had been covered up in Delhi ruptured in Lahore when the government of Punjab filed a case against Manto for his story 'Boo'. Manto asked me to come from Delhi to Lahore as a defense witness. The lower courts pronounced their judgment against Manto but he was acquitted after an appeal. Whatever little fear Manto may have had disappeared after this and he started writing obscene articles with complete abandon. The elderly Chowdhary Mohammad Husain, then the Press Advisor to the government of Punjab, was a peculiar person. He used to hang around with Allama Iqbal but he suffered from an exaggerated sense of self-importance and had convinced himself that he was instrumental in making Iqbal eminent. He began to hound Manto in every way possible and, one after another, filed many lawsuits against him. He soon became so intoxicated with a sense of power that, along with some other writers, he began to snare publishers and booksellers in his net. Manto was left with no option but to come from Bombay to Lahore in connection with these cases. I, of course, was not spared either and used to travel from Delhi to Lahore with my separate group of the accused. Our arrival triggered a great deal of flurry among the literary circles in Lahore. As far as the lawsuits were concerned, a penalty was imposed on the writers for their stories but, mostly, everybody was cleared after appeals. This, of course, generated much chagrin from Chowdhary-saheb. Manto too did not forget it and, in the preface to one of his books, he wrote an account of his trials and dedicated the book to Chowdhary-saheb.

It was extremely interesting to listen to Manto. He considered himself to be the best among writers and never acknowledged any other writer as being even close to him. The moment anybody tried to flaunt their conversational skills, Manto was sure to block their flight and make them fall flat on their faces. He kept poor health and his continuous battle against ill health had left him with very little patience. He got easily irritated and picked quarrels over minor issues. Those who had figured him out practised a great deal of caution while interacting with him. Manto would often say that no doctor had been able to successfully diagnose his illness. Some doctors, he said, had confirmed that he was suffering from tuberculosis; others had established a malfunction of the stomach; still others claimed that his liver had slowed down. One of these fellows had gone to the extent of announcing quite casually to Manto, 'Your stomach is too small for your intestines, which are too big.' Manto, however, remained impervious to all this information regarding his illness and studiously turned a blind eye to the list of dos and don'ts.

'Fraud' was Manto's favourite catchword and recurred like a leitmotif in his conversations. Meeraji had developed his own distinctive style of holding two iron pellets in his hands. If I ever happened to ask him, 'What's the use of holding these pellets all the time?' Manto was sure to say, 'It's all a fraud.'

Once Meeraji started eating dry sewaiyaan mixed with curry. I was surprised and asked him, 'What are you doing?' And it was Manto who responded. 'Fraud,' he said. If Upendranth Ashk wrote something, Manto's pet response to it was, 'It's fraud.' And if Ashk protested a little, however meekly, Manto would comment right away, 'You are a fraud.'

I can also clearly recall that there was a gentleman called Devendra Satyarthi. Actually, 'was' is the wrong word to use. I must say that Devendra Satyarthi is a well-known Hindi and Urdu writer. He has many books to his credit, including an English book on folksongs. Those were the days when the Satyarthis had just arrived in Delhi, and the fancy for writing short stories had taken hold of him. He was a pretty experienced and worldly wise man but still the comments he made and things he said somehow sounded very naïve and innocent. He was a tall, heavily built man. Most of his face was covered by a thick beard. The truth is, he had taken great pains to make himself look like Tagore. He had even got himself photographed with Tagore. He had preserved this photograph and below it one could clearly read the words guru and chela (master and disciple). In this photograph was the fair and classy guru, elegant like a heron, with an extremely dark and gawky disciple standing next to him!

So then Satyarthi-saheb started writing and reading out his short stories. In the beginning, people listened to him out of sheer decency but they soon started avoiding him. People would slip away when they spotted him in the distance. Manto listened to one or two of his stories and started abusing him roundly. Manto began to directly say to him, 'You are a big fraud. Even your beard is not a simply a beard. That too is propaganda. You get your stories altered and modified by us and publish them in your name.'

Manto would hurl the choicest of abuses at Satyarthi. But what wonder! Not even a tiny frown would appear on Satyarthi-saheb's face. He would continue to smile and make his naïve comments. In fact, people often used to say that Satyarthi had the qualities of a saint. Manto, in response used to say, 'He's Rasputin. He is Iblis.'

The fact of the matter is that Manto hated pretense of all kinds. And as far as he himself was concerned, there existed no contradiction between his inner and external selves. Naturally, he never misled or deceived anyone. In fact, he was honest to a fault, expressing whatever he felt in a direct and straight manner. He was frank to the point of being offensive.

Once Maulana Ahmed Shah Bukhari told him in a very patronizing manner, 'Look here, I consider you to be my son.'

To which Manto responded in an irritated tone, 'But I don't consider you to be my father.'

One incident we really enjoyed was the confrontation between Chirag Hasan Hasrat and Manto. It happened at All India Radio. By sheer coincidence everybody had gathered there to have tea. Hasrat always tried to impress others with his wide range of knowledge. Somerset Maugham, Manto's favourite writer, was the focus of this particular discussion. Maulana cut short the discussion on Maugham, dragged Arabic and Persian into the conversation and said in his loud quarrelsome voice, 'It is written in *Mukamate Hariri*. You of course would not have read it. The book is in Arabic. If you had read *Diwan-e-Hamasa*... But of course, you don't know Arabic...'

And in one breath, Hasrat rattled off the names of many Arabic and Persian books. Manto was sitting silently, his anger slowly mounting. When he finally spoke, he only said, 'So what if we do not read enough of Arabic and Persian? We have read a lot of other things.'

The situation would have probably turned unpleasant had Krishan Chander and others not intervened and changed the topic.

The next day, when everybody got together again, Hasrat's entry was followed by an earthquake.

'So Maulana, have you read such and such book? But you of course would not have read it. It is in English. And such and such book? You perhaps would not have even heard of this latest writer.'

And, in the list that Manto quoted, there was hardly any book that was well known. Manto reeled out about fifty titles and compelled Maulana to admit that he had not read even a

single one of them. Maulana broke out into a sweat when he saw himself being slighted thus among friends and companions.

Manto then said, 'Maulana, if you have studied Arabic and Persian, we have studied English. Don't consider yourself to be matchless. Don't try to impose yourself on us ever again.'

After Maulana left, somebody asked Manto, 'Yaar! How do you know the titles of so many books?'

Manto smiled. 'Last evening, after I left, I went straight to Kutab, the English publisher. I took a catalogue of their latest publications and mugged up the titles.'

I learned later that the dispute was settled in a cocktail party organized by friends. After a few rounds of drinks, Manto and Hasrat were coaxed into hugging each other.

Manto declared, 'Maulana, you are a fraud and I too am one.'

Maulana said, 'No, you are Maugham.'

Manto responded, 'You are Ibn Khaldun.'*

And the two hugged each other.

Manto was a very sharp and intelligent man. He took it as a personal insult if anyone crossed their limits in front of him. It made him feel as though he was being treated as an idiot. Moreover, Manto was no admirer of keeping things close to one's chest. The person who could do this very efficiently was Upendranath Ashk. He was truly a secretive man and never opened up in front of others. Manto used to write thirty to forty plays and features in a month and Ashk would write only a couple and that too after a great deal of effort. But Ashk was brazen enough to go around saying that two plays written by him were worth more than the salary he received. Manto used

---

*Ibn Khaldun was an Arab historiographer and historian from the fourteenth century, acknowledged as one of the greatest philosopher of that age.

to openly mock him in front of others. He often showered his favourite abuses—'fraud' and 'bastard'—on him. Ashk would come close to tears at such times. He never forgot Manto's words and stored them in some corner of his memory. Later, in the film industry in Bombay, he did whatever he could to dislodge and uproot Manto.

Manto detested bragging of any sort and derived immense pleasure in taking the wind out of a bragger's sails. I once told Noon Meem Rashid, 'I don't really enjoy your free verse. What is so special about it after all?'

Rashid delivered a short lecture on rhythm and rhyme. Then he started reciting his poem 'Ye meri hum rakhs mujhko thaam le,' and declared, 'See, I have taken care to maintain the rhythm of dance in this poem.'

I listened to him dutifully but how long could Manto have tolerated this! He chipped in to enquire, 'Which dance? Waltz, Rumba, Sambha, Kathakali, Kathak, or Manipuri? You fraud!'

Poor Rashid just smiled shamefacedly and fell silent.

Manto's mind continuously churned out innovative and creative ideas. I have never seen such mental fecundity in anybody else. He once looked at the shapely legs of a fashionable lady and said, 'If I ever get hold of four such legs, I will get them sawed and turn them into legs for my bed.'

Manto was once sitting at All India Radio looking quite exasperated. I walked up to him and asked, 'All is well, I hope?'

'The people here are totally uncivilized and uncultured. When I receive a phone call and say, "I am Manto," the caller from the other end asks in a surprised voice, "One two?" If I then say, "It's not one two, it's Manto", the caller asks, "What? Bhantu?"'

Manto was very proud of his impeccable prose. Manto's writing was truly precise and polished. In one of the stories he sent to me for publication, he had described the stomach of a woman and written that her stomach had 'shikan' (wrinkles) after she had delivered a baby. I replaced 'shikan' with 'chursen'. When the story was published in *Saqi*, Manto saw the word and leapt excitedly, 'When I was writing the word "shikan", I did feel that it was not apt but at that point no other word came to mind. Actually, this is the most appropriate word. It is this word that I was looking for.'

After that he would say quite candidly in front of everybody, 'I accept changes made by only two editors—one is you and the other is Hamid Ali Khan. Nobody except you two have permission to alter even a single word in my writing.'

It is quite clear that Manto gave the impression of being a very stubborn and impolite man but the truth is that he had a very sensitive heart. The world gave him a great deal of pain. He was the pampered child of a rich family. He was spoilt beyond all limits. Everybody, including friends and family members, wounded him in some way or the other. This had made Manto a very bitter man yet his humanity remained intact all through his life. Manto's son, a healthy, playful child, passed away suddenly after a minor illness. I went to his house when I learned about this. Taking percaution, I took a hundred rupees with me, thinking that he may need the money. Safia was devastated and wept inconsolably. It was a house of mourning, so my wife had taken some food with her. She tried to console Safia. This was the first and the last time I ever saw tears in Manto's eyes. The child had been interred. I offered Manto the customary consolation and then quietly offered him the money. Manto did not take it but for a few moments he almost forgot his grief and kept gazing at me in wonder. He later mentioned the incident to many friends and never failed to express surprise that somebody could offer money without being asked.

Only God knows when Manto got into the habit of drinking. His drinking remained within limits while he was in Delhi. After he went to Bombay, he earned a lot of money and also drank a lot. He came to Lahore after the creation of Pakistan. Since there was no film-related work here, he had to depend entirely on his pen. Only a person like Manto could have managed to generate a profession, as well as his bread and butter, from the barren land of our literature. His health was not too good to begin with, and was destroyed further by alcohol. He reached the verge of death many times. He may or may not have food, but he needed to spend twenty rupees every day on alcohol. And he wrote profusely, both good and bad, to earn money for this. It had become routine for him to write one or two stories every day. He used to take his stories to some or the other publisher. To begin with, the publishers paid Manto for their own profit, and then continued for some time even though they knew they would not make much money out of him. After that they started avoiding him. If they saw him walking towards them from a distance they would slip away from their offices. Eventually, Manto was in the same state that Akhtar Shirani and Meeraji were in the final stages of their lives. He used to quite casually put his hand into people's pockets and pull out whatever he found in there. None of it ever reached home.

People tried hard to save him from alcohol. Manto too tried hard to save himself from it and got himself admitted into a lunatic asylum in an attempt to do so. Manto had actually managed to free himself of this kafir, but one day some friends, God help them, got him drunk. The result was that he vomited blood that night. He was taken to hospital where he stayed for many months, and another chance to live was granted to him.

I went to Lahore in August 1954 after a gap of many years. Many prominent writers and publishers from Lahore had gathered together for a party when, quite unexpectedly, Manto too made an appearance and walked up straight to me. His condition was really bad. I told him, 'You are very ill. Why did you come here? I would have come to you myself after finishing with the party.'

'Yes,' he said, 'I am ill but I could not stop myself when I heard that you are here.'

Just then, an ill-fated publisher came close to us. Manto called out, 'Oye! Come here.'

The publisher stopped a bit and then crept close hesitatingly.

'What do you have in your pocket? Take it out.'

He took out five rupees and offered it to Manto but of course, Manto would not have taken merely five rupees.

'Haramzade! Take out at least ten rupees,' Manto said.

He then put his hand into the publisher's inner pocket, extracted ten rupees, and continued talking to me as though nothing unusual had happened. The publisher also thought he been had let off cheaply and immediately vanished from the scene. Manto sat and talked to me for about fifteen or twenty minutes and then began to get increasingly restless. After some time, he made some excuse and went away. As far as I am concerned, that was his final parting from me.

Five months later, it was through newspaper reports that I found Manto had bid goodbye to this world. He had drunk alcohol on the sly and continued to throw up blood until he died.

We, of course, recognize Manto's uniqueness but what is equally true is that Manto too was fully conscious of it. The epitaph he wrote for his grave very clearly indicates it:

*Yahan Saadat Hasan Manto dafn hai*
*Uske seene mein fane-afsana nigari ke saare asrar-o-ramooz*
    *dafn hain*

*Woh ab bhi mano mitti ke niche soch raha hai ki woh bada afsana-nigar hai ya Khuda?*

Saadat Hasan Manto lies buried here
In his heart are interred all the secret techniques of writing
It is as if he lies under the cover of earth, wondering who, between him and Khuda, is the better writer.

# Let's Take a Bottle to Manto

## Ibrahim Jalees

ON 18 JANUARY 1955, FINALLY, SAADAT HASAN MANTO became thanda gosht and his flesh turned cold.

As far as Manto's death is concerned, I feel death decided to take him away from this world at the right time. If death had not obliged him, I am certain he would not have left behind such a radiant name, loved by all, because Manto had started exploiting his name like a silver coin since he came to Pakistan. This silver coin had begun to circulate from one hand to another hand very quickly and layers of sweat and grime from the palms of people had begun to cover the coin and tarnish it. If the circulation of this coin had continued at the same pace, Manto's name would soon have become worthless, counterfeit, and be used for deception.

It was in the last phase of his life that Manto had set up the shop that sold his name. He used to sit in this shop and hawk his name for fifteen, twenty, twenty-five, fifty rupees. His name was becoming defunct due to excessive use. Death too must have loved Manto and must have disapproved of his actions. That is perhaps why it decided to take Manto away while there was still some shine and glitter left on him.

I was very distressed when I heard that Manto had departed from this world but it did not surprise me. My last meeting with Manto was in Karachi where he had been summoned in connection with the obscenity case. When I saw him there, it became apparent that his time to bid farewell to the world was fast approaching and that I should prepare myself to receive the news of Manto standing at the door of either hell or heaven, knocking, and calling out, 'Khol do...'

I cannot claim to be an intimate of Manto's and neither can I be counted as one of those sitting around his grave to collect cash. However, I can certainly say that two years ago, when I had gone to Lahore for six months, there was hardly any evening when Manto did not take either me, Naseer Anwar, Ahmed Rahi, Munir Nyazi or A. Hameed along with him on a tonga to wander around the streets of Lahore that bubbled with life.

Most of his evenings were spent in the hotel where I was staying. In those days, Manto's family had strictly forbidden him from drinking and so he had turned my room into his refuge and drinking hole. These daily get-togethers with a bottle in the middle had made me informal to the extent of becoming shameless. In short, during these meetings there were moments when I felt that I was looking at a Manto who did not have even a shred of clothing on him.

My proximity with Manto cannot be termed a close friendship. However, it can be described as that last stage of familiarity from where friendships begin. My familiarity with Manto had evolved into friendship also because whenever he met me he would leave Manto behind and approach me only as Saadat Hasan. And whenever I went to him, I never went as Jablees. I was only Ibrahim Hasan. I can clearly recall that during the period of our companionship, we had an unseemly discussion about literature only once.

Those were the days when Manto's book about the film actress Noor Jehan, titled *Noor Jehan–Suroor Jehan* (Noor Jehan–Intoxication of the World), had been published. After having read it, I told Manto, 'Your book is complete rubbish. Why do you no longer write stories like "Hatak", "Gopi Nath", "Khol Do", and "Mozel"? Why have you started chasing the likes of Noor Jehan?'

Manto replied, 'Yaar, Noor Jehan sells much more easily than Gopi Nath these days.'

I said, 'Saadat, you are the one being sold more than Noor Jahan. I am pained to see that instead of installing unforgettable statues like those of Gopi Nath, Khushiya, Sugandhi and Mozel on the highway of literature, you are now calling out like the slave merchants of ancient Baghdad, first introducing your friends and then auctioning them openly in the market.'

Manto was shaken by what I had said. It was Manto's habit to lose his temper and brace himself for a quarrel if his ideas were criticized. He had developed a weakness for flattery in the last phase of his life. Many people praised him in his presence to reap under served benefits for themselves—and continue to do so. Yet when Manto entered a room after a span of time, he would walk up straight to me and say, 'All this business about literature is complete rubbish. Only human beings are important. Come along, pick up your glass and let's kill time.'

It was when I spent time in close company with Manto that I painfully discovered that he was trapped in a kind of a negative superiority complex. At all times—while getting up, walking around or writing—he found it necessary to say, do or write something that would startle people and make them think of him as being different or better than them. I call recall many incidents that can be traced back to this feeling but there is one specific episode I remember very clearly.

Whenever I would travel on the streets of Lahore with Manto in a tonga, he would always sit in the front with the tongawala, and Naseer, Anwar, Muneer Niazi or I would sit at the back. I had never attached much importance to his sitting in the front or at the back but one day, when Manto was quite animated, he said, 'I am ahead of you not just in story-writing but also on the roads of Lahore.'

What he said was true and so I felt it was not out of place. Still, a mischievous idea crossed my mind. Once when Manto got off from the tonga for some work, I quickly stepped down and went up to the front. When Manto came back, he asked, 'Why did you come and sit in my place? Go, sit at the back.'

'You go and sit at the back. Now I am going to sit here.'

Manto was very angry but I had made up my mind to not budge. The two of us continued to bicker for quite a long time. Manto finally hired another tonga, sat beside the tongawala, and said to him, 'Overtake that tonga in front of you.'

Manto was thrilled when his tonga overtook ours and turned back many times to look at me victoriously.

Many people who did not know Manto personally based their judgment of him on his writings and had many misconceptions about his character. They imagined him to be a depraved drunkard and a debauch, fond of dissolute women. I too had the same opinion of Manto before I met him. I was also quite surprised when I met Manto, not just the first time but later as well, because I found that he was a very heavy drinker. On days when the sky was overcast and it was raining, he used to pour the mornings, evenings and nights into empty bottles.

Along with the bottle, one quite often finds the presence of immoral and naked women in Manto's stories. In his stories, one can clearly hear the cacophony of filthy streets. A dirty room with a soiled bed on which lies a shameless, half-naked woman, and a man standing nearby, drenched in sweat. An open bottle of alcohol stands on the table. Cigarette smoke fills the room which is bursting with commotion. But just step out of Manto's story, go behind Lahore's Hall Road and knock on the door of Lakshmi Mansions, the corner apartment. The Manto who will emerge from within will be a Manto dressed in clean clothes. He lives in a well-furnished house, the devoted husband of a courteous wife, and the father of three adorable daughters. When you sit in his drawing room, you discover that he cannot tolerate people who ignore the ashtray and scatter cigarette ash on the floor instead. Once, when I did this, Manto handed me a broom and asked me to clean the floor.

I believe that it was this contradiction between Manto's personal and mental existence that was the primary cause of the conflict from which a Manto was born out of Saadat Hasan.

Alcohol was probably the most important thing in Manto's life. And I am inclined to believe that, for Manto, life itself was a bottle of alcohol from which he kept drinking with great relish and kept distributing its intoxication in the form of stories. But Manto was always in a rush to finish all jobs and, much like the manner in which he drank alcohol from the distillery, Manto finished the bottle of life too in great haste. Manto drained the bottle of life, which holds the potential of intoxicating one for sixty, seventy, ninety, or even a century, only in forty-two years. And, instead of tossing this empty bottle on the garbage heap, Manto's family decided to bury it with due respect under a mound of earth in the Miani Sahib graveyard. The bottle has been buried but the intoxication known as Manto continues to hold sway and shall always do so.

When Manto used to drink, he would claim that he was the master of alcohol and not the other way round. The truth, on the contrary, was that Manto failed to realize that alcohol had taken a grip over him and was decimating him gradually until, finally, on 18 January it finished him off completely.

Manto has gone so far away. He would be struggling to come back into this world unless he, with his fragile body, has already begun to rejoice with Bari and Shyam, the film star. He must be quarrelling with the angels and creating quite a scene there.

While it is true that Manto is dead, still, when I read

and write late into the night, I often feel that he has walked stealthily up to my room and is peeping through the keyhole.

Anyway, Manto belonged to that special group of people in Pakistan and India who have died but are still alive. And I never feel the need to bid him a final farewell. Instead, these words come to mind: 'So long, Saadat Hasan Manto, I'm off!'

# The Minister of Literature

Ahmed Nadeem Qasimi

THE STORY OF MY RELATIONSHIP WITH MANTO SPANS over eighteen years. I have preserved every letter, even one-liners, that Manto wrote to me during this period. My reason for doing so is obvious: I loved Manto's personality and I had full faith in his art too. Glimpses of a writer's personality and his art come together in his letters and blend in such a way that it becomes impossible to separate them. (I had once published an open letter to Manto in the magazine *Sangmeel*. Naseer Anwar had told me how Manto, without reading the letter, had brought a bundle of personal letters written over ten years and burnt them one by one).

It was in 1937 that Akhtar Sheerani* introduced us to each other 'in absentia'. We kept writing to each other for four years and our letters established the foundation of such sincere attachment that, until 1949, Manto remained apprehensive that the relationship would come to an end if we physically met each other. I could never understand why Manto should have entertained such negative thoughts. He had perhaps made some conjectures about my perspective regarding life and morality, based upon which he may have concluded that we may not be able to go far walking next to each other. And therefore, when Manto came to Delhi from Bombay in 1940, and invited me from Multan to Delhi, I recalled all those letters in which he had written about the potential danger of our imminent meeting.

I got off at the Delhi Railway Station, went to a tongawala and told him where I wanted to go. A smile touched his lips

---

*A well-known Urdu romantic poet.

as soon as he heard me. I thought that it was the way I was dressed that amused him. I was wearing a Patiala shalwar and my coat—which ought to have been worn with trousers—hung over the shalwar. My physique in those days was like that of a wrestler and the tongawala looked quite fragile. So, I also began to think that it was probably the stark contrast in our physiques that had brought a smile on his lips. However, the enigma of the tongawala's smile was unravelled only after we neared my destination.

It was my first visit to Delhi and I was entirely at the mercy of this tongawala. To begin with, I suspected that he was a total ruffian and that because he knew I was new to the city, he had brought me to a bazaar that echoed all around with harmonium music. People with dishevelled, unkempt hair and lips covered with thick layers of lipstick were casting their dark shadows all around. Women sitting at windows looked like village headmen in a public meeting place or like wrestlers being carried on the shoulders of friends and fans. The environs resonated with jaded laughter issuing from gaping jaws, paan-spit and wilted flowers strewn around.

The tongawala asked me, 'So mian! Is this your first time in Delhi? This is Chawri Bazaar. This is where you asked me to bring you. Where would you like to get off?'

Manto had given me this address in Chawri Bazaar. I was astonished that Pandit Kripa Ram, in all of Delhi, could not find a better place than Chawri Bazaar to set up *Movies*. I was hesitant to ask anybody about the whereabouts of the office. I expected them to turn to me and say, 'Here? The office of a magazine? The offices here are of a very different kind.' But then, my eyes suddenly fell on the signboard. I got off the tonga and walked inside.

I recognized Manto immediately. He was looking through a railway timetable, trying to locate the time of the train I

had travelled in but of course, by then I had got off the train
and reached Chawri Bazaar. This was my first meeting with
Manto. His health looked somewhat fragile but his eyes had a
sparkle and his complexion was suffused with a golden glow.
In the evening, we were relocated to the fourth storey of an
ultra-modern cinema hall where we arrived in a lift. It was
here that I embarked on writing the dialogues and lyrics for a
move based on the story 'Dharam-patni' by the Marathi writer
Khandekar. Manto took the responsibility of typing them out.
We would keep busy with this creative and technical enterprise
all through the day and then go to the bazaar in the evening.
Manto used to drink while I munched on potato chips. After
two or three days Manto said to me, 'Ahmed Nadeem Qasimi,
it is not at all fitting that you eat potato chips while I drink.'
And the very next day he asked Shahid Latif to accompany us
in the evenings and put an end to my 'lonely' status. Shahid
Latif was an M.A. student in Aligarh at that time. We lived
on the fourth storey of the cinema hall for about ten or twelve
days.

I kept wondering why Manto should labour so much for
me. In any case, the story was Khandekar's and the payment for
the lyrics and the dialogues would of course be mine. So why
did Manto sit all day typing out dozens of pages, often guiding
me about film technique? In fact, he had actually written out
some long scenes entirely on his own and typed them out too.
He probably wanted to help me because I got only seventy-two
rupees for my job as Excise Inspector but I was also fully aware
of the fact that Manto himself received a meagre fifty rupees
from *Musavvir* in Bombay. So what was the passion which
was pushing Manto to do such back-breaking work to help
me out? It is obvious that he possessed a great deal of selfless
sincerity, a quality that was common to both of us. We had
mutual respect for each other but, despite it, there came many

situations in life when we could not support each other. Our personalities were very different but this did not come in the way of our friendship that remained intact through our lives. We had grievances against each other, and we expressed them too, but whenever we happened to meet, we were transformed into the Nadeem and Manto of seventeen years ago.

My second meeting with Manto took place the following year when Manto had left Bombay and come to Delhi for good. He was an employee at All India Radio in Delhi and stayed in a flat in Hasan Building on Nicholson Road. At that time there was a congregation of many Urdu writers like Chirag Hasan Hasrat, Meeraji, Upendranath Ashk and Noon Meem Rashid at All India Radio.

I stayed in Manto's house for a few days. The degree of cleanliness and order that existed there is often missing in even rich homes because of an absence of a sense of the aesthetic. A clean white sheet used to be spread out on the floor in Manto's study. His manuscripts were safely stacked inside a one-and-a-half-feet high desk. His typewriter too was kept at this height. Books were neatly arranged on the shelf. Manto, with his fair complexion and spotless clothes, was often seen busy typing away. He used to hide his whisky bottle too in this same desk.

The beautiful simplicity of Manto's house brings to mind an incident that occurred in 1948. Manto had dropped in to see me. He entered my room and said in a startled voice, 'It looks like the room has just been whitewashed.' I informed him that he was right; the room had indeed been whitewashed just about a week ago.

He then said to me, 'You are a poet. How can you bear to be surrounded by such hideous whitewash?'

I informed him, 'I have done this myself so there is no question of not being able to bear it.'

Manto sat quietly for a while and then got up and took

me to his house. We entered the drawing room where he announced, 'See, this is what you call whitewashing.'

The third time I met Manto was when he called me to Delhi. Manto and Krishan had written a story for the film *Banjara*. They wanted me to write the lyrics for the film. This time I got the opportunity of staying in Manto's house for a month. Manto persuaded me to write a long opera and four poetic dramas during this time. He argued a lot with the radio officials to get me suitable payment for my work. When he was finally able to extract a respectable amount on my behalf, he took me to Chandni Chowk. He bought cloth for my coats and trousers from an Amritsari shopkeeper and within two or three days my new clothes had been stitched. And thus I wore trousers and a tie for the first time in my life.

My fourth meeting with Manto took place when legal proceedings against his story 'Boo' were going on. Manto was in Bombay and I was the editor of the monthly *Adab-e-Lateef* in Lahore.

The fifth meeting happened incidentally in Anarkali bazaar. I had gone to Lahore in connection with the case against the magazine *Savera*, and Manto had already permanently shifted there. A few days later, he came to Peshawar where he stayed with me for about fifteen days. It was in Peshawar that our disagreement over ideological issues became apparent for the first time.

We would spend the entire day at the radio station and, in the evening Manto would turn up with someone or the other. This was followed by drinking rounds and discussions about realism and sex in literature. Manto had complete and authoritative information regarding all legal cases against obscenity in literature in all prominent countries of the world. He cited examples of writers and writings in such a forceful voice that he could have been easily mistaken for a firebrand orator.

One day I remarked, 'Tolstoy has commented on one of Maupassant's stories and written that if he had to show his heroine naked, would it not have been enough to say that she was bathing? Or perhaps he could also have added that she had just finished with her bath and her body was still covered with drops of water. Why did Maupassant feel the necessity to describe the colour of the drops as being the same golden or pink as the colour of the heroine's skin? It is precisely at this point that the spice of sexuality makes its entry into literature.'

Manto was furious when he heard this and said, 'What do you know about mysteries of the woman's body? You are not married. In fact, you have not even tasted alcohol yet. That day in Chawri Bazaar you looked like a crow that had entered a group of royal swans. How can you understand why Maupassant felt the need to describe the colour of water drops? The woman would have remained flat and unidimensional if he had not mentioned the colour of her skin. It is the presence of pink drops that infuse her with the beauty of a flower in full bloom. You write stories about farmers but that does not in any way indicate that you can understand the psychology of a farmer woman. One has to become a woman when writing about them. Have you ever turned into a woman in your creative moments? Has somebody ever teased you? Has a stranger ever laid his hand on your body? Has somebody's touch ever sent a tremor through you? Has your body ever quivered and chimed, even at a stranger's touch? So my dear, there were times when Tolstoy too became a Gandhian but do you think that he would not have felt the same sensation that Maupassant had felt while watching the pink drops of water on his heroine's body? So then, Ahmed Nadeem Qasimi, the fact is that you are the external-affairs minister of literature and I am its internal-affairs minister. Both of us have our own paths and our own destinations. Nadeem cannot become

Manto and Manto cannot become Nadeem. Tolstoy is Tolstoy and Maupassant is Maupassant! I think I have had a drink too many. Come now, let's sleep.'

Those days I resolved to myself to leave no stone unturned in my attempt to make Manto accept that some parts of his stories were obscene. I dug in my heels and refused to spare him. Finally, Manto's comments became nastier than I could ever have imagined. One day in Peshawar, when I tried to stop him from drinking excessively, he became exasperated and said, 'This is my private affair. It is true that you are my friend but I have not appointed you the imam of the mosque of my consciousness.'

The very next day, the realization of the bitterness in that beautiful sentence dawned on him and the manner in which he spoke to me made it quite evident that he was trying to mollify me.

I have always seen Manto dressed in spick and span kurta-pajamas. He would also wear suits in winter. He used to write his stories on very expensive sheets of paper. Manto started each story by writing the number 786 on top of the sheet and say, 'This is Allah's phone number.' There used to be about a dozen well-sharpened pencils in front of Manto when he sat down to write. I once even asked him, 'Why so many pencils?' Manto said, 'The pencil point becomes blunt with writing and then it takes a while to sharpen a new one. In the meantime, my train of thoughts is interrupted. So, what I do is that I keep aside the blunt pencil and pick up one that's sharpened.'

I had written the lyrics for *Banjara*. Manto, Krishan and I had to go to the seth, the owner of Manoranjan Pictures, with the lyrics. We were to receive a single cheque for the story, dialogues and the lyrics. Even a single rupee had great value in those days. We were to receive a consolidated amount of two thousand rupees for the story, dialogues and lyrics, which was considered pretty high. Manto advised me, 'If the seth argues with you over a certain word, or interrupts you somewhere, simply agree with him. You poets have a huge ego. Just don't argue with him or else our payment will be in jeopardy.'

The seth was a young man but had such thick layers of fat all over his body that it looked like a swollen dome had been placed between his chin and his knee. I recited the lyrics to him. He liked them, except for one word that he paused on and said, 'Forget about tamanna, just write asha. People from the lower classes will not able to understand the word tamanna.'

I was just about to agree with him when Manto spoke up. 'Seth-saheb,' he said,'tamanna is the most apt word here. One should not comment about things one is ignorant about. This is poetry, not a box where you can throw in whatever you like. This business of throwing in asha is not acceptable. Tamanna is fine here and if you disagree, please allow us to leave.'

The seth became nervous and said, 'You talk too loudly Manto, and your eyes begin to bulge out so much that I get scared. Fine, let it remain tamanna. Now let's go ahead.'

As soon as we walked out of the seth's bungalow with a cheque for two thousand rupees, Manto said that we should encash it immediately. Krishan said, 'Why is the rush? We will get it cashed tomorrow. Nadeem still has three or four days to leave.'

Manto, however, insisted, 'You are not familiar with the mindset of these seths in films. Who knows, he may change his mind. Delaying this even for a minute is a serious risk. And moreover, we have to help Nadeem get rid of his ungainly shalwar and his long sherwani, which looks like that of a a maulvi's. When he walks with us in his flowing, fluttering shalwar, he looks like a big landlord, and we like his farm hands.'

The cheque was encashed in a bank in Chandni Chowk. When it came to the issue of dividing the money, Manto said, 'Krishan and I are local. Each of us will take six hundred and sixty rupees. Nadeem has come from Multan so he will get six hundred and eighty rupees.' The three of us then went to a shop and bought material for my coat and trousers, which was then handed over to a tailor for stitching.

When we reached Manto's house, we found the seth's munshi waiting for us. He informed us, 'The seth has said that he has postponed his plan to make the film. Please return the cheque. There are reports that Japan has jumped into the war and it has demolished American ships in Pearl Harbour.'

Manto looked at us with a victorious gleam in his eyes and then, turning towards the munshi, he said, 'Go and tell your seth that the Pearl Harbour of that cheque has also been attacked and demolished. It has already been encashed and blown away.'

Krishan and I could not get over our amazement and admiration at Manto's foresight.

All India Radio had once organized a poetry conference. Patras Bokhari, the then Director General, had hosted a lunch as a part of the celebrations. Rashid, Krishan, Manto and I were sitting at one of the tables. Manto suddenly started talking about Hafeez Jalandhari* and said, 'He is swollen with self-pride; I am going to smash his pomposity and conceit to smithereens. He addressed me in front of a large number of people as though I was a schoolchild. He could have addressed me as Mantosaheb, but instead of that he spoke to me in a

---

*A well-known poet who supported the British Government during the Second World War. He also composed the national anthem of Pakistan in 1952.

patronizing tone: "So then, barkhurdar Sadaat, how are you?" Just you watch now how I set him right.'

He said as much and getting up from his chair, walked over to the table at which Bokhari-saheb was seated with Hafeez-saheb and some other well-known people of the city. As soon as he reached the table, Manto said, 'Hafeez-saheb, one of your shers has really put me in serious trouble. There is such depth, along with such heights, in it that despite my best efforts my mind is not able to grasp its full significance. I think it is a deeply philosophical couplet. Please be kind enough to explain its full import to me.'

Hafeez-saheb was overjoyed. He was impressed with Manto's manner and said, 'Yes, of course, barkhurdar Sadaat! Tell me, which is the couplet you have in mind?'

Manto responded, 'There is a very profound couplet in your book *Shahnama-e-Islam*. It goes like this:

*Yeh ladka jo leta hai, yeh ladki jo leti hai*
*Yeh Paigambar ka beta hai, yeh Paigambar ki beti hai*

This boy, lying down, this girl, lying down
He is the son of God's Messenger, and she his daughter

Hafeez-saheb immediately caught Manto's intention. He stood up in a huff and started blaming himself for being there. It was with great effort that Bokhari-saheb was able to pacify him. Manto walked back to us and said, 'So then? Did you see the skill that barkhurdar Sadaat possesses!'

Manto once planned to tease Maulana Chirag Hasan Hasrat. Manto, Krishan and I went to the Maulana. He showered praise on us and ordered tea for us. Manto addressed him very politely and said, 'Hasrat-saheb, do you think Iqbal's poetry is really poetry in the real sense of the word? To me it seems to be nothing but preaching and sermonizing.' That was it! Hasrat-

saheb was furious with us and gave us such a tongue-lashing
that we had no option but to immediately leave the room.

In another instance, Manto harassed Hasrat quite a lot.
It so happened that Faiz-saheb was taking his students from
M.A.O. College, Amritsar, on a visit to Aligarh University.
They stopped in Delhi on the way and Manto organized a
get-together in a hotel to welcome him. Hasrat-saheb, who
was also there, suggested: 'There are such good poets here
this evening. How about a ghazal from each one of them?'
When that round of ghazals ended, Hasrat said once again,
'Let us have another round of ghazals.' However, Manto said,
'No, we must now hear nazms.' Hasrat thundered in response,
'No! We will have only ghazals.' Manto thundered, 'No, only
nazms!' Both were seething with anger. Then, despite being a
Kashmiri, Manto said, 'If I had a pair of sharp forceps in my
hand, I would have plucked all the proverbs of Ratan Nath
Sarshar* out your mind. And after that will not remain a
Hasrat or anything but pure and simple Hatu.'

Everybody at All India Radio loved Manto but he could not
resist teasing people around him. He would say to Noon
Meem Rashid, 'You talk about holding your dancing partner
in your poetry. Have you ever even tried Western dance? I
have. Come, take me as a partner and we will dance a few steps.
All your illusions will be immediately shattered.' Whenever his
eyes fell on Krishan Chander, he would say, 'This man wants
to make everybody happy. Look here, bhai, you should be in a
state of some tension with someone or the other. Krishan, you
are the true Mahatma Buddha among writers.' And whenever
he would spot Upendranath Ashk, he would put on a heavy
Punjabi accent and call out, 'Ashke! Oye Ashke!'

---

*Ratan Nath Sarshar was a Urdu writer, originally from Kashmir. Hatu
is a term of insult.

One day, I was sitting with Manto in his house when a well-known poet of the times, Vishwamitra Adil, turned up to meet me and said, 'When I found out that you are here, I decided to come to you to confirm the pronunciation of one word. Do tell me please which syllable should be emphasized in the word gandiri. Should it be pronounced gandiree, or ganddiri with the stress on "d"?'* Manto asked him, 'Where do you want to use the word?' Adil said that the word appeared in one of his nazms. Manto responded in a very casual tone, 'You buffoon! Can any writing in which this word appears ever be called a nazm? Why don't you forget about poetry and start selling gandiree on a cart?'

One day I found Manto looking quite pleased with himself. He narrated the following incident to me:

'There is this person who visits me everyday and smokes all my cigarettes. When I heard his voice at the door today, I threw down a packetful of cigarettes on the floor. As usual, he asked me for a smoke as soon as he entered. I told him, "I finished the packet just now. See, there it is, lying on the floor." "Never mind," he replied, "I must sometimes have a conversation with you even without smoking." He continued to talk for some time and then got up to leave. When he reached the door, he suddenly turned around, picked up the cigarette packet from the floor, put it into his pocket, and said, "The children will play with this."'

The two of us laughed at the incident for quite a long time. Later, Safia-bhabhi too joined us in our mirth.

Those were the days when I had just started writing stories. I had brought my story 'Assalam-alaikum', published in the monthly *Saqi*, with me on my visit to Delhi. Manto read

---

*Gandiree are small pieces of sugarcane, peeled and diced. Ganddiri is the word for branch.

through my story but started arguing with me about the last paragraph. 'Is this the way to end a story? Is this the way to wrap up a story? Should such a good story be ruined like this? You have completely destroyed it in the end.' Safia was very displeased with Manto's manner: One, I was their guest, and two, I was Manto's contemporary in age. Safia was ready for a spat with Manto. I too tried to present my point of view but Manto did not give in to either of us. He sat down, rewrote the last page of my story, and said, 'Here, read it now.' I read through it and found that as far as the impact of the story was concerned, it had increased manifold.

One day Manto came to my house for some work. At that time, Abdul Majeed Bhatti was reading out a part of his novel to me. Manto talked to me and as he got up to leave, Bhatti said to him, 'Manto-saheb, why don't you sit for a while longer. I am reading out a section of my novel to Nadeem-saheb. Why don't you also listen to it and give me your suggestions about whether my style is suitable or ...? '

Manto replied, 'Bhatti-saheb, I know very well that when you start reading you forget to stop. You should know that I am not an idiot like Ahmed Nadeem Qasimi to fall into your trap.' Manto \fired his salvo and left, leaving me behind to offer a lengthy apology to Bhatti.

Manto once rang the doorbell of my house and, when I opened the door, he asked me for fifteen rupees, saying that he needed the money to buy medicines for his daughter. I was completely bankrupt those days. I said to Manto, 'Right now I have only a rupee or so. Why don't you sit for a while? I will go get the money from someone or the other.' But Manto did not wait. 'I know you are speaking the truth,' he said, 'and so I will not allow you to beg for money from someone else. I will arrange for it somehow.' And left.

Almost immediately after that, Shabab Keranwi, the editor

of the film magazine *Director*, came to my house. He took out twenty-five rupees from his pocket and, keeping them on the table, said, 'I am bringing out a special issue of *Director* and need a story from you for the issue. To which I replied, 'Shabab-saheb, firstly I don't have a story, and secondly, even if I had one, I would give it for publication to some literary magazine. Why would I get it published in a film magazine?'

Shabab did not give in. 'I am leaving an advance and will come back again next week,' he said and left. He probably had not have even crossed the road from my house when Manto entered my house once again and said, 'I just saw Shabab leaving your house and I began to wonder what business he could have with you. All he could have done was to ask you to write something for his magazine and leave behind an advance.'

'You are absolutely right,' I told Manto. 'He has left behind those twenty-five rupees lying on the table. You take them.'

Manto replied, 'No, not all the money. I need only fifteen rupees. You take the rest. You will need it.' Manto picked up fifteen rupees and left.

A Progressive Writers' Association Conference was held in Lahore in 1949. A resolution boycotting many well-known writers and poets, including Manto, was passed at the conference. I was the Secretary of the Association but the resolution was passed despite my opposition to it.

Manto was deeply hurt by this boycott. It was bad enough that his friend was made the Secretary of PWA at this conference but what was worse that it was at this same conference that Manto was branded an obscene as well as a reactionary writer. I was put in a situation where I had no courage to face Manto.

Soon Manto, along with Hasan Aksari, started editing the Urdu magazine *Urdu Adab*. In the very first issue, he published an article by Yusuf Zafar in which he had criticized my poetry. He did not stop there and went on to target my photograph too. The fact that I was not looking straight at the camera was interpreted as evidence that I did not have the courage to confront reality and the real world. When I met Manto quite by chance, I raised the issue of this absurd criticism. Manto replied, 'If you get absurd boycotts passed, then we too will publish absurd criticism against you.' I tried very hard to convince Manto that despite being the Secretary, I was against the resolution and that it was still passed with majority vote. Manto, however, could not be persuaded. It was only after the PWA withdrew the resolution in 1952 that Manto's anger was mollified and we started meeting once again.

Manto once came to the office of the daily, *Imroz*, and said, 'I have written the first Punjabi story of my life. You bring out a special Punjabi page in your paper. Publish the story there.' When I read that story, written with a pencil, I felt that Manto's art had touched its pinnacle. I got the payment sent to Manto from the office and planned to widely publicize the story as 'Manto's first in Punjabi' before publishing it. However, just a few days later the police turned up without warning to search the office and turned the papers upside down so heartlessly that Manto's story was forever lost in the chaos. I persistently tried to look for Manto's story in all the files for as long as I worked at *Imroz*. However, I could not find it anywhere. It probably went into the hands of the police.

There was a time when the Punjabi facet of Manto's personality raised its head quite strongly. Shahid Ahmed Dehlvi once invited both of us for a party in Delhi. Almost all the prominent writers of Delhi were present. Needless to say, all discussion regarding literature was happening in Urdu but whenever Manto and I spoke to each other, we did so in

Punjabi. Shahid-saheb did not take kindly to this and told us, 'You are Urdu writers. And while you use Urdu when you talk to us, you insisting on talking to each other in Punjabi...This is unacceptable. You must use Urdu.'

Manto found this very objectionable and said, 'Shahid-saheb, Punjabi is a much older language than Urdu and its vocabulary is richer than Urdu's. For example, if I drop an aluminium bowl on a cement floor, the dent it gets is called 'chab' in Punjabi and the act of the bowl getting dented is known as 'chab padana'. What is this kind of dent called in Urdu? And denting of this kind?' Friends suggested more than one word as a substitute for chab but none of them really served the purpose as well as chab does. And Manto was ecstatic. It was as if he had achieved a great triumph and was holding the flag of victory in his hand.

Whenever Manto would sense a story lurking somewhere within anyone he met, he would build a rapport with that person. He would then try to closely observe the person's routine and when he felt he had gotten under the person's skin, he would construct a story based on this character. One such character of his is based on the well-known politician Khan. Manto spent a few days with Khan and then constructed his story around him. When Khan discovered the story, he came to me, breathing fire, and asked, 'Manto is your friend, isn't he?'

'Yes,' I answered.

Khan could not hold himself back and declared, 'He has written a story against me. I am going to break his teeth.'

I pretended to be ignorant about the whole issue. I knew that Khan-saheb was in a temper and I wanted to warn Manto before he managed to get his hands on him. So I told him, 'We are not on talking terms these days. And moreover, I have heard that he has also changed his house.'

Khan-saheb was still furious but decided to leave. After a short time, the same Khan-saheb came back to me smiling and said, 'That friend of yours, that Manto, I happened to meet him. I was going to Zaheer Kashmiri to get his address when I suddenly met Manto himself on Bedian Road. I caught hold of him and said, "You come here. So? You have written a story against me?"

'Manto replied, "No, I have not written against you. I have just written about you."

'So I asked him, "What have you written about me?"

'And he then told me, "All I have written is that Khan drinks and visits prostitutes."'

I got really concerned when I heard this and asked him nervously, 'And then? What happened then?'

'Then what?' Khan saheb responded. 'What could have happened? What he has written is of course true.'

Finally, one day Manto came to my house with a publisher and told him, 'Take the bottle out of the bag and keep it on the table.' After the publisher did so Manto told me, 'Get up, Ahmed Nadeem Qasimi-saheb, and unfasten the window that opens onto the street outside. Get me a glass and a jug of water. I will sit and drink here today and spread the stench of alcohol in the whole neighbourhood.'

I opened the window and got the glass and jug of water from upstairs. I kept these in front of him and said, 'Bismillah kijiye.'

He looked at me with his large eyes. The pallid and unwholesome face that surrounded the eyes made them look even larger. He sent off the publisher and then, turning towards me, he said, 'I could never understand you. Neither were you ever able to understand me. How come we still continue to be friends?'

It was clear from his voice that he was trying hard to get a grip over his emotions.

That was the first time I saw an unshaved Manto. It was also the first time that the crease of his pajamas was crumpled in some places along the fold.

I said, 'Drink. Should I open the bottle?'

Manto laughed, 'What's the point of you opening the bottle? Your whole neighbourhood will hear the boom of you opening it.' He then stood up and said, 'Come with me. Hide the bottle in your coat.' I did so and went out with him. On the way, he asked, 'You profess to be a great leader of the Progressives, don't you? If any of them somehow get to know that Manto has a full bottle of whisky, they will start trailing me like beggars.' I kept completely silent.

He reached home and, after placing the bottle on a stool, went inside to get some water. Just then Safia-bhabhi came to me for a few moments and said, 'Nadeem-bhai, for God's sake, stop him from committing suicide. You are the only one in the world who can stop him from doing this. He has great respect for you. He cannot live long if he continues to drink like this.'

Manto entered the room and said, 'What is being whispered between brother and sister?' Safia went off inside.

I did what Safia had wanted and tried to persuade Manto. I pleaded with him to stop drinking. I talked of his wife and his daughters. Manto had already drunk two or three pegs in the meantime. He turned to me and repeated, 'I have not appointed you imam of the mosque of my consciousness.'

Then there were times in Lahore when we did not get a chance to meet for months together. During that period he once came to me and said, 'Just note down what I say, my dear. It is quite possible that after a few days you may be asked to write something "in memory of the late Manto".'

I lost my cool when I heard this. It went against the grain of my character, but I forgot about his drunken state and said, 'If my friendship is precious to you, you will have to stop drinking. You drink as though you were mad. Do you even realize that Nakhat-beti, also stays in the same house where you drink? She is the same child whose photo you had sent to me from Bombay. I still have that photograph. You are the minister of internal affairs of literature but can you not understand what must be happening to Nakhat, internally? What impression are you making on Nakhat's heart and mind? What image of her father will she carry into the future? If you cannot understand this, then you should call yourself a minister without a portfolio. If a writer blocks himself away from everybody else...'

Manto responded, 'There is no need for all this fraud.' And after that, he told me in very clear words that I had absolutely no right to interfere in his personal matters. I left but did not mind what he had said since I was convinced that he would he would regret his words the next day after coming back to his senses. But I was wrong. Manto did not express any regret. On the contrary, when we met by chance a few days later, he impressed upon me quite plainly that what he had said that day was a clear declaration of his position. He also made it clear that he had voiced it when he was in full control of himself and not in a state of inebriation.

After that, I accepted defeat. I did meet him occasionally during that period. But what was also true is that Manto could not accommodate my presence with the extremes to which he had gone. And I did not have the strength to see him slowly but surely killing himself and not say anything about it. I had already spoken and had seen the consequences of doing so.

But I now feel that I have been a coward. Why did I not guard him like a sentry? I would have had to bear his abuses, his chiding, but at least I would have continued to make an effort to keep him alive. His family and some of his friends would have supported me. We could have worked towards saving this invaluable treasure from being destroyed so soon. Manto had once written to me that he would always need me.

A few days later, I was walking along with some others who had also loved Manto. We were on our way to offer our shoulders to carry his dead body.

So now, there are two things left for me to mourn in my life. The first is Manto and the second is the sham of my self-respect.

# Manto-saheb

## Mohammad Tufail

I HAVE A SEVERE HEADACHE AND FOR SOME STRANGE reason I wish it to further intensify. It is perhaps this mood that is goading me on to write something about Manto right away. I must do this without even a moment's delay. There is no knowing when both this pain and this mood may evaporate, for reading Manto's stories puts the dagger in my heart and not the head. I am certain that other readers of Manto's stories too have experienced this same agony, though their reasons may be very different. It is possible that Manto's piquant style and expression may have troubled some while others may have been aggrieved not just by his style of writing but also by his formidable articles which possess the power of making heads reel with the force of their attack. I often wonder about where, among the range of Manto's readers, I can locate myself but I will come to that later. That is mainly because at this point I want to talk about Manto's personality and not his art. I hand over the responsibility of commenting on Manto's writing to the critics and humbly submit that I have no doubt that what I offer in terms of critical comments is bound to be inadequate.

One day I happened to see a gentleman walking down the streets of Anarkali Bazaar in a very unusual fashion and, for some incomprehensible reason, I felt that he was Manto. Or perhaps the thought came to me because I already knew that Manto had left Bombay and was in Lahore. A few days later, I saw the same gentleman cycle across our office on a brand new bicycle. I saw him peer inside the office in a peculiar way and the idea once again flashed through my mind: 'There goes Manto!'

Barely a few minutes later Ahmed Nadeem Qasimi entered our office and said, 'I would have reached dot on time but for the fact that I happened to meet Manto-saheb on the way and spent half an hour talking to him.'

A few days later, Nadeem-saheb came to the office once again. Accompanying him was the same gentleman I had first seen in Anarkali Bazaar and then cycling across our office.

Nadeem-saheb made the introductions.

'This is Sadaat Hasan Manto.' And then, gesturing towards, me he said, 'This is Tufail-saheb.'

Manto is a man of many talents and the most distinctive of them is that no one can say a single word in his presence despite trying one's best. Of course, conversations with him are, no doubt, interesting as well as enlightening.

That was the first time he had visited us but he started talking as soon as he arrived. In fact, I did not get the opportunity of serving him even a glass of water. He was talking continuously but I still managed to somehow chip in and ask, 'Manto-saheb, would you like a cup of tea?'

Manto-saheb was in his 'non-stop' mood at that time and so something that should have been seen as courtesy somehow ended up being distorted as incivility. He shot back, 'Forget it man! This discussion is far more sizzling than tea...'

The thread of conversation had snapped however, and so he strayed off on a different course and, addressing Nadeem-saheb, said, 'In Hyderabad, in the south, many people were deeply concerned, and continue to be so, that I should have married Ismat. I just can't understand why such things come to people's minds. My wife became green with jealousy when she heard about it. She was literally on fire, she became a kebab when she heard of it, and I fully understand her response because first and foremost, Ismat is her very close friend. And secondly, this was a threat to her prerogative of wife-hood. So her turning into a kebab is fully understandable.'

He then moved on to something else.

'Oh! What can I say about Bombay, my friend! Ek teer mere seene mein mara ki hai hai. Those were really good days! An income of about two thousand and great esteem! Everybody had Manto's name on their lips. And after I came here, to God's special country, I find that I am the one who has to approach publishers and request them to publish my books. I have often had this irresistible desire to stand in the middle of the road and scream, "Pakistan zindabad" but then better sense prevails and I realize that if I did so, people would think I am mad.'*

This speech seemed to distress Manto and it was probably to rid himself of it that he produced a beautiful cigarette-case and offered one to Nadeem-saheb. He then took out another cigarette and held it between his thin lips. He was about to pull out the matchbox from his pocket when it suddenly struck him that I too was present.

'Apologies,' he said, and pushed the cigarette case towards me.

Nadeem-saheb took the pressure off me by saying, 'Ye nahin peete.' (He does not smoke.)

Manto caught hold of 'peete', drink, and took off! Hai kambakht tune pee hi nahin; cigarette peena is nothing compared to real drinking...'**

---

*A line from the couplet by Ghalib:

*Kalkatta ka jo zikr kiya tune hamnasheen*
*Ek teer mere seene mein mara ki hai hai*

The mere mention of Calcutta by you, my love
Is like an arrow piercing my heart

**A line from a couplet by Jigar Muradabadi:

*Lutfe maiy tujhse kya kahoon naaseh*
*Hai kambakht tune pee hee nahin*

How do I tell you about pleasures of drinking, my dear preacher,
When you yourself have never even drunk?

After that, he asked Nadeem-saheb, 'Have you read my article, "When My Eyes Opened in the Morning?"'

Nadeem-saheb made his habitual response, 'Yes.'

'Forget it man,' Manto-saheb said in Punjabi. 'There's not much in that article. It's complete nonsense.'

This is Manto-saheb's consistent response when he heard somebody praise his writings. Or sometimes he merely says, 'That's it. That's enough.' And after that he started praising his article himself, that too with specific references and examples. He sometimes quoted from the article and added: 'Let me tell you how wonderful some sentences are. For example, listen to this: It was a morning suffused with an amazing enchantment. The shops had still not been opened, except the one which sold sweets. I walked towards the shop and when I reached it I saw that it had an electric table fan. It was rotating, but it had been turned towards the wall. I asked the shopkeeper, "What is the point of fanning the wall?" He glared at me and said, "Can you not see it for yourself?" I looked again and saw that the fan was facing the photograph of Mohammad Ali Jinnah and cooling it.

'All of a sudden, a great commotion started. I heard a lot of noise and saw some young boys holding bundles of paper, blindly running around and screaming at the top of their voices. I got to hear many, many varieties of speeches in all the shrieking and screaming. Newspapers were being sold—the latest news, hot off the press. Brawl in Delhi; dogs attack such and such in a house in Lucknow; an astrologer in Pakistan predicts that Kashmir will be independent in two weeks!'*

He could not decide where to stop. He went on. 'I am in a strange frame of mind these days. I start to write a story but it

*Here Tufail adds: Manto had narrated the above in broken and disconnected sentences but I have quoted these from his book and reproduced these here as a continuous dialogue.

turns into an article in the end. When I plan to write an article it ends up becoming a drama.'

I am not sure what came over me at that point but I interrupted him. 'You will surely become a question mark if you try to write a drama, a story and an article at the same time.'

Manto-saheb enjoyed my remark and replied in a clear Punjabi accent, 'Good! It's good!'

But since he could never accept anything that was remotely uncomplimentary about himself, he pondered for a few moments and then added, 'What you just said is certainly interesting but I find myself incapable of responding to you since I am still not on informal terms with you.'

Nadeem-saheb of course knew the kind of response that Manto was capable of giving. He smiled and said to him, 'Please don't react. He is an unusual type of a person.'

I wondered what Nadeem really meant when he said that I was an 'unusual' person.

But Manto himself had moved on and his mind had begun to ponder over the word 'type'. He asked, 'Have you read my article, "Types of Noses"? Yes, yes, that same one that says, "Once his nose started to run, it kept running." I have catalogued different types of noses in this article.'*

Manto wore thick glasses over his large eyes. He turned them towards Nadeem-saheb and asked, 'Would you like to stay here longer?'

Nadeem-saheb repeated his usual: 'Yes.'

Manto stood up and said, 'Fine then, bhai. I should leave.'

After that, I met Manto almost every day. But these meetings were also quite erratic. Manto would meet us regularly and

---

*Aaye jo unki naak to aati chali gayi* (Once his nose started to run, it kept running). The line is a parody of the lyric, *Aayi jo unki yaad to aati chali gayi* (Once I thought of my beloved, the memories kept coming.).

then suddenly disappear. This usually happened because he was preoccupied with quite different things in those days. His disappearance act generally continued for just a few days, or at best, a few weeks. These meetings began with Manto's loud 'Assalam-alaikum', while still getting off the tonga. He would follow this up by saying, 'Just give me ten or fifteen rupees for medicine.'

One had no option but to shell out the money. People take medicines to remain healthy but Manto took them to destroy his health. His medicine is called 'alcohol'. To begin with, he was the one who drank the medicine but now it is this medicine that is draining him completely. I am quite certain that one day we will suddenly get the news that Manto-saheb has passed away.

It is an established fact that Manto is one of the foremost writers in Urdu. Some people, however, refuse to accept this fact and I am in total disagreement with such people and their refusal to grant Manto his rightful status. Nonetheless, it once so happened that Manto-saheb had written a story titled 'Nutfa' (Sperm) for *Nuqoosh*. I did not like the story much and communicated this to him, though after a great deal of hesitation. Manto-saheb did not mind this at all. In fact, he wrote a new story instead. I, however, felt that the second story was no better than the earlier one. When Manto got to know of my opinion he said, 'I will write a new story tomorrow and will continue writing stories till you discover the one you do.'

After that, he handed me two stories within four days. I really liked two of them, 'Mozel' and 'Sadak ke Kinare'.

My purpose in recording this incident is to establish how Manto was not just a writer of immense stature but also truly courageous, tolerant and liberal. Writers have a soft corner for even their most insignificant writings and cannot tolerate the slightest disapproval of them. But a writer like Manto, who is a great artist and is blunt to the same degree, did not in any way try to impress upon me his eminence as an artist or his ability to become extremely brusque.

Actually, nothing in this world has the power to block or silence Manto's words. He sometimes turns up when he is drunk and says, 'What nonsense have you gone and said to so and so, my dear? My relationship with him is on a completely different level. Pardon me for saying this but he is a bastard and so am I. But what is it that compelled you to communicate to him what I had told you in complete confidence? Not that I am afraid of him! What can he do to me, after all? But my dear, you too are a strange man. Pardon me, but you don't realize what a shameful thing you have done. I was smouldering and seething when I found out. My...'

I keep quiet on these occasions or sometimes merely smile a bit because what Manto says when he is drunk is completely inconsequential. It is actually not Manto but the bottle that speaks.

There are times, too, when Manto and the bottle become inseparable. And when Manto speaks then, one feels only love for him and all that he says. Such moments, however, are quite rare. What generally happens is that he gets drunk and starts talking rubbish, and it is because of this that he has had to go twice to the mental hospital.

It was Manto's own decision to go to the mental hospital the first time. The second time, it was his family that forced him. When he came out of the hospital the second time, I asked him, 'What is it, Manto-saheb? Why do you keep going in and out of the mental hospital?'

To which he replied, 'The first time, I went in the fond hope that it would help me give up drinking. I had heard that they have some methods of treatment which help people give up drink easily. But it is difficult for me to describe what happened after I reached the place. The second time, my family forced me to go back. I pleaded hard with them but they would not be dissuaded. After I was admitted, I asked the doctors to conduct a thorough investigation of my mental state since I was convinced that I was perfectly fit and fine. They, however, paid no attention to what I said. Yesterday, a friend of mine had come to visit me—I just left the place and came away with him. They must be hunting for me. Let them. Mad people!'

The most interesting discussions we have with Manto are the ones that deal with the issue of obscenity. He says, 'I am quite baffled by the fact that people have hardly paid any heed to my innumerable stories that do not have the slightest mention of sex. Actually, very few of my stories deal with sex. The people who brand my stories vulgar are the ones who go from shop to shop enquiring if I have published a new collection. I think my readers can be divided into those who love my writings and those who have serious objections to them. The latter read my stories only to condemn and criticize them heartily. I too settle the score as soon as I find a suitable occasion. It is because of this that I have the following dedication in one of my books: '"For the editor of *Deen-o-duniya* who has abused me the most."*

'Now I feel like dedicating a book to the respectable Maulana Majid Dariyabadi since this gentleman too has increased the significance of my stories by consistently criticizing them. If I fail to do this during my lifetime, then it is possible that Maulana Majid may end up reminding me about this unpaid obligation on the Day of Judgment. That would be really embarrassing for me.**

---

*Mufti Shaukat Ali Fehmi, who edited the monthly *Deen-o-duniya* for more than fifty years.

**Maulana Majid Dariyabadi was the editor of *Sach*, published from Lucknow.

'Oh! Forget about these other respectable people, my friend Qasimi-saheb has also written an open letter to me. I felt like I too must write something, seal it, and send it for publication but refrained from doing so because Qasimi-saheb is essentially a decent person. Just because Askari has written the preface to my book *Siyah Hashiye*, people have started saying that I am under his influence. He, on the other hand, is such a simple and straightforward person that, forget influencing me, he is not capable of exerting any influence even on himself.

'To begin with, the Progressive writers used to promote my writings and assert with great pride that I was one of them. Now they say that he is not one of us. I did not believe their earlier claim and neither do I believe the current statements. Earlier, PWA writers used to say that Manto belongs to us. I had no objections and said, "It's fine." Now, 'Halqa-e-Arbab-e-Zauq'* has declared that I am their member. I have no objections to it either and have said, "It's fine."

'If somebody asks me which party I belong to, I will tell them that I am alone. I am completely alone in all ways. I will stop writing the day somebody who writes like me is born. However, I have no objection if some party adds my name to its list of members with the hope of increasing its prestige.'

These days Manto-saheb has developed a special kind of weakness. Everyone he meets gets to hear from him reports about how such and such were going into raptures while praising his stories.

'Some gentleman, I don't know his name, turned up day before yesterday and started saying, "Manto-saheb, I have read all your books and I can say with confidence that I consider you the greatest Urdu story writer."

---

*A literary circle in Lahore.

'Yesterday such and such person sent two containers of pure ghee to my house from Sheikhupura. He considers me a great writer.

'I had given two of my photographs for framing to a shopkeeper at Mall Road. Some gentleman turned up at the shop and his way of expressing his admiration was to pay for the frames and take away my photographs.

'I had lost a cigarette case. The very next day a gentleman turned up with it and said, "Manto-saheb, assalam-alaikum. Here, keep this cigarette case. I found it in such and such place." I asked him, "How did you find out where I stay?" He replied, "Wah! Who doesn't know you?"

'Here Mumtaz Shiri is writing a book on me and the English translations of my stories are being published somewhere else.

'One day it so happened that a gentleman living in Lakshmi Mansions swallowed a heavy dose of opium. The doctor was called and he prescribed some medicines that would help the person vomit it out. He, however, refused to take the medicine and said he would prefer to die. This created such a commotion that I too went there. I told him, "Bhai, take the medicine." He asked me, "Who are you?" I said, "I am Manto." He was in a poor condition but still said, "It's fortunate that I have met you before I could die. I consider you to be a really great writer." I ordered him, "You must take the medicine!" And he took it.

'One day I fainted and passed out somewhere between Anarkali Bazaar and Mall Road. I have no idea what happened to me. All I recall is that I felt as if someone had struck me on my neck with an axe and I blacked out. I regained consciousness in about half an hour and realized that I was sitting on an iron chair at a cycle shop. A large number of people had crowded around me and all of them were saying, "Manto-saheb! Manto-saheb!"

'I asked, "What happened?"

'They said, "We hope you are not hurt."

"'Why are my clothes wet?"

"'How do you feel now?"

'I was a bit edgy and said, "What rubbish are you talking? Why have you turned me into such a spectacle?"

'It was only later that I learned that I had fainted and these people had splashed water on my face to try to bring me back to consciousness. I also discovered that some people were convinced I had had an epileptic fit and that I had been made to smell lots of shoes.

'I was alarmed when I heard that I had been made to smell shoes. I got really worried and touched my nose to ensure that some tiny shoe had not entered my nose. It made me a little nervous so I stood up and told the people who were standing around me, "I want to go home. Get a tonga for me."

'The tonga arrived and people started arguing about who would accompany me home. I started my journey home in the company of three people. One of them said, "Manto-saheb, it is my good fortune that I got to meet you today in this dramatic manner. I consider you one of the foremost story writers of the world. I have read Western story writers but they are pygmies compared to you."

'I told that gentleman, "I am not exceptional. I am an ordinary story writer and now I am not even that. I am a writer when I hold a pen in my hand. I am nothing when I don't. Where are the stories that I can write? The stories have all gone away. The ones that stayed too were thrown out and forced to leave for elsewhere. There too they must have suffered a similar fate. I used to stumble on many stories, even on a single road, but here I don't come across one story even after walking on many roads."

'Now, my dear, it is not fiction that Manto had fainted near Mall Road and the people greeted me by splashing water and making me smell shoes. My dear, how can I write a story about things like this?'

Once somebody mentioned his story 'Mozel' and Manto-saheb declared, 'Actually, I am not the one who has written this story. It is Mozel herself who made me write it. I don't have a conscious plan that I follow while writing. My modus operandi is to start by organizing my pen and ink-pot. I put these in order, write 786 on the blank sheet of paper in front of me, and then begin to ruminate, "I have to write a story. What should I write?" Suddenly an idea crosses my mind. For example, the fragment of a thought like "she was standing under a tree" flashes through my mind. After that I put down my pen. I smoke a cigarette, or go out to relieve myself, or for a paan. I come back after the break and then begin to talk to "her". My first question is: "So then, what is it you want to say?" And then I just keep writing whatever she tells me. I follow her wherever she goes and, from the corner of my eyes, I try to see what she looks like. What is special about her? What does the swell of her breasts look like? Does she get dimples on her cheeks when she laughs? What is her style of walking? Does she steal hearts with her smile?

'The next stage is an extremely delicate one for me. When she steals a heart, does she herself get robbed as well? It is this fact that I am not able to understand at all. When I begin to approach the end of the story, I address all my characters and ask them, "Look here, tell me, what do you want? Who among you must be killed and in what way should the others be treated?" Some characters refuse to get killed and so I spare them and declare, "Go, I grant you life." After that, I hold discussions with other characters and go along with their wishes. I snuff out life from those who express the wish to die. Actually, I just don't get in the way of what these hoodlums, both men and women, wish to do. Nevertheless, Manto is the one who decides what the final sentence should be. He puts it down, signalling the end of the story. For example, let's look at the first sentence of "Mozel": "It was after many years that Trilochan...had looked up and set his eyes on the sky at night." And the last sentence of the story is: "Take your religion with you. That which is left over is mine." Only these two sentences, the first and the last, are mine. Everything else belongs to Mozel.'

This was usually followed by a discussion on the identity and personality of Mozel. While talking about Mozel, Manto would say, 'She was a bold and brash Jewish woman from Bombay. She had fat and fleshy thighs and did not wear anything under her skirt. She materialized in my mind while writing the story but I had forgotten her name. I then remembered that a Jewish woman used to live right across our flat too, and her name was Mozel. The image of the woman with fat, fleshy thighs emerged in my mind simultaneously along with the name Mozel. So, then, the story had happened! What is my credit in all this? If anybody can claim any credit for it, it is Mozel. ...'

By the way, Manto has written a bit about this himself too. You must know about it and I am sure you will enjoy reading it. Here is what Manto has to say about himself: 'Now, it is difficult to explain "how" I write. It's a real dilemma! And if I try to illustrate to you the process of "how" I write, then I can do that by saying that, to begin with, I go and sit on the sofa in my room. I pick up the paper and the pen, and in the name of Allah start writing the story. My three daughters continue to create a racket around me; I also keep talking to them and sorting out their quarrels. Along with that, I extend hospitality to guests who turn up; but all the time I continue writing the story. When I don't write, I feel as though I am stark naked or as if I have not bathed. Actually, I am not the one who writes the story, it is the story that writes me. I am a man of meagre education. While it is true that I have written more than twenty books, there are moments when I get flabbergasted and begin to wonder, "Who is this man who has written such amazing stories and gets challenged in court every other day?" I am plain and simple Saadat Hasan Manto when I don't have a pen in my hand; a man who does not know either Urdu, Persian, English or French. Sometimes my wife persuades me and I pick up a pen and start writing. At these moments, my mind is totally empty but my pockets are full. One or the other story leaps out of my pocket on its own. In that sense, I consider myself not to be a story writer but a pickpocket who picks his own pocket and delivers all the booty to you... Do you think there lives another man in this world who is a bigger fool than me?'

I once signed a bail bond for Manto. You have already heard about it from Manto-saheb himself. The difference between his and my account is basically that he is a great writer and I don't figure anywhere in that list. If I had been a writer, then I too, like many prominent writers, would have considered all other writers inferior to me. I would have passed judgment on each one of them, challenged everything they wrote and made comments like, 'What rubbish do they write; his language is poor; so-and-so lacks the ability to observe; so-and-so is uncivilized...'

So then, going back to what I was saying: I had signed a bail bond for Manto-saheb.

My middle brother was critically ill and I had gone to a doctor to seek advice regarding his treatment. I was reporting the condition of my brother to the doctor when I received the message that Hajra-bahen had come to my office and wished to see me.*

I felt that I should not make a lady wait in my office and so decided to meet her first. I thought I would come back to the doctor for medicines after finding out what she had to say to me.

I told the doctor that I would soon be back.

I was deeply distressed and worried about my brother's illness but, out of sheer formality, I had to smile and talk to Hajra-bahen. I also insisted on serving tea, though she repeatedly refused.

This is when Manto-saheb suddenly arrived. He was sitting in a tonga and, without getting off it, he gestured towards me and said loudly, 'Come here.' I walked towards him. He too got off the tonga and took a few steps in my direction. We found ourselves standing in front of each other in between my office and the road.

Manto-saheb said, 'Come with me. You have to bail me out. I had gone looking for some other friends but could find no one.' (It was difficult for me to determine at that point of time if he had come to me because he considered me a friend or an enemy.) He also added that the bail amount was five thousand rupees.

I tried to slip out of this on the pretext that my brother was very ill and that I had to buy his medicines and take them home. I suggested he ask someone else. I also added that there was the risk of the bail being rejected despite my putting up the five thousand rupees.

Manto-saheb's response was that I would be able to finish the whole thing and return in about half an hour. Along with this he also asserted, 'You have your own house. You would certainly have the bail amount in your bank.'

---

*Hajra Masroor, the feminist writer from Pakistan.

When I responded in the negative he said, 'Come along! There's no doubt that you will be able to put up the bail. Do you think a bail of five thousand rupees by the owner of such a big publishing house will not be accepted?'

Hajra-bahen too put in a word, 'Why don't you go? Where's the harm?'

So I sat in the tonga with Manto-saheb. My heart was palpitating and my mind was burdened with domestic anxieties. Naseer Anwar and Hanif Ramey were already sitting in the tonga. The tonga moved through Anarkali Bazaar and reached Nisbat Road. On the way, I found out what had happened.

Manto-saheb said, 'The head constable who had come yesterday to my house with the warrant was a very well-mannered man. I told him that I would come to the police station today along with my guarantor. I then asked him to leave so that I could rest. He did what I told him and I rested through the night.'

Naseer Anwar chipped in some times, 'Manto-saheb, why do you write the kind of stories that drag you into lawsuits?'

I too told him more than once, 'Manto-saheb, make me sign the bail bond only if you are certain that you will reach the court at the appointed time. Please don't trouble me if you think you won't go.'

When we crossed Nisbat Road and reached McLeod Road, Manto-saheb said, 'I would have been in deep trouble had Tufail-saheb not been here.'

Naseer Anwar responded to this, 'Your problem has been solved but you are now creating problems for Tufail-saheb.'

Manto-saheb smiled when he heard this and said, 'Absolutely not! I do need to eventually go to Karachi at least once to put an end to this matter.'

By then the tonga was turning from McLeod Road towards Quila Gujar Singh and finally halted in front of the police headquarters of the district. We went in and communicated the purpose of our visit. There I happened to meet an acquaintance. When he found out the reason for our visit, he began to make a sincere effort to get the bail accepted as quickly as possible. Although my ardent desire at that moment was that he would do something to ensure that the head constable refused the bail. He, however, could not see through the depths of my emotions and understand that I was there out of sheer obligation—because I could not bear to see a great writer suffer this agony.

Moments after the bail was accepted, Manto-saheb announced his decision and said, 'I will not be able to go to Karachi. I am not well. I will send a medical certificate.'

I was astounded to hear him say it, especially because I had never seen him looking as well as he did that day.

I was very angry with Manto-saheb though I should have actually been angry with myself. But what would have been achieved by it? We eventually got on to the tonga and started heading towards my office. The tonga was stopped at the offices of *Pakistan Times* and *Imroze*. When we went upstairs, I discovered that whoever heard about my signing Manto-saheb's bail bond had declared with complete confidence that he would not reach the court at the appointed time. Manto-saheb kept smiling when he heard these remarks and kept repeating, 'No, my dear friend, why will I not go?' And this despite the fact that he had already declared to me that he would not go to Karachi.

Finally, I thought of a plan and asked Manto-saheb, 'If I book two seats for tomorrow morning, will you and Naseer Anwar go to Karachi?'

Manto-saheb considered my offer as though it was some formal communique and then decided to accept it. After that I requested Manto-saheb to go home. I, of course, decided to try to book the two seats.

I walked from the office of *Pakistan Times* to my own. When I got on my bicycle, I suddenly remembered my brother's illness and his medicines. Soon, my mind was spinning as fast as the bicycle wheel.

It was not easy to book the tickets. To begin with, I found out at the reservation office that all seats were booked for the next four days. The crux of the problem was that Manto-saheb had to record his presence in the court the very next day. Finally, I decided to go to Shaukat Thanvi at the radio station. He first severely reprimanded me and said afterwards that the seats could be confirmed if we reached the station by seven the next morning.

I apprised Manto-saheb about the situation and also requested his wife and his sister to ensure that he got ready in time so that I could be freed of further responsibility.

When I finally reached home at night, I had to endure the bitter onslaught of my family members for being completely unconcerned about my brother's illness and not finding time to even buy medicines for him. I was deeply embarrassed but had no way of communicating to them what I had gone through that day. I spent the night intermittently worrying about my brother's illness and the immense goodwill that Manto-saheb had shown towards me! I have a strange habit of counting my injuries rather than stars in the sky. That night too, I spent the hours of darkness in the same hectic activity. My family members were further troubled when I left the house at five in the morning—in the winter months I generally went to sleep late and never got out of bed before nine in the morning. Quite understandably, my family members were deeply concerned and anxious about the aberration. I, however, pacified them by saying that a friend was going to Karachi and I had to be at the railway station to see him off. I also assured them that I would return soon with medicines for my brother. After I reached Bhati Darwaza, I thought that I could go to Manto-saheb's house in a tonga but then I remembered that it was still quite early and that Manto-saheb would be inconvenienced if I reached his house that early. But I was equally anxious that if I got even slightly delayed, Manto-saheb might just go off somewhere. I finally decided to walk the distance. Clearly, I was more concerned about him than about myself.

On the way, dogs welcomed me with their barking. They must surely have been wondering who this stranger was. In one or two places, when people sweeping the road told me, 'Please move away a bit,' I felt like stopping for a few minutes and asking them, 'How are you? How is your family? Your children?' But I lost courage and moved on. I hardly lost any time on the way but despite that, the sun was up by the time I reached Manto-saheb's house. I knocked at the door and his wife opened it. Manto-saheb was awake. He entered the room rubbing his eyes and welcomed me with an 'Assalamu alaikum.' A long warm shawl was wound around his neck like a muffler. After some time, Naseer Anwar too arrived. A tonga was called. His sister, wife and daughters bid us farewell with prayers for our safe return.

The seats had been reserved in the train. The luggage was safely placed and after that, Manto-saheb took out whisky bottles and placed them in such a way that they could be easily seen by people entering the train. When I asked Manto-saheb to not do this, he pulled out a small green piece of paper from his pocket and said, 'I have a permit for the whisky.' He had just about said this when the train chugged out of the station.

It was only after the newspapers reported the next day that Manto-saheb had appeared in court that I finally heaved a sigh of relief.

There was also a phase when Manto-saheb would be sitting around as usual and then suddenly burst forth and say, 'Listen!

Just listen to this! Tana tan tana tan tana tom tana tom' (Some such stuff.) People sitting next to Manto-saheb would be quite confused and wonder what had suddenly gone wrong with him. Manto-saheb would then look around and ask, 'What do you wish to hear?'

After that he would say, 'It's the radio, what else? What did you ask? How can the music be heard?'

Soon he would provide the answer himself: 'Come here. Place your ear next to mine. Glue it to my ear. Now, you can hear it, can't you? Wow! What an amazing voice the fellow has!' He would then move his hands in many different directions, as though he was keeping tune with the beat. He would sometimes suddenly stand up or sit down, appreciating the music. It would be peppered with comments: 'Oh! What a killer! Well done man, well done! Wah woman!'

Sometimes, out of sheer mischief, people would tell him: 'We cannot hear anything. Why don't you keep writing what you hear?' He would then pick up paper and pen but also offer advice, 'Get your ears cleaned and put a little oil in them. Get your head massaged.' And at the same time, he would begin to write. He generally first wrote two or three Punjabi songs. After which he would announce, 'Now listen to the Urdu songs.' The pen and paper were put to use again and Manto-saheb would write down three or four Urdu songs. This radio continued to play in Manto-saheb's ear for two or three months. Of course, he was the only one who could hear it. As far as others were concerned, Manto-saheb would write down the songs and sing them himself for their benefit. Then, all of a sudden, the valves of his 'ear radio' became defective and the radio stopped playing.

Around this time I decided to visit him one evening. I spotted Manto-saheb while I was still outside his house. He was singing. Like a professional singer, he would sometimes take his hands close to his ears, and sometimes he would shake his head, seemingly along with the beat. I remained standing there, watching this performance for quite a long time. Finally, I got tired, went in and announced my presence.

When his servant came out, I told him, 'Please call Manto-saheb.'

He went in and told Manto-saheb, 'A gentleman is waiting to see you.'

Manto-saheb said, 'Go and tell him that Manto-saheb cannot see him now. He is singing.'

But then, he appeared on the scene on his own. He came close to the door, adjusted his spectacles and asked, 'Who's there?' After he spotted me, he said, 'Oh! It's you! Forgive me, my dear, I was singing. Come, why don't you listen to it too?'

'Who all are there?' I enquired.

'Nobody,' he said, 'just the family.'

The ordeal of lawsuits has forced him to get a grip over himself. The trouble is that now what seems to be slipping out of his grip are the stories. It is because of this that what he has written during this period is not good enough when compared with his earlier work.

He often says, 'The lawsuit begins even before my story gets written.'

Time and again he also says, 'I feel like giving up reading and writing and going somewhere far away from both Hindustan and Pakistan, where I can write freely to my heart's content, without any hitch. And then I will send all those stories here for publication so that publishers are thrown behind bars and I am spared of all the trouble. I can't help but call white white, a spade a spade, but I have been directed to describe white as black and black as white. And in case I happen to set my eyes on both black and white simultaneously, I have been directed to simply seal my lips, just maintain silence, smother myself and, if nothing helps, to pour melted lead down my throat, or commit suicide...

'The penalties imposed on me continue to be exactly the ones that were meted out during British rule and I am quite bored of the charges and penalties being repeated over and over again. I would have preferred Islamic penalties to be inflicted on me in Pakistan so that at least I would have had the comfort of variety. However, the situation here continues to be exactly as it was. The English as a race are certainly very shrewd. They have physically left this country but have managed to leave behind their spirit. I sometimes feel like writing a very hiptulla kind of story, exposing all the gangrenes in society and state; perform a thorough surgery with deep cuts, and then rub salt into those cuts. After which I will shoot myself, convinced of having achieved my goal.'

Manto speaks Punjabi effortlessly. He often tells the person conversing with him, 'I hope you understand Punjabi.'

It is obvious that even if the person being addressed does not understand Punjabi, he would nod his head in agreement and respond in Urdu saying, 'I can't speak in Punjabi but of course I understand it.'

Manto-saheb then carries on the conversation and says, 'Do forgive me please but when I speak in Urdu my mouth feels like it is full of blisters, or as if the blisters are just about to start erupting. My jaws begin to hurt when I speak Urdu. My tongue clacks in protest each time it touches my palate. So my brother, do forgive me but I will speak only in Punjabi. This of course does not in any way imply that I have a grudge against Urdu. But I think, since I write in Urdu anyway, I must use Punjabi at least when I am speaking. Nonetheless, if you desire, I can put you in trouble even if I speak in Urdu.'

One often gets to meet Manto-saheb either in his house

or on the tonga. If you happen to see a person stretched out on the rear seat, his face turned away, please don't make any assumptions. Wait for the tonga to draw closer. It is quite possible that this person will turn out to be Manto-saheb. If one or two of his companions and fellow drinkers are with him, he sits in the front seat and keeps announcing to his fans and admirers: 'I want to write an extraordinary, a truly remarkable story, but I am scared that it will certainly invite legal action. But, at the same time, I will be deeply pained if it fails to do so and will begin to feel, perhaps rather unjustifiably, that the government has become indifferent towards its obligations… Or I may be compelled to believe that the story itself is so poor and ineffective that the government feels no need to take any action against it.'

Manto-saheb is a man of many talents but his personality is somewhat flawed due to excessive consumption of alcohol. Earlier, I used to get angry with him but now I just feel sorry for him. I have no idea how others feel about this fact but I can turn a blind eye to all his weaknesses when I think of his exceptional talents. During his last years he cherished the wish that a magazine bring out a special issue on him while he was still alive. He must have approached other publishers, and discussed the idea with me as well. This was the conversation we had:

'Bring out a Manto number, my friend.'

'Yes.'

'What I am saying is that you should publish a special Manto number of your magazine *Nuqoosh*.'

'Today you seem to be saying odd…'

'You think that I am drunk and am talking rubbish.'

'What is the great rush? It will get published anyway.'

'I cannot wait for death to strengthen my case, and ensuring that the number is published.'

'Don't talk of dying. You still have...'

'What will I achieve by living? Now even I have agreed that I should die.'

'All right. Tell me what should be included in this special number.'

'It will have all the abuses that have been showered on me. Tributes paid to me by some dim-witted people will go in the last pages. The pages in between will be filled by three or four of my unpublished stories and sketches. Anyhow, there is no need for you to worry about this. I will edit this special number myself and hand it over to you.'

'What will I do if you edit the special?'

'You will twiddle your thumbs.'

'If this is what it is going to be, then it would better if you edited the collection yourself and published it as a book.'

'I want a *Nuqoosh* number to be published as a Manto special.'

'In that case you will have no role to play in its editing. I refuse to accept even suggestions from others.'

'Who the hell do you think you are? Do you think you are more capable than me?'

'This has nothing to do with capability. The issue is that of accountability.'

'Forget accountability. The issue is one of ability.'

'I refuse to accept your expertise in the matter.'

'Well then, if you have made up your mind to destroy me, then it is better that you do it during my lifetime.'

Manto's passing away has been described by writers as a literary catastrophe. And it is indeed fitting to call it so. His immense contribution to the treasured world of short stories can never be forgotten; neither at present, nor in the future.

Like some other journals, I too published a special number

on Manto and it was widely acclaimed as being better than many others. The issue had twenty unpublished stories by the departed Manto. The ten representative stories were selected by Manto himself. People like Mumtaz Shiri, Viqar Azeem, Mohammad Hasan Askari, Abid Ali Abid, Abdul-lais-Siddique, Ibadat Barelwi and Mumtaz Husain had written on Manto's art.

People who wrote on Manto's personality included the likes of Ismat Chughtai, Upendranath Ashk, Ahmed Nadeem Qasmi, Hajra Masroor, Abu Saeed Qureshi and Ghulam Abbas.

When I began collecting articles for the Manto edition, I invited Qudratullah Shahab too to contribute. He promised to send his article soon. He added that the article would be in the form of an imagined letter written to me by Manto from his heavenly abode. I liked the idea because I felt that it could be a good technique to successfully grasp Manto's complete personality as well as all the thorny problems that had confronted him.

However, Shahab-saheb had a very busy schedule and he could not find time, so I decided to write something in the same format. The letter has been published as 'Manto ka Ek Khat', a letter from Manto in the Manto special edition. I have tried to emulate Manto's style in the letter but I am not sure how successful I have been.

My dear brother,
Assalam-alaikum,

I arrived here about three and a half months ago but could not write to you earlier because of the unfamiliar surroundings. However, the atmosphere here is definitely much better than the one in which I squandered away forty-two years of my life, under threat and intimidation.

Neither Safia, nor Nuzhat, Nakhat or Nusrat have made

any demands on me since I entered this world. I was otherwise so often pestered with, 'Abba! Get this!' or 'Abba! Get that.' You know, of course, the unbounded love I have for my little daughters and that is why I have often shed tears of blood when I was not able to fulfil their wishes due to my extreme poverty. In fact, there have been occasions when the birthdays of my dear daughters have come and gone without my having even a single paisa in my pocket.

How could I have gone on living in a world like that? The plan that destiny had for me was to make me live on for much longer in that ruthless, inhumane world. But I devised really ingenious methods and managed to slip out of that hell of yours. As long as I was there, I was consumed with the anguish of each one of you. Not only was I consumed by this anguish, it disintegrated me and finally finished me off altogether.

Here, I raise my hands in prayer every day and wish that all my friends and contemporary writers, as soon as possible, partake the experience of my life here. The kind of lives I have seen them living are much worse than the one I had. When I have had to come here, it makes little sense that they should continue to live on there.

You are acquainted with a large number of writers in Lahore. You could verbally inform the writers in Lahore and write to those who live outside Lahore that they should all come here with their families. I have made arrangements for everything they would need on their arrival and so they will not be inconvenienced in any way.

Neither society nor the times we wrote in expressed any appreciation for me or my fellow writers. Do you realize that if people like us had not been there, you would have had everything in society except literature, art and knowledge?

All those who are here are quite content with their lives. I often come across writers and find that they too, like me, are nursing one or the other grudge in their hearts. Some of them have written such strident satires about that hypocritical world of yours that one has to toughen one's heart to even as much as listen to them. If they ever get published, rest assured, at least some crazy people are sure to get thrashed in the bazaar.

Anyhow, this collection of satires has still not been published. I will send you a copy when it gets published. You can review it for *Nuqoosh*.

The writers in your country, as well as the neighbouring one, have great hopes from those ruling the countries. Let me tell you, this is not faith but sheer foolishness, illusion and misconception.

Politics in your country is truly dhadan takhta.* Someone who is a minister today may find himself in jail tomorrow. On the other hand, a person in jail, on a charge of conspiracy against the country, suddenly becomes a minister. Believe me, I get deeply embarrassed when my friends here discuss the politics going on in your part of the world.

As you already know, there were five cases of obscenity against me though the truth is that I had not written a single obscene piece. You know the tortures that were inflicted on me and the ordeal I had to live through. I was served warrants, I was imprisoned. At times I had to borrow money from friends to pay the penalties imposed on me. Despite all this, I continued to express my faith in law and justice. If I had stayed on for any longer, it is possible that I would have been falsely charged with murder, robbery and rape. Which idiot would like to stay in a place where he gets punished for crimes he has not committed?

If by good fortune, one happens to escapes the anger of the government, he is sure to be pursued and trapped by the critics. I have tried to steer clear of critics all my life. It is equally true that some critics have also stayed away from

---

*The term is of Manto's creation. Its closest meanings are chaotic, or disorganized.

me. Actually, these people are failed poets and failed story writers. They are transformed into custodians of criticism after they realize that they are deprived of even a touch of creativity. I have had some kind of an innate antagonism against them and that is because once they sit with a pen in their hand, they can demolish the best writing. They, however, are completely blind to the failings of their own writing. For God's sake, save yourself from these highly educated people. My absence should not embolden them to sharpen their pencils and slaughter the untouched and pristine quality of my art.

In present times, any development in literature can happen only if one does the exact opposite of what the critics recommend. Actually, the truth is that this is the real intention of the critics as well but nobody besides me has been able to see through this.

I sincerely hope to meet a critic here and have a critical discussion with him. The rules of the game will be that one who uses the three words, 'if', 'but' and 'however' in their correct forms will win.

It is only when the critics are infused with creativity that their writings will achieve any degree of equilibrium, truth and sincerity. Only when the talents and emotions of an artist and a critic merge can one repose full faith in what is written. Sharaab-e-Tahoor is easily available here.* There is no need to drink water. You can just drink Sharaab-e-Tahoor. One gets really inferior quality alcohol in the place I lived in and only I know the extent to which I had to go to procure it. At times, I was also humiliated because of it. I lost my esteem among

---

*A drink that one receives only in heaven. Mirza Ghalib mentions it in the following couplet:

*Vaa-iz na khud peo, na kisi ko pila sako,*
*Kya baat hai tumhare Sharaab-e-Tahoor ki.*

O Preacher! You can neither drink it nor offer it to anyone
What a drink your Sharaab-e-Tahoor is.

friends. They turned their backs on me. Sometimes they even changed their usual routes to avoid me. They had become strangers. If somebody did come face to face, he took false oaths just to convince me that he had no money. I, of course, knew he had enough money in his pocket to buy several bottles of this destroyer of homes, these bottles of alcohol, for me. I call alcohol the destroyer of homes because it has plundered and disturbed my home many times.

I am going to reveal a very well preserved but dangerous secret to you. Hide it carefully and be careful not to even mention it because if you do, I assure you that you will be badly beaten up. What I want to tell you is that all the women here are thousands of years old but what nubile bodies the wretched women have! They can destroy the strongest pledge of celibacy. However, I am a complete idiot to discuss this with you because you I know that you are a total chugad in this field of activity. Despite my great admiration for your idiocy, I cannot help but say that the girls in your world are not a patch on the ones we have here.

That is not all. The men here are very handsome too. In fact, they are so good looking that a poet from your world will possibly swoon at a mere glimpse of them. Come to think of it, I am pretty sure that some of them would not be able to survive it and give up the ghost.

All my life, I never felt humbled in company of any of my co-writers because I knew that I had no equal, but Ghalib has been making my life very difficult here. He makes really hurtful comments whenever he meets me. He once confronted me and said, 'You are a thief. You have stolen your titles from my couplets. Just because you could not think of suitable titles for your books you decided to mutilate my couplets. And that story which you wrote for the film on my life is a disaster. Not only did you not express your gratitude to me, you did not even have the decency to mention the qualities I possess. Instead, you spelled out my failings: that I was a womanizer and that I had many other flaws, including the fact that I was a gambler who had been sent to prison for gambling.'

You of course already know that I consider Ghalib to be head and shoulders above all other poets. So, when he showered all those accusations on me, all I could do was silently curse myself, 'Shame on you, Saadat Hasan Manto! Shame on your attempt at becoming realistic!'

Nonetheless, Ghalib is a truly lively and energetic man. We are close friends, as thick as thieves despite the injustice I have done to him. We often drink together and the funny thing is that whenever we do that we seem to once again acquire our essential flesh-and-blood traits. And what follows next is a clash of egos. Ghalib says, 'I could have been a much better story writer than you but I decided to keep away from it because I thought it was worthless.'

In response I tell him, 'What is so great about composing couplets, Mirza-saheb? There lurks not just a couplet but a complete ghazal in every line of my prose.'

We realize that both of us are wrong but then managing our egos is beyond us!

Uncle Sam's increasing influence is intensifying terror and panic all around your world by leaps and bounds. Congratulations!

One should have respect for elders but deference does not mean that you put your precious little life in danger. I have heard that these days Uncle Sam decides how your jobs should be done and you people are just sitting there twiddling your thumbs and waiting for darkness to descend. It is not good to have such a laid-back, comfortable life. You are bound to regret it soon but you people have degenerated to the point of abandoning all your self-respect and locking it up in a dark cupboard so that you never set eyes on it.

The problem is that I cannot write a letter to Uncle Sam from here. Otherwise I would have requested him to stay within his limits. Just pray that he comes here on his own so that you are freed of his presence. I can deal with him quite easily. Only a fraud has any chance of vanquishing another.

I have also heard that there has been an unending outpouring of grief in your world since I came here. I swear by God this information had burnt me inside out. It made a kebab out of me because, as long as I was there, everybody had ganged up against me, literally ostracizing me. Now that I am here, due to attempts of some of these people and of course, due to my designs as well, why are announcements about my disappearance being made on the radio? They are the same people who did not allow me to come anywhere close to them. Magazines and newspapers seem to be lamenting the fact that I have gone underground. They too have treated me like Hazrat Yusuf was treated by his brothers. Given the situation, you all should be really ashamed of your hypocrisy.

I have got a few new fans here. They have given me the responsibility of presenting the quarterly report. They took this decision because, in their opinion, I am the best realistic writer there ever was. I have also written down everything in my usual vein. It's a truly hiptulla report. I have severely criticized a friend of mine and have exposed his secret love affair. I have crossed all limits by writing that the practice of growing beards in this world is something that irks people with sophisticated temperaments. It is therefore important that the decision of either growing or not growing beards be left to the individual. It was not easy to express such an opinion in front of a powerful ruler. Still, I have done exactly that. Had I said something as blunt as this in your world, in front of your inconsequential prime minister, my tongue would have been wrenched out by the very root.

I must also inform you that my book *Ganje Farishte* is very popular here. People have really liked it. If possible, do take care of my wife and children.

Yours humbly,
Saadat Hasan Manto
20 April 1955

# A Solitary Soul

## Balwant Gargi

### (1)

I first heard of Manto in 1944. I had come to Delhi in search of a job. Everybody with a B.A. or an M.A. was being hired because of the War. I found employment in All India Radio for a salary of two hundred rupees a month in the department that broadcast news about the War.

There were six of us. Our job was to sit around a large table in a big room, translate for half an hour and make a ten-minute broadcast. We had no other work for the rest of the day, but the army had given us a clear diktat that we must not leave the room.

We would often shut the door and crack jokes. Hari Chandra Chadha would narrate interesting anecdotes about political and literary events, peppering them generously with swear words and name-calling. He frankly recounted stark, unvarnished stories about prostitutes and girls in the army battalions. Sometimes he would climb on to the table and start dancing while we drummed on it. There was, however, an intellectual and literary tinge to all this.

It was winter and there was a light drizzle. A strange lonesomeness and gloom had gripped our hearts. Chadha had taken leave to go and drink and so we were feeling very desolate and down in the dumps. We seemed to have lost interest in everything. However, Chadha had left behind the story issue of *Adab-e-Lateef* for us. I started flipping its pages. It had Krishan Chander's famous story 'Annadata', which deals with the most severe famine of Bengal. It was a lengthy story. I read through ten or twelve pages but then dropped it and glanced through the other stories but nothing fired my interest. Suddenly my eyes fell on the name Saadat Hasan Manto. What an odd name! Like Lord Minto or Pinto. It struck me as a really phony and absurd name. And then I read the title of the story: 'Boo'.

I began reading and finished in one sitting. Every sentence was beautifully crafted and the relationships between the characters were magical and immaculately communicated. The sentences, the similes, in fact the very feel of every breath described in the story are fresh in my mind even today. Its impact on my mind was so deep and so immersed was I in the story that I lost all sense of time. I realized it was five o'clock only when all my friends stood up to leave for home.

The story glowed and was suffused with bodily odour. It had a complex psychological depth and flavour. The simplicity of short sentences was evidence of a mature and polished artist.

The hero of the story is Randhir who spends a night with a ghaatan girl. The story describes a bored Randhir sitting at the window of his room when his eyes fall on the ghaatan girl who works in a rope factory. She is standing under a tamarind tree to protect herself from the rain. Randhir clears his throat and coughs a little to attract the attention of the girl. Successful in doing so, he gestures to the girl to come up to his room.

There is hardly any conversation between the two. Their dialogue is carried on through the scorching waves of their physical passion. Randhir sees that the girl's clothes are soaked and offers his dhoti to her. The girl removes her wet clothes and wraps herself in the dhoti. She then tries to unstring her blouse. However, the knot is worn out and tangled because it is wet. She merely says, 'It isn't opening.'

Randhir gives it a strong tug with his brawny hands, the knot comes unfastened, and he finds himself holding the ghaatan's dark breasts.

Manto describes the dark glow of the ghaatan's body and breasts as the cups of unbaked clay that a potter has just shaped from the wet mud on his wheel; as two earthen lamps glittering on the surface of a filthy pond.

Randhir devours the odour of the ghaatan's body through the night. The odour courses through his veins, spreads across his body and settles down in every nook and corner of his mind. The memory doesn't leave him even after he gets married. His wedding night and the beauty of his newly married wife appear to be entirely colourless and washed out, like the white crumbs which float on spoiled milk. The red silk string of her shalwar has left a deep mark on his wife's fair, soft body. The marks fail to wipe off the memory of the night spent with the ghaatan and the healthy, strong odour of her body. The throttled love of the middle-class and the ritualistic ardour for his wife seem completely jaded and listless when compared with that dark odour.

It was after reading the story that I began to think of contemporary Urdu literature in an entirely new way.

I had already read Krishan Chander's stories set in Kashmir and was filled with the agony of love and poverty. I had the opportunity to read short stories by some other writers as well but after I read them, I would feel that I too could have written such stories. This was just my personal response. It is of course possible that I could not have written like Krishan Chander and Rajender Singh Bedi but, whenever I read them, I always got the feeling that my creative energy could touch much higher leaps and flights.

When I read Manto's story I felt I would never be able to write like him. I *knew* that I could never ever have written such a remarkable story.

One day the peon in the office came after lunch and left an envelope on my table. For some unknown reason, I felt that the envelope was carrying something dangerous, a cruel command, a disturbing message. I can still vividly recall the tension I felt before opening the envelope. Sure enough, when I opened it I discovered that my job had been terminated. I took the envelope and went to Major Bakshi, who declared, 'We are under no obligation to cite any reason for terminating your job. Here is your advance salary for a month.'

He brought out crisp ten-rupee notes from the drawer and handed them to me. I took the money and came back to my room.

I was terminated because the government had got my earlier activities scrutinized by their secret police. They had discovered that I had been jailed for participating in the freedom movement of 1942. That crime was strong enough reason for them to terminate me.

I went to my room and informed my friends about the decision. One of the Hindi writers broke into tears of commiseration. I took one of the crisp notes I had received as salary and ordered tea and pastry for everybody.

Chadha presided over this small farewell party and announced in his own distinctive style, 'Oh you motherfuckers, you will continue as bonded labourers while this bird has been freed from the cage.'

He gave me a collection of Manto's stories when I left. He had worked with Manto at All India Radio and often talked of him. He used to say, 'Manto was a cut above everybody else. He worked here in All India Radio for a year and a half and then went off to Bombay. He left behind a hundred and fifty dramas and features. Upendranath Ashk kept hankering all his life to become his friend but Manto did not allow him to even come close to him.'

Manto had a stately circle of literary friends that included Krishan Chander, Ismat Chughtai and Rajinder Singh Bedi.

Upendranath, however, was never able to step inside this charmed circle and kept hovering around its margins. Though he worked at the radio, he was not able to come anywhere close to Manto's creative genius. Obviously, he nursed an inferiority complex and continuously bragged and blew his own trumpet to get over it.

Manto was like a lofty tower of Indian literature.

Even back then, I was conscious that Manto was a unique literary miracle. I knew that a few years later people would enquire about which café he had spent his time in; where he lived; what kind of pen he used; which room he would sit in and write at All India Radio.

During this time, I made a special effort to meet people who had worked with Manto. I talked to them to get an idea about everything that Manto used to do. There was a restaurant on the second floor of the radio station. It was run by Sanoober Khan. Manto used to come to drink there. Manto carried a small Urdu typewriter in his bag when he came to the radio station. He used to directly type out his dramas on this typewriter.

He was extremely proud of his art and would often write his plays after accepting a challenge. Once he announced to his friends that he would write a play on any subject they wished to propose, the only condition being that they keep a dozen bottles of beer ready for him.

One of his friends said, 'The hen pigeon; come now, write a play about it.'

Manto immediately rolled the paper into the typewriter and soon wrote a play about the kabootari, which went on to become extremely popular.

Once when he was betting about writing a play with his friends, somebody stood outside the room and asked, 'May I come in?'

One of Manto's friends said, 'Manto, what will be real fun is if you write a play with this title.'

The wager was immediately laid: beer bottles!

Manto of course soon handed over a play with the title, *May I Come In?*

A writer once cancelled a confirmed programme that was to be broadcast on the radio. This resulted in complete chaos as there seemed little chance of the programme being finalized. Manto was requested to write some feature or a play. He was furious and said, 'I can't write it. Machines too need some time.'

People tried to cajole him to write a play. One of his friends rolled the paper into the typewriter and pleaded, 'Come on friend, do write now! We will sit outside and wait.'

Manto kept sitting for a while, staring at the blank sheet of paper, and then he typed out the title: 'Intezaar', The Wait. The play is still considered one of his finest. It is evidence of the technical and psychological experiments that Manto undertook. The story revolves around a young man writing to his beloved that he is sitting and waiting for her. He expresses himself at two simultaneous but distinct levels: the conscious and the subconscious. The dialogues at both levels mutually conflict with each other and generate a great deal of fascinating suspense. The subconscious persona of the young man gets in the way, obstructs, debates, converses and peels off the layers of his conscious personality.

The creation of this kind of dramatic emotion and character was Manto's distinctive trait. Once, the Director of the Radio Station, Mr Advani, raised an objection to one of Manto's dialogues and asked him to change it. Mr S.A. Bokhari was the Director General. Advani was a very assertive and well-connected man, but even in that big gathering, Manto declared: 'Advani-saheb has no idea about writing plays. Moreover, he cannot read plays written in Urdu and he has the cheek to point out errors in my play.'

Advani-saheb bristled with anger and wanted to take action against Manto. The whole issue was brought to Bokhari's notice. Manto told Bokhari, 'What I said is absolutely true. How can a man with a name like Advani know anything about Urdu?'

Bokhari-saheb broke into a laugh. And thus the whole incident was over and done with.

I went away from Delhi to Lahore and was jobless for a few months. Then, my play *Loha-Kutt* was published in 1942 and afterwards I was employed as an artist by the Lahore Radio Station.

Rajender Singh Bedi used to work at the Lahore Radio Station, as did Shameem Aapa (Mohini Das) who had a really melodious voice. Imtiaz Ali Taj and Rafi Pir would come to produce plays.* Mallika Pukhraj would sit in the studio, chewing paan and singing. The atmosphere was truly creative. Manto was often mentioned in these gatherings.

Chaudhary Nazeer Ahmed was the editor and owner of the Urdu journal *Adab-e-Lateef.* He belonged to some village in Punjab. Barely educated till Class 4 and completely uncultured. He was a muscular man of medium height with sparkling teeth. He was called Nazeera and he spoke unadulterated Punjabi. He and his uncle Barkat Ali together laid the foundation of Maktaba-e-Urdu. This became the most popular publishing house in the whole of Hindustan and along with that, Nazeera became, first, Nazeer Ahmed and, then, Chaudhary Nazeer Ahmed.

Chaudhary Nazeer used to read and assess every single story himself. Manto was the only writer for whom he cared to

---

*Imtiaz Ali Taj was known for his drama *Anarkali*, the source of the legendary films *Anarkali* and *Mughal-e-Azam*.

wait, sometimes even to the point of delaying the journal. He used to persistently write to Manto, send him telegrams, and when his story arrived from Bombay, he would chuckle with delight and say, 'Now my journal is complete.'

A lawsuit was filed against Manto's story 'Boo' after its publication, and Manto had to come to Lahore to appear in court.

Tall and slim, Manto's body seemed to have the suppleness of a flexible cane. He had a wide forehead, a sharp Kashmiri nose and piercing eyes behind spectacles. He was dressed in a white shirt, sherwani, cotton shalwar and shoes. He held his head high with pride and gave us a cursory, careless look.

Manto was standing next to Ismat Chughtai and all of us waited for the call from the court. Professor Kanhaiya Lal Kapoor made the introductions but Manto did not utter even a word of formal courtesy or thanks. Neither did he express any pleasure. Just then, Chaudhary Nazeer turned up and said, 'Come along. Our names have been called.'

The crowd of writers entered the room of the judge. They described the literary and artistic qualities of 'Boo', asserting all the time that there was nothing objectionable in the story and that it was a literary masterpiece.

Sardar Gurbaksh Singh Preetladi was the most respected writer in Punjabi. He was a writer of love stories and had raised the flag of social protest. When he was asked to give evidence in Manto's favour, he refused to do so and said that the story was obscene. Ismat and Manto were quite surprised when they found out about this. Manto said, 'It is astonishing that there are such writers in Punjabi too. Only God can protect the fate of literature in this language.'

The evidence was recorded and the judge fixed the date for the next hearing. Manto was fed up of the environment of the district court and had become quite despondent.

Broken benches scattered around, iron chairs, dust, dirt, the bargaining with lawyers and clerks. A strange kind of tension and nervousness prevailed all around. All writers had begun to look like criminals.

Manto said, 'I want to go home, Nazeer. Ask for a tonga.'

'Does anybody else want to go? Just one...'

I was standing close by. I immediately stepped forward and took the seat in front.

We had a little conversation on the way.

Manto said, 'These people are making a hero out of me for no reason. I am afraid of prisons. It is very difficult to come from Bombay each time. And very expensive too. The penalty is too high.

'I was writing the screenplay for a film when I received the telegram from Chaudhary Nazeer. What are you doing now?'

I told him a bit about myself. I was in complete awe of him.

I got off when we reached the Neela Gumbad.

He said, 'I will go straight home. Safia has come too. I have to go and finish a story for Chaudhary.' And then he suddenly added, 'You come to our house in the evening. I would have finished the story by then.'

He went off after that.

I began to recall and examine all that had happened. He had talked to me in Punjabi. His voice was thin and warm. It represented the intensity of his whole personality. His voice was neither like that of a leader nor that of a saint. There was an impetuosity which was communicated when he spoke.

I went to meet Manto in the evening. He was staying in a relative's bungalow on Ferozpur Road. The servant told me that I must sit in the drawing room and wait because Manto was busy writing a story. This was the story that was published as 'Raja Bhaiyya' in *Adab-e-Lateef*. It was later published under the title 'Mera Naam Radha Hai'. Manto has satirized Prithvi Raj Kapoor's stern and strict mannerisms in the story.

Manto entered the room after about ten minutes and asked me cheerfully, 'Will you have some tea?'

He then said loudly, 'What are you doing, Safia? Come here.'

His wife came into the room and Manto made the introductions. By then, some other writers had also arrived on the scene. Chaudhary Nazeer had come too. There was a social gathering in somebody's house later and he had come to take Manto with him.

Manto told me, 'So then, let's meet tomorrow. I will be at Maktaba-e-Urdu.'

Manto wrote not with a pen but with a sharp knife with which he used to slash the nerves of society to bleed out dirty and diseased blood. He was a surgeon, not a physician. His incisive vision functioned as double-lenses when he looked at society through them. His narrative was sensuous and one could experience the intensity that suffused it. Everybody knew that he wrote much better than any of them and accepted his supremacy.

I met Manto again.

He was sitting at Maktaba-e-Urdu, looking at the blurb of his book which declared: 'Manto, the prominent and best writer of our times, on an equal footing with Chekhov, one who draws out emotions, breathes magic into them, his stories touch the very heights of creativity.'

Manto said, 'Oye, Chaudhary! What rubbish have you written?'

He removed all words of praise and wrote the blurb of the book himself. And this is what he wrote, 'Manto writes rubbish. People say that Manto is obscene but if you start reading Manto, you cannot leave the story unfinished.'

The words 'rubbish' and 'obscene' were in bold letters.

He pre-empted his opponents and wrote what they would to jolt everybody.

He detested sweet, conventional words, articles and sentences. Once, somebody introduced Manto to a very prominent person who said, 'Manto-saheb, it is a pleasure to meet you.'

Manto replied, 'It's no pleasure for me to meet you.'

This style, this bitterness of truth was an integral part of Manto's temperament.

The next day, Chaudhary Nazeer informed me, 'Manto is in Kailash Hotel. He is calling you there.'

Kailash Hotel was on Anarkali Street and it was three minutes away from where I was. I climbed up the stairs of the hotel and reached the first floor. Manto was drinking with three other writers.

As soon as he saw me he said, 'We will leave soon. Will you have a drink?'

'No,' I said.

One of the writers said, 'Manto-saheb, your stories are outstanding. "Hatak" and "Kali Shalwar" touch great heights of creativity.'

Manto said, 'Stop this rubbish. You wanted to drink. That's done. Now get lost.'

I became a bit fearful and anxious but the others quietly got up and walked away.

Manto said, 'I was waiting for you when these three bastards left their table and came to sit here. They started losing control after two drinks. They began praising me in the hope of having a third drink. Let's go.'

I began to walk with him.

I asked him on the way, 'Where are we going?'

'To meet Abdul Bari.'

I cannot fully recall whether we went to Abdul Bari or he met us somewhere else.

I had seen Abdul Bari on many literary and political

occasions. He was somewhat dark. He was a well-read
journalist and would refer to a range of readings from all over
the world in his lectures. I had never desired to meet him after
listening to his dry and uninspiring lectures. Manto, however,
always sought him out. He also told me that Abdul Bari was
his literary mentor and guru.

The three of us sat in an elegant Peshawari tonga. Abdul
Bari and I sat on the front seat next to the coachman and
Manto, as was his wont, sat on the rear seat, his legs stretched
out and his feet shod in gold-embroidered shoes.

The tonga began to move quickly along Mall Road. It
crossed the main post-office and came to a halt. Bari stepped
down from the tonga. Manto took out his wallet and handed
a green-coloured note to him. Bari went to Bhola Nath's shop
while the two of us sat in the tonga. Ten minutes went by and
Manto said impatiently, 'This oaf is wasting my time. Why is
he taking so long? What is he buying? Diamonds? Rubbish...'

Bari appeared. He walked to the tonga with swift steps and
climbed up. There was a tall bottle of Johnny Walker in his
hand.

Manto asked, 'Is it good?'

'Yes,' Bari replied.

The tonga started moving once again. We crossed the
Museum and the Government College and reached Ravi Road.
I wondered if the two of them were heading out for boating. I
had absolutely no idea that their destination was Hira Mandi,
the district where the prostitutes lived.

The tonga stopped at the bazaar near Shahi Masjid.

Bari paid the coachman and the three of us entered the
bazaar of delight and beauty.

I had never come to these parts before. Not because of any
social compulsion but because I was scared of the environment
in which the prostitutes and pimps functioned and carried

on their profession. The image I carried in my mind since childhood was that these people were quarrelsome and cared for nothing but money. People got knifed here. I also nursed a fear of entering an unknown territory. But at that time, Manto was with me and so I was not afraid at all. In fact, I felt as though I was sitting on the back of a crocodile and meandering through the ocean.

The bazaar was glittering and bustling with activity. There were seekh kebabs, paan, gajras and a mass of onlookers. In the commotion, one could sense the goings on of strange whispers, unspoken gestures, and being watched by unblinking eyes. The bargaining was shrouded in silence.

I saw that Bari had off gone to one side and was talking to a Pathan in a soft voice. The Pathan had henna-coloured sideburns. The two of them then came to us and Bari asked Manto to settle the rate.

Manto was angry. 'You settle all of this yourself. Idiot. Go now...'

Manto disliked bargaining.

Bari and Pathan came close to us.

The Pathan then said, 'Come along. There is good maal inside that kotha.'

The four of us climbed up the staircase. We crossed a balcony and entered a room where we found a Pathan prostitute. She was around thirty-five and had thick-set features. She had tucked in some buds of the chameli in her hair, which was generously oiled. She wore a satin shalwar and a cheap silk shirt with blue spots. Her mouth was stuffed with paan.

'Come, sit.'

The Pathan also sat down next to us.

The sideburns framed the Pathan's face, which had begun to take on a gentle expression. His whole demeanour was polite and deferential, giving the impression of a man ready to do the master's bidding. He was the chief pimp of this adda.

Manto threw a glance at the sagging body of the prostitute.

A servant walked in with three glasses and placed them in front of us.

Manto said, 'Get some soda and some tikkas and kebabs.'

'What will you eat?' Manto asked me.

I did not eat meat in those days. I had tried it a couple of times but each time I felt like I was chewing something rubbery.

I said, 'I will have an omelet.'

Manto pulled out crisp ten-rupee notes from his pocket and handed them to the Pathan. About ten minutes later, the Pathan and the servant walked in with plates of meat, kebabs and the omelet, along with soda bottles and ice. There were slices of lemon and onions in another plate. When they handed over the change to Manto, he said, 'Keep it.'

Bari opened the bottle, poured out the whisky into three glasses and topped it up with soda and ice.

'I don't drink,' I said.

A smile touched Bari's dark face for the first time, 'Drink it, bhai. Alcohol is a thing of virtue.'

'He doesn't drink,' Manto added.

Manto then thumped the prostitute on her thigh and said, 'Drink it, my love.'

She threw a sidelong glance at Manto and smiled a thick smile. She then picked up her glass and started drinking.

Manto and Bari, emptied their glasses almost at once and prepared the next double peg.

Manto knocked back a swig and said, 'Now show us the maal'.

The prostitute gestured to the Pathan and he soon returned with a dolled-up prostitute. She came up to sit right in front of us. Manto looked at her closely. I too gazed at her with interest. She was thin, with layers of red stuff on her face and an excess of kajal in her eyes. She was wearing a purple georgette sari.

She smiled at us and asked, 'Where have you come from to grace our place?'

'From your mother's village!' Manto said. 'Where are you from?'

Manto asked a few more questions and then rejected the prostitute.

The Pathan gestured to her and she went away.

The Pathan brought in the second prostitute, and then the third one. Manto did not approve of any of them.

And then, the fourth one walked in. She had sharp features and a sexy smile played across her face. She was wearing dark glasses. She sat in front of us as though she was about to offer namaz.

Manto approved of her style. He asked a few questions and her coquetry was in full play when she answered them. Manto was clearly getting interested but other thoughts, too, were crossing his mind.

He asked her, 'Why are you wearing dark glasses at night, my love?'

'So that you aren't dazzled by the blaze of my beauty.'

Manto said, 'It will be good fun to be in bed with you but at least I must get to see what you are like.'

And then he suddenly took off her glasses.

The prostitute blinked. She was crosseyed.

Manto said, 'I would definitely have loved you had you come without the glasses. I would have given up all I have for your crossed eyes, but I can't tolerate deception.'

She too was rejected.

It was around eleven o'clock by then. Meat, kebabs and omelets had been brought in and demolished thrice. Manto had had five drinks and his pupils appeared distended but his words continued to carry the same spark and enthusiasm.

Manto was about to pour out the sixth drink when the

older prostitute caught hold of his hand and said, 'I beg you, on my life, don't drink anymore.'

I too said to Manto, 'Yes, don't drink any more. She is right. She cares for you and is concerned about you.'

'Concern!' Manto swore. 'Saali, she is an utter fraud. She wants to save the whisky for her pimp. I would get a full bottle for her if she was honest about it but this wretched woman is only pretending to be concerned.'

He filled up his glass and drank from it with evident pleasure.

The prostitute held Manto's hand and said, 'God is my witness. He knows how much I like you.'

Manto thumped her thigh and said, 'You are the most beautiful woman in the world, my love! You are Cleopatra! Helen!'

Manto kept handing out crisp notes to the Pathan without accounting for any of them, and each time the Pathan brought anything, he would keep the change for himself.

I could see Babu Gopinath in Manto—the character Manto created in his story with the eponymous title.

Babu Gopinath frequents the lodgings of prostitutes and recklessly spends money despite knowing the whole truth about these dens. He is as comfortable in the world of prostitutes and pimps as he is with dervishes, saints and mazaars of religious men. However, Gopinath himself remains detached from all that surrounds him.

Manto was another name for Gopinath—or perhaps it will be more appropriate to say that the humanity which is such a dominant characteristic of Gopinath is actually a reflection of Manto's soul itself.

Manto's soul had a perplexing solitariness. Manto spent a great deal of time in the world of prostitutes and yet he remained detached from them. Manto's eye pierced though these dens and discerned the humanity and compassion that lay there, tucked away in corners. He had caught sight of the woman hidden in the heart of the prostitute. He saw the prostitute in the woman and the woman in the prostitute.

He was a trader of souls in the bazaar of bodies.

(2)

The following day, Manto came to the radio station at eleven. Jugal Kishore Mehra was then Station Director. He was very authoritative and the entire staff was scared of him. He would come to the radio station in his own special style. He had an actor's voice, a supple body, and eyes like a hyena's in a face full of pockmarks which had somewhat lightened with time. He would arrive wearing a tweed coat and with a cigar in his mouth; his Alsatian would accompany him to office.

I was sitting in my room and working when the peon came to tell me, 'Manto-saheb is calling you.'

I had Manto's wallet with his money in it. He had handed it to me the previous night.

When I came out, I heard Manto say in a loud voice, 'Jugal, I am leaving.'

Just then, Mehra-saheb came out of his room and said, 'Wait a bit more, my friend. We can leave together.'

Manto replied quite casually, 'You go for the races. I have no interest in them. They are boring. I am leaving.'

I returned Manto's wallet to him. He did not count the money. He just ensured that the tickets to Bombay were there and told me, 'I am going back this evening.'

I reached the railway station in the evening. There were two seats reserved in the Frontier Mail since Safia was also travelling with Manto. He placed a suitcase under the seat. The shopping done in Lahore was packed in bundles and he put them too under the seat.

Manto and I were standing on the platform. Manto said, 'Chaudhary has still not come. The signal has gone down but there is no knowing where he is.'

He was quiet for a while and then said, 'This ass has no sense of time. He came to Lahore straight from his village. Totally uncivilized! Uncultured! He has still not come. I made a serious mistake by giving my clothes to him for washing. Six shalwars, six shirts and my achkan and the nincompoop has still not turned up.'

The guard blew his whistle and Manto grumbled, 'The ass! He has no brains!'

Just then Chaudhary Nazeer turned up huffing and puffing, 'I've reached with such trouble! I had to stand there and get the clothes ironed.'

Manto glared at him in anger, 'The train is just about to leave and it is now that you turn up.'

Chaudhary quickly kept the clothes in the train and just about managed to step down when it started. When the train puffed out of the station, he wiped the sweat from his forehead and said, 'Just look at the way he orders me around, as if I am his father's slave.'

After that, both of us began to slowly walk away.

He began to speak once again. 'He thinks he is the scion of a royal family. He takes the clothes from me and then rebukes me as well. When he arrived, I gave him an advance of two thousands rupees to write a novel. He frittered away one thousand right there, in front of me. He is always the first one to offer to pay all the bills. The money, after all, comes from people like me.'

He kept grumbling for quite a long time. Finally, when he had cooled down, he said, 'Balwant, I tolerate all the airs of this man only because he is Manto. I don't care about any other scoundrel. Important judges, directors and professors keep approaching me to get their books published but I don't entertain them. I publish only what I personally assess as worth publishing. Manto, however, is the God of the short story. I may perhaps be remembered in the future only for carrying the bundle of Manto's clothes to the railway station when he was leaving. As a writer, he belongs to a class of his own. He is completely different from anyone else.'

And Chaudhary went off to Maktaba-e-Urdu.

Manto once came came to Lahore without notice. He was sitting in Maktaba-e-Urdu with his legs crossed one above the other. He was wearing a silk kurta, a tapered cotton shalwar and shoes with golden embroidery on them. Fikr Taunsvi used to sit in a room at the rear end and proofread. He said to Manto, 'You did not inform us about your visit this time, Manto-saheb.'

Manto ignored him completely and, hitting his heel on the floor, said, 'Nargis had come in a white saree and juttis with golden embroidery. She was sitting on the chair and hitting her heel on the floor exactly like this. She had no idea that juttis are not supposed to be worn with sarees. I was quite mortified. I got a kurta-shalwar stitched, and bought the juttis after I came here. Now I will go and tell her, "Look here, this is the way embroidered juttis are supposed to be worn."'

His personality and taste had this kind of a royal opulence.

Manto used to completely submerge himself into the ethos of places where he spent time and authentically recreated them in his stories. I had become familiar with the police station at Nagpara in Bombay, the prostitutes on Foras Road, and the film studios of the city without ever stepping out of Lahore. The prostitute Sultana from 'Kali Shalwar' used to live in a brothel on G.B. Road just next to Ajmeri Gate. Right in front of her room was the railway yard with the network of rail tracks spread all around. These days there is a row of brothels there but both the setting of the place and the emotional state of the prostitute continue to be the same as described by Manto in the story:

'The railway tracks gleamed in the sun and Sultana looked down at her hands with blue veins protruding like rail tracks. Engines and trains kept moving around in that wide, open ground. All the while they kept moving around here and there. The huffing and puffing, the clamour of the engines and the trains echoed all the time... Sometimes she saw train bogies moving on all by themselves after they had been pushed by engines and then abandoned.'

The above lines have come to represent what is considered classic in Urdu literature.

Manto went to Pakistan after Partition and wrote extensively about the riots and the violence that occurred as an aftermath of the division. He never hesitated to confront, express or swallow the poison of truth. He was a blunt man who had no qualms in telling the truth, however harsh, to people. He never allowed emotional concessions to change his track.

A friend once asked him, 'Manto, how much of a Muslim are you?'

Manto replied, 'My heart skips a beat with joy if Islamia College scores a goal in a football match against D.A.V. College. I am certainly a Muslim to that extent.'

However, there is no evidence of the above fact as far as Manto's friendships were concerned. His closest friends were Shyam, Ashok Kumar and Mukherjee and he talked about them over and over again.

He probably made the comment regarding the football match because there were many Hindu writers who, despite claiming to be progressive, internally remained religious bigots. They, however, did not have the courage to plainly accept this reality. Manto has written about those thoughts and emotions that remain embedded in our subconscious and defy all control of the conscious mind over them and by doing so, Manto manages to bring us to the point where we have no option but to confront profound and unfathomable truths.

Manto's take on death was completely unique. He used to say, 'The death of one person is seen as a tragedy but the death of one lakh people is passed off as an act of nature.'

He has written stories about the killings and rapes that occurred during the Partition of Punjab. All of us are familiar with his remarkably impressive stories 'Toba Tek Singh', 'Thanda Gosht' and 'Khol Do'.

He has described the senseless slaughter of communal riots in his collection of stories, *Siyah Hashiye*. These are dark jokes, stories that are very short, pungent and sharp, like those from the *Panchatantra*. He has satirized hooliganism, murder and human idiocy. It was for the first time that this form of dark humour appeared in Indian literature.

It was after many years that Feletti was recognized for this kind of dark humour in his films and Faulkner in literature. In truth Manto was first one to position himself on the path of international literature and carve out new routes and channels.

Many of Manto's characters have names of real, flesh-and-blood individuals. They are so compelling and interesting that there remains no difference between their fictional and 'real' personas.

Manto also uses meaningless, nonsense words in his descriptions and conversations.

Manto was once going to Filmistan studio on an electric train in Bombay when he happened to read the name Baraktullah or, perhaps, Hanifullah. Manto, however, could read the word only in bits and pieces like Hepa-hip-tulla and he liked the sound of it. Manto reached the studio and was soon sitting with the director and discussing a story. After a while Manto said, 'It is a fine story but it is not hiptulla.'

Ashok Kumar agreed with Manto and added, 'The story of course must be heptulla.'

It was a nonsensical, meaningless word but Mukherjee had got the sense of it. After that, the term hiptulla became current for film, dialogue and situation in the world of films in Bombay.

The bazaar of murder and bloodshed heated up in August 1947. I left Lahore and came to Bhatinda with nothing except a shirt and a pair of trousers. I learned later that the train I had travelled in was the last to have safely crossed the bridge over the Sutlej. When I reached Bhatinda, I found that riots had broken out there as well. I did not want to live in the bloodied surroundings where my childhood friend Fazal and his sister Maaran had been butchered.

I went to Delhi but the bloodshed had reached there as well. I struggled there for a month without a job and an uncertain future looming large. I therefore decided to go to Bombay.

I remembered Mulk Raj Anand's address. I reached his house and stayed there surrounded by his warmth, hospitality and sincerity.

There used to be frequent literary and cultural gatherings in Mulk Raj Anand's house. People like Krishan Chander, Ali Sardar Jafri, painters and dancers from Bombay, and many other progressive intellectuals used to regularly come to these gatherings and discuss the possibility and hope for peace.

It was, however, not difficult to see that a deepset, unseen fear had begun to swell and surge at the fall of dusk. The Muslims were going away after the creation of Pakistan. Occasionally, one heard of some or the other murder as well.

I rang up Manto and he asked me, 'When did you come?'

I told him about myself and said that I wanted to meet him.

'Come home this evening,' he told me. 'You know my house, don't you? It's in Byculla on Clare Road.'

He told me the house number and described some major landmarks.

That evening, Krishan Chander and some other friends dropped in to meet me. We started a tete-a-tete and it became dark before any of us realized how late it had become. When I told them that I was to go and meet Manto, they cautioned me. 'You still don't know the roads here very well. It is dangerous to go out in the dark. Go tomorrow.'

I too was afraid and so I did not go to see him that evening.

When I rang up Manto the next day he said in a loud voice, 'Oye! I was waiting for you last evening. Why did you not come?'

'Krishan Chander and Mulk Raj Anand had come,' I told him. 'So I could not.'

His voice was still loud and heated. 'Oye! Who the hell do you think Mulk Raj and Krishan are? Did you not know that Manto was waiting for you here?'

I apologized and promised to visit that evening.

He then said, 'Have dinner with me and then stay over for the night. The whole house is empty. Safia has gone away. I too will go.'

It was dark by the time I reached Clare Road that evening. I climbed up the stairs and knocked on Manto's door. I heard his loud, animated voice asking, 'Who's there?'

I called out my name. Manto's cook opened the door after some time. I went in and saw that Manto was sitting on the chair with his knees folded. He was writing. A bottle of whisky was on the table.

'I am writing a letter to Safia,' he said. 'Just a couple of words more. Just sit here.'

Manto kept sitting in the same pose with the board on his knees and continued to write.

After finishing the letter, he turned to me. 'It's good that you came. I was alone. I get very unnerved when I am alone. Will you have a drink?'

'No,' I said.

He poured the whisky into a glass, took a sip and said, 'My cook has roasted chicken. Have you started eating meat?'

'Yes.'

'Should I read out the letter to you? Safia had sent me a letter saying that she has got a very good flat in Lakshmi Mansions. Top-quality furniture, fridge. She is very happy. Oh woman! You good-for-nothing creatures, what is it that you are so happy about? Manto is here, and what is the point of having a fridge when I am not there? Rubbish! I am green with jealousy. I am on fire! I've become a roasted kebab.'

And he read out the letter he had written to Safia. It described his loneliness. It talked about the cook, the condition in Bombay, and included abuses flung at the fridge in Lakshmi Mansions. The letter then turned into a complaint about leaving his world in Bombay, his life with films, and about letting go of his love for friends. He was giving up all this and coming to Lahore for Safia and his daughters. But her response was limited to going into raptures over the refrigerator! The letter was suffused with feelings of a husband and father, as well as the gloom of a devastated home. His flat had been his companion and the witness of his emotional state. His wife and children were in Pakistan and he was here...in Bombay.

He refilled his glass. His eyes and his expression became more incisive and sharp.

'My friends ask me the reasons for my decision to go to Pakistan,' he said. 'Am I a coward? Am I a Muslim? But they will never be able to understand what I feel. I am going to

Pakistan so that there is a Manto in Pakistan too. A Manto who will rip open the façade of politics and expose corruption. It is certain that the future of Urdu is going to be dismal in Hindustan. One can already see the spread and ascendancy of Hindi. I want to write and I can do so only in Urdu. I want to be published so that I can reach the wider public. Language has a philosophy of its own and many a times language is thoughts and ideas as well. It is connected with blood... One Manto has lived in Bombay, the other will live in Pakistan.'

He talked until late in the night.

That night I slept in Manto's room. I stayed back the next day too. And a week later, I came away to Delhi.

I later found out that Manto had gone off to Lahore.

He wrote countless stories after he went there. He challenged the government and wrote against communal people. His letters to Uncle Sam are an avalanche of criticism. He was a born rebel with an innate fearlessness, coupled with the talent to expose the falsehood and hypocrisy of society.

He could have accepted any challenge posed by society but did not possess the strength to endure attacks by friends.

In 1950 in Pakistan, the Progressive writers accused him of being a conservative and obscene writer. They did not stop here. They went on to publish a circular stating that no journal must publish Manto's stories. The most painful and regrettable fact about this was that Manto's dear friend Ahmed Naseem Qasimi was the General Secretary when the decision was taken.

Manto was deeply hurt and distressed. He had become an outsider in his own world.

Financial constraints and neglect by friends pushed Manto towards drinking more heavily. He began writing stories for a bottle of whisky as payment. There were times when he even wrote as many as three stories in a day and sold them to publishers.

A collection of his stories was published. He had put a date to all his stories. He wrote in the preface of the book: 'What I want appreciation for is the fact that my mind entered my stomach and performed amazing miracles.'

He had become very thin. He could digest nothing except alcohol. A strange kind of obsession seems to have gripped him at that time. He was even admitted to a lunatic asylum for treatment but that did not impair either his creativity or the speed at which he continued to write. His story 'Toba Tek Singh' represents the essence of his personal experiences in the asylum. The story deals with partitioned humanity and remains a masterpiece in the world of literature.

Manto knew that he was an exceptional writer. He has written his own epitaph in which he says: 'Manto is buried here. The talent of writing stories died with him.'

His prediction has proved to be true.

# My Father, Saadat Hasan Manto

## Nuzhat Arshad

ABBA PASSED AWAY IN 1955. I WAS JUST SEVEN AT THE time. My elder sister was nine and the youngest was five. It is self-evident that we were not old enough to be either influenced by our father or remember much about him. None of us were fond of reading or writing—something that became a source of satisfaction and solace for my mother. Our mother's opinion was unambiguous: It is better for people not to write.

My mother's experience of life as a writer's wife was far from pleasant. She never accepted Manto-saheb's habit of drinking excessively. And to top it all, he gave away money without hesitation; he was exceptionally generous, and gentle. He could easily gift away whatever he possessed. It was not unusual for him to hand over a hundred-rupee note to a tongawala if he did not have change. My mother used to often complain to him about his habit of frittering away money, especially when there was not enough to run the house.

Manto-saheb had infinite compassion and love for the poor. Whatever little generosity we have is an inheritance from our father. A Hindustani writer once came to Lahore to meet us. He told us that he wanted to bring out a collection of our father's unpublished writings. We handed over all of father's stories to him but it is a matter of deep regret for us that despite repeated reminders he did not return the original script to us. He just vanished into thin air after taking possession of all the stories. Dozens of collections of Manto-saheb's stories have been published after his death but my mother did not ever receive even a single rupee as royalty.

Ammi-jaan always lived under the stress of not having enough money but she still made sure that we were educated well and then got married well. Nonetheless, how can I ever forget the problems that my mother had to face all her life! Ammi-jaan's brother gave us immense support in these difficult times. It was because of him that we did not feel orphaned even after our father's death. Ammi-jaan has told us how Manto-saheb had become so addicted to alcohol in his last days that he used to sell off his stories for even five or ten rupees. He came to Pakistan after the Partition but, in the literary circles of Lahore, he did not attain the kind lofty position and status that he had enjoyed in Bombay. The popularity of his writings has somewhat diminished in the last ten years, too, because of the propaganda that Manto-saheb was an obscene writer.

The policies of the government have also had a negative impact on the popularity of Manto-saheb's writings. Many of Manto-saheb's stories were dramatized for Pakistani television between 1970 and 1980. These dramas enjoyed immense popularity too but they were never screened after that. Father did not write much for films after coming from Bombay to Lahore. The film made on his story 'Katari' was very successful. It also won an award. Similarly, the film *Ek Gunah Aur Sahi* too won an award. The story 'Ek Gunah Aur Sahi' was inspired by my mother's personality and the film producer paid five hundred rupees for the story. Much like the publishers, the producers too don't want to give either payment or royalty to the writer.

Ammi-jaan used to be the first reader of father's stories. She has told us about father's exceptional talent. There were times when he would verbally dictate three different stories to three different people, asking them to simultaneously pen them down. And then there were times when he would continue to chat with guests and write his story as well.

# Manto-mamu's Death

## Hamid Jalal

I SOMETIMES WONDER WHAT I WOULD SAY TO MANTO-mamu if he decided to rise up from the Miani graveyard and walk into the house. I am quite certain that I would not be impressed with the miracle of his resurrection and would simply say to him, 'Manto-saheb, you have done many irresponsible things in your life but the most irresponsible of them all has been your act of dying.'

The second match in the series between India and Pakistan was going on at Bhawalpur in Pakistan. I was sitting in Dring Stadium, assisting Taley Yaar Khan with the running commentary of the match, when I got a trunk call from Lahore informing me that Saadat Hasan Manto had passed away that morning. At the outset, the news, instead of making me crazy with grief, ignited an uncontrollable anger within me. I was extremely angry with Manto-mamu for treating his wife and children so shabbily. I, however, did not express my anger and when I did speak, my voice clearly communicated my deep concern.

'Where was he when he died?' I enquired.

'At home,' I was told.

The response gave me some consolation as I was afraid that he had gone out of his house and then suddenly died in some strange spot. I also knew that it was a distinct possibility that he could have breathed his last while sitting on a tonga, or in some restaurant, or in the office of some publisher, or a film studio....

When I went back to my seat, my companions who were giving a running commentary on the match gestured to me to enquire about what had happened. I handed them a slip of paper on which I had written: 'The umpire has finally given an "out" to Saadat Hasan Manto, who passed away this morning.'

Several appeals had already been made to the umpire to give an 'out' to Manto-mamu. All earlier appeals had been rejected but his reckless and shaky innings was finally over. If he had been a cricketer, I could have said with a fair degree of confidence that he would never have been a cautious and astute player like Hanif Mohammad—whom he was very eager to see playing in the third test match. I discovered this only after I reached home, twenty-four hours after his death. In fact this was one of the two desires in his final wish-list. Just a day before he died, he was sitting in a restaurant where he had told his friends, 'Let Hamid Jalal come back. I will go with him to watch Hanif play the test match.'

His other desire was to write a story about the helpless woman whose naked, dead body was discovered on some road in Gujarat. According to the newspaper reports, the woman, along with her little daughter, had been kidnapped from the bus stand. Around half a dozen depraved men had ruthlessly satisfied their lust. When the woman eventually managed to escape from their clutches, there was not even a shred of cloth left on her body. The mother and daughter soon died in the freezing cold. Manto-mamu was deeply distressed by this tragedy. That very day some people from Gujarat had visited him and reported further details about the incident which must have made him extremely angry and restless. My guess is that after listening to them, Manto-mamu may have had more than his usual quota of alcohol, which probably proved fatal for him.

That day he got back home quite late in the evening and soon after began to vomit blood. My six-year-old son, who was standing next to him at the time, drew his attention to the stream of red blood but he evaded the issue by telling him that it was merely the spatter of paan that he had coughed up. He also told the child not to mention it to anybody else. After that, he had his dinner in much the usual way and went to sleep. Nobody in the house had even the slightest suspicion that anything abnormal had occurred since my son kept Mamu's secret to himself. It is possible that even Manto-mamu did not realize that this was something he ought to be concerned about. Moreover, he preferred not to let family members know of such matters because it invariably gave them a chance to start demanding that he give up drinking.

The night had reached its last phase when Manto-mamu woke up his wife and told her his pain had become unbearable and that he had lost a great deal of blood. He believed that his liver had ruptured. When his wife realized that she would not be able to handle the situation all by herself, she woke the other people in the house. Soon after that began the struggle to wrench Mamu out of the jaws of death. He had been in a critical condition on many earlier occasions but had managed to pull through and so the thought that he would probably be with us for only the next few hours did not cross anybody's mind. The truth, however, was that the umpire's finger had begun to gradually rise up into the air from the moment Manto-mamu had first vomited blood.

Whatever I have heard about Manto-mamu's last moments makes me believe that for quite a time, he too had not realized that those were his last moments. He had not lost hope till about an hour or two after the doctors had given him the injections, which brought no improvement in his condition. His pulse was continuously fading, his pain steadily increasing, and he had not stopped vomiting blood. The following morning the doctor advised the family to admit Manto-mamu to the hospital.

Manto-mamu was completely in his senses at that time and as soon as he heard hospital being mentioned he said, 'It is too late now. Don't take me to the hospital. Just let me lie here in peace.'

The prospect was unbearable for the women of the family and they began to weep. Manto-mamu got furious when he saw this and thundered, 'Look, no one must weep.'

After the proclamation he covered his head with a quilt.

This was the true Manto-mamu. No aspect of his life had remained veiled from the eyes of the general public until then. He now found it difficult to accept that people should watch him die too. Manto-mamu had become an embodiment of anger from head to toe. We will probably never find out whether he was angry with himself or with alcohol—which was responsible for his untimely death.

He had removed the quilt from his face just once or twice before the ambulance arrived. He had also said, 'I am feeling very cold. Perhaps I won't be so cold even in the grave. Cover me with more quilts.'

And after a while a strange glow had lighted up his eyes and then he had said softly, 'There are three-and-a-half rupees in my pocket. Add some more money to it and get some whisky...'

He persisted with his demand for whisky, so a quarter-bottle was brought for his satisfaction. He looked at the bottle with very strange and contented eyes and said, 'Make two pegs for me.' And shuddered with a fit of unbearable pain as he said this.

There was not even an iota of self-pity in Manto-mamu's eyes at that time. He had realized that his end was near but not even for a moment did he allow emotions to get a grip on him. He did not ask his children or anybody else to come close. He was not a proponent of either writing a will or casting that last, sentimental glance at his loved ones. The difference between life and death is rather blurred and fuzzy for people like him. And it is only proper that it should have been so because his life and his soul had already been taken out of his body and transferred into his stories. Once housed in the stories, both life and soul are certain to achieve immortality; they live on eternally; they talk, they laugh, they love.

Manto asked for nothing besides alcohol on his deathbed. He had known for quite long that alcohol was the main scourge of his life. It had become synonymous with death for him and he knew that he could not have battled and triumphed against it. Just as a human being is helpless when confronted with death, Manto-mamu was powerless when confronted with alcohol. All the same, he remained the rebel that he had always been and as was his wont, remained defiant in the face of death. He hated to be defeated, even if it was at the hands of death. That was probably the reason why he wanted to confront death in complete seclusion, where nobody would see him dying, where nobody would witness the spectacle of him being defeated by death.

I am certain that a person much inferior to him in every way would have taken pains to organize and coordinate a much more dramatic death for himself to provide people enough fodder for discussion; for articles to be written; and grant adequate opportunity for friends and relatives to declare that though they did not much approve of the way he had lived, he had expressed deep regret and turned over a new leaf before he died. But Manto-mamu was not a hypocrite. He firmly stemmed down all desire for drama, except one, which was the spectacle of his demand for alcohol. That too was done not for effect. It was to satisfy a need that only he could have understood.

I am quite certain that he would have, to some extent, revealed his internal state to me had I been with him at the time. I am also sure that he would have done this quite effortlessly for all that he would have told me is the following: 'Don't ever forget the story of the snake and the man.'

I would have nodded my head to say yes and, after that, I would have offered him his last drink. That one sentence of his would clear all the cobwebs from my mind. The story of the snake and the man is really simple. There was a man who kept a poisonous snake as a pet despite the objections of his friends. One day the snake emptied all his poison into the man's body. After that, the man too caught hold of the snake, chopped off its head and threw it away.

As soon as the ambulance arrived to stand at the door, Manto-mamu demanded alcohol once again. A spoonful of whisky was poured into his mouth but a mere drop is what must have trickled down his throat. The remaining whisky spilled out as he became unconscious. This was the first time in his life that he had lost his senses and it was in this condition that he was put inside the ambulance.

The ambulance reached the hospital and when the doctors arrived to see him, they found that Manto-mamu was already dead. He had not regained consciousness after leaving home and had passed away on the way to hospital.

# NOTES ON THE CONTRIBUTORS

**Abu Saeed Qureshi**, a childhood friend of Manto's, was a poet and an author. He wrote, among others, a popular biography, *Manto: Sawaneh*, and *Faizan-e-Faiz*.

**Ahmed Nadeem Qasimi** was one of the most wide-ranging and prolific authors in Urdu in the last century, writing fifty books in the genres of poetry, fiction, literary criticism, journalism, drama and the short story. He edited and published the literary magazine, *Funoon*, for almost fifty years. He received the Pride of Performance Award and the Sitara-i-Imtiaz, both given by the President of Pakistan, and the Lifetime Achievement Award given by the Pakistan Academy of Letters.

**Ali Sardar Jafri** presided over the first ever Progressive Writers' Conference to be conducted and remained connected with the movement over much of his early literary career. He was a lyricist, a writer of stories, poet and critic. He edited and published *Guftagu*, a leading Urdu literary magazine and his published work includes *Khoon Ki Lakeer*, *Amn Ka Sitara*, *Asia Jaag Utha* and *Sarhad*. Jafri also edited very popular anthologies of Ghalib, Kabir, Mir and Meera Bai

**Balwant Gargi**, playwright, theatre director, novelist, short story writer and academic, was one of most prominent Punjabi writers of his time. Gargi wrote several plays, including *Loha Kutt*, *Kesro*, *Kanak Di Balli*, *Sohni Mahiwal*, *Sultan Razia*, *Soukan*, *Mirza Sahiba* and *Dhooni di Agg*. His plays have been widely translated into many languages and performed all over the world. Gargi was awarded the Sahitya Akademi and Sangeet Natak Akademi awards and the Padma Shri award.

**Hamid Jalal**, cricket commentator and a civil servant in Pakistan, was Saadat Hasan Manto's nephew.

**Ibrahim Jalees** was a journalist, writer and satirist. Over the course of his journalistic career, he worked for *Jang*, edited *Musawat* and *Anjaam*, and also launched his own weekly *Awami Adalat*. His also wrote *Nai-Deewar-i-Chin*, an account of his travels in China.

**Krishan Chander** was a prolific writer of satirical short stories in Hindi and Urdu, as well as a well-known screenplay writer. He also wrote over twenty novels and radio plays. His writing addresses social and political themes such as the partition of Kashmir, the Partition of India and Pakistan, and the Bengal famine, and is known for its fundamental humanism and idealistic approach. He was a dedicated member of the Progressive Writers' Association and an ardent socialist. His short story 'Annadata' was made into the film *Dharti ke Lal* by K. A. Abbas.

**Mehdi Ali Siddiqui** was a poet, translator, author and judge, first in Hyderabad state and, after Partition, in Pakistan. He was a professor of law at the Islamia College and the Sindh Muslim Law College and also edited *Muslim News International*. His published work includes *Qurbani*, a translation of *A Tale of Two Cities*, and his autobiography *Bila Kamo Kaast*.

**Mohammad Tufail** was an editor and publisher, and calligrapher, who ran *Nuqoosh*, a literary magazine which enjoyed great prominence and prestige in the world of Urdu literature. He also set up and ran two publishing houses, Maktaba-i-shear-o-adab and Idara-i-farogh-i-Urdu.

**Naresh Kumar Shaad** was an accomplished poet who wrote mostly ghazals and was considered a master of the quat'aa and rubai forms of Urdu poetry. He published a number of collections of poetry, among them *Lalkar* and *Dastak*.

**Nuzhat Arshad** is Saadat Hasan Manto's second daughter.

**Shahid Ahmed Dehlvi** was an accomplished musician, prolific translator and chronicler. His sketches of Delhi, its people and the city itself, are collected in *Dilli ki Bipta* and *Ujra Diyar*. He was the lifelong editor of *Saqi*, the prestigious literary magazine which published the work of leading authors in Urdu of the time. He was also one of the founding members of the Pakistan Writers' Guild.

**Upendranath Ashk**, novelist, short story writer and playwright, wrote both in Urdu and Hindi. A contemporary of Krishan Chander and Saadat Hasan Manto, Ashk worked for All India Radio in Delhi as a writer of radio plays and for Filmistan in Bombay. Ashk's literary output through his lifetime was immense, with over a hundred published works to his credit.